French Leave

First published in 2011 by
Liberties Press
Guinness Enterprise Centre | Taylor's Lane | Dublin 8
Tel: +353 (1) 415 1224
www.libertiespress.com | info@libertiespress.com

Trade enquiries to Gill & Macmillan Distribution
Hume Avenue | Park West | Dublin 12
Tel: +353 (1) 500 9534 | Fax: +353 (1) 500 9595
sales@gillmacmillan.ie

Distributed in the United States by
Dufour Editions | PO Box 7 | Chester Springs | Pennsylvania | 19425

ISBN: 978-1-907593-13-0
2 4 6 8 10 9 7 5 3 1
A CIP record for this title is available from the British Library.

Cover design by Sin É Design
Internal design by Liberties Press
Printed and bound in the UK by CPI Mackays, Chatham ME5 8TD

French Leave

An Irishwoman's Adventures in Normandy

Liz Ryan

ACKNOWLEDGEMENTS

'Are we nearly there yet?'

Yes, *mes amis*, we are! The long and rocky road has been much shortened by your stalwart support and fabulous friendship.

Anna, Philip, Annie, Mary and the lads, Michael and Eileen, Rita, Marcelle, Danielle and Michel, Helen and Patrick, Sheila and Dominique, Gill and Lyndon, Ken and Wanda, Libby and Dave, Helen and Lahcen, Beryl and Ralph; you will never know just how wonderful you have been or how much your encouragement has mattered.

To Tim, my eternal thanks for the cheerful patience, endless generosity and invaluable computer expertise without which France would be a very different story.

To my mother Lil, *mille mercis* for what can't have been easy but has, I hope, been worthwhile.

And to Seán, *chapeaux* for faith.

1.

Why?

Maybe my father had a French mistress. Maybe there's something my mother has yet to tell me. Because the answer doesn't simply trip off the tongue when people ask: 'why France?'

What is it about this particular country that draws people in their droves, makes them dream of living in a way that seems impossible anywhere else? Long the traditional Mecca of those in search of a discreetly civilised 'quality of life', today it has competition. Spain is sunnier, is it not, and the golf great? Italy is livelier, South Africa is cheaper, Dubai is ritzier, Florida is fantastic, Poland is revving-up like a Harley Davidson and Australia has it all, if only it could be moved nearer.

But France . . . ah. Offering a hint of romance with a tint of magic, France continues to charm, to seduce, to enchant. Contrary to popular belief, the French are not strutting peacocks: *au contraire*, they suffer from twittering insecurity, spectacularly low self-esteem and the firm belief that their country is going to hell in a handcart. *Eh oui*, it was once a great nation, but today – *bof!* No confidence, no sense of direction at all. And yet it beckons, it draws, it lures people from more supposedly prosperous and dynamic nations.

Today, foreigners put far more faith in France than do the French themselves. Their reasons for moving to Brittany, Provence, Burgundy, Alsace or the over-subscribed Dordogne are myriad, but they all share one common pursuit: *le bien être*. Well-being, or feeling good in one's skin. There's even a popular cologne of that name, a long-running best-seller still on the shelves today.

I wanted to feel good in my skin. Like so many others, I woke up one morning suddenly sick – almost literally – of commuting twelve hours a week to work. The joke about renaming Ireland 'the car park' was wearing thin, and I was en route to an office woefully demoralised by budget cuts and Machiavellian intrigue, by rows, rivalry, sexism and psychological warfare. As in companies worldwide, 'rationalisation' had reduced facilities to a pitiful level, and going to work each morning felt like embarking on the *Titanic*. My job, once a joy, had degenerated into a farce. Arriving in the office one day to find myself hot-desking with a complete stranger, I suddenly experienced that Reggie Perrin moment: No! Enough! Stop the wheel, I want to get off! Just one more midlife crisis, amongst millions – but I was lucky. I could do something about it. For some, life begins at forty with a Porsche or an affair or an assault on the Himalayas; for me, it would entail quitting my job, selling my house, ditching my comfortable lifestyle and abandoning some very good friends. But as the saying goes, you can't make omelettes without breaking eggs.

The early twenty-first century was, for many, Ireland's finest hour. The economy was booming, transforming the former famine country from pauper to prince. But ironically, wealth was proving to come expensive, on a wave of drugs, crime, political corruption, material greed and spiritual erosion. Southfork-style mansions were mushrooming in every hamlet, huge jeeps were congesting every tiny crossroads, small children were riding to their rites of religious passage in stretch limos, many of them bedecked in designer garb and sporting sunbed tans. As it hurtled along the fast track to prosperity, Ireland seemed to be losing touch with its once easy-going nature, the atmosphere mutating from mellow to manic, propelled by consumer pressures that were thrusting mobile phones into the fists of infants, whirling everyone off on endless exotic holidays which did not appear to be generating any sense of relaxation whatsoever. Gradually, inexorably, the country seemed to be turning into a triumph of show over substance, and the stress of intense social competition was showing. Alcoholism, always a problem, was reaching new heights, stag parties were spewing out onto city streets and teenagers were spending entire weekends in cocktail-induced stupors, victims of a new syndrome: TMM. Too Much Money. Traditionally a cheery, chatty country, Ireland was still fun in many ways, but its soul no longer seemed to be singing.

Mine wasn't singing either, sitting in traffic jams or waiting for non-existent buses (the boom had yet to produce a decent bus service), battling a macho culture at work, banging its head against the glass ceiling of office politics and watching its back with increasing unease. Dear old Dublin had become dangerous; as a woman I felt unsafe even at home unless the burglar alarm was on, and distinctly unsafe on the streets. One day, an aggressive backpacker bumped into me in Henry Street, slamming me up against a wall with such a violent volley of oaths that bypassers turned to stare (but not intervene) as he screamed and spat a tirade of abuse. A few days later, an enraged biker, ranting and bellowing, flung his helmet at the windscreen of my car. Road rage was rampant, the cost of living was rocketing and litigation had become the new career option. Tribunals clogged the courts, half the clergy seemed to be up on paedophilia charges and no amount of money could maintain a decent health service.

The entire nation seemed obsessed with flash goodies, fake tans and (con)fusion food, and it was speaking in an increasingly American accent: 'Mum' had become 'Mom'. The airwaves were squawking endless advertising of pension plans, financial 'products' and bulletproof insurance against the terrifying prospect of one unplanned, unprotected moment anywhere between cradle and grave. Musing during the twenty-kilometre commute that now took seventy-five minutes each way, I realised with a jolt that my job was costing five thousand euro a year in petrol and parking. Like many people, I'd been mugged and burgled more than once over the years, my car had been vandalised and sometimes it all felt like one long battle for survival.

Enough of this, I thought. Ireland may not be the worst place in the world – we're hardly talking Iraq or Afghanistan – but it's just not me any more. Not at the moment, anyway. Maybe later, when it simmers down. Meanwhile, I am going to jump off this crazy carousel.

And all the signposts were pointing to France. I'd adored that beautiful country all my life and suddenly here was the chance to experience it close up and personal. This wasn't about putting a Band-Aid on a blister, it was about elective surgery. Selling up, jumping ship and trying on a whole new way of life for size. I didn't have any children to worry about, nobody would have to study Pythagoras in French or eat tripes. At worst, I might end up on the wrong end of a few smouldering bridges, with my job, house and pension up in smoke . . . so, let's do it. Let's cut loose.

And besides, there was Serge. I could almost hear him singing already. Many years earlier, on my very first visit to France at the age of eighteen, I'd been hopelessly, irrevocably seduced by a man called Serge Reggiani.

He was Italian, he lived in Paris and he was nearly twenty-five years older than me. We met in a friend's apartment in Ivry and it was love from the first moment his recorded voice caressed my spine like fingers on a piano, wistfully singing a song called *Le Déserteur*, of which I understood scarcely a syllable. But – whoooh! – at a stroke I was felled like a sapling, dizzily, hopelessly in love. Once you'd heard Serge sing, there was no going back. Overnight, the Stones, the Beatles, the entire British-based culture of my youth faded from my mind. 'He luvs ya, yeah yeah yeah' just didn't cut it as a lyric any more. Whereas Serge Reggiani sang the haunting, poetic lyrics of Boris Vian in a way that made me wish he would come galloping into my parents' Dublin semi-dee, scoop me up over the saddle of his prancing steed and whisk me off, permanently, to Paris. Serge notoriously considered himself an ugly chap, but I'd happily have set up camp with him on top of an Alp, at the bottom of Lac Léman, anywhere, just so long as he kept on singing in that black-velvet voice about anarchy, and sedition, and that poor dead soldier with the bloody wounds, and the river eternally rolling under the Pont Mirabeau . . . I'd have done jail for Serge, had he asked me. It was unrequited love, but it was to last a lifetime. Sometimes, crossing O'Connell Bridge, my mind would duck under le pont Mirabeau, floating away to France where Serge was now rising to the status of national treasure, beloved of the entire French nation.

Over the years, the French bug bit repeatedly, burrowing deeper under my skin like one of those inexplicable infections that makes doctors reach, frowning, for their *Gray's Anatomy*. I tuned in to French radio stations like a patient wired up to a drip, and Serge began to amass rivals for my affection: Jean Ferrat's voice could crumble cathedrals, shoot stars from the sky. When he sang the poetry of Louis Aragon, I prayed to God to take me now, since life thereafter could hardly have much point. One sunny day in

Skerries, as I sat propped against a friend's wall overlooking the sea,
I heard Charles Trenet sing *La Mer* and was all but washed away on
the rippling romance of it. And then Serge and Jean and Charles
were joined by Piaf, Barbara, Gainsbourg, Leo Ferré, George
Moustaki, Marc Ogeret; later, Julien Clerc, Pascal Opisbo, Isabelle
Boulay, and – no, no apologies – Johnny Hallyday. (Anyone in the
throes of divorce should listen to *Ne Reviens Pas*, in which Johnny
invites his ex never to darken his door again.) I really had it very
bad. The only schmoozers I wouldn't let into my sound system were
Sacha Distel and Charles Aznavour, since they sang in English,
missing the point entirely. Let Charles and Sacha be snapped up
by the ladies of Limerick or Leeds or Louisiana: me, I took my
Frenchmen *neat*.

However, one does not move to France merely for sexy warblers
who, by the time I finally arrived, were either pensioners or dead.
There have to be *valid* reasons too. A million immigrants can't all
simply be seduced by Serge.

Today, many of those who move to France are economic
migrants: people on the run, not only from Third World countries,
but from collapsing economies in places as near as Britain,
Holland, Ireland, Belgium, Spain, busily buying *maisons de maître*
on a couple of acres in the Languedoc or Limousin for half the price
of their bungalows back home. But money is not the only motivat-
ing factor. For many, France offers another, unspoken incentive, a
dark and shady secret: it is intelligent. Candidly, unrepentantly
intelligent. Articulate and erudite, a refuge of sense and sensibility.
Almost alone in a Europe culturally dominated by the likes of Lady
Gaga, it is not ashamed of its education, its literacy or its nakedly
philosophical turn of mind. It doesn't rate beer over books, go tribal
about football or dumb down its social communications to kindergarten level. Even if its self-styled *intellos* rarely read Sartre any

more – or indeed anything more complex than the film reviews in *Télérama* – it remains literate, cultured and eloquent. To a Frenchman, the term 'intellectual' is a compliment, not an accusation, and the France I'd come to know and love over so many years would never 'go oik', never turn into a braying yob.

Would it?

Oh yes it would, some people muttered darkly. It's got *Desperate Housewives* on television now, *Who Wants To Be A Millionaire*, all those cheap imports and amateur contests! Okay, maybe the teenagers don't behave like gangsters, raves and discos are still relatively rare, but McDonald's is everywhere, as are Pepsi, popcorn, all the hallmarks of Americanisation. As for that lovely language . . . they do 'business' now, they have a 'manager'! A *rendezvous* is a 'meeting' these days, people say 'top' and 'cool' and 'bad boy' and 'stress' . . . you might as well move to Manhattan or Merseyside. Ten years from now, it'll be exactly like Ireland, just one more united state of America.

Oh no. Not my France. Even if globalisation was rampant, I couldn't envisage the French wearing baseball caps backwards, slurping Red Bulls or digging gangsta rap in their puffa jackets. Not the country that produced Voltaire, George Sand, Escoffier, Debussy, Victor Hugo, Marie Curie, Monet and Rousseau . . . good grief, Flaubert would spin in his grave. Monsieur Eiffel would throw himself off his tower.

If France went oik, it would simply be the end. Civilisation would have no hiding place left.

❧

Changing countries is not a popular thing to do. Many see it as changing allegiance, denying one's flag, questioning one's entire history and culture. Even if it's quicker to fly to Paris from Dublin than to drive to Cork, for many people, 'foreign' is still synonymous with 'France' in the worst possible sense. The EU stands for European unity primarily in business terms, and moving voluntarily abroad is viewed almost on a par with divorce, a last resort implying you are finally washing your hands of a marriage that just wasn't working. Your motives and loyalty will be questioned, and people will make well-intentioned attempts to talk you out of going.

'You'll be sorry.'

Perhaps you will. Very. Which is why you should think long and hard before doing it. It can be risky, difficult, exhausting, expensive and frustrating. It may cause resentment. Friction. Heartbreak. Confusion. Loneliness. Bankruptcy. Estrangement. Bitter regret. Or the whole lot.

'You'll be bored.'

Well, there are those who might argue that you can only be bored if you have no imagination. But bored some people soon become, if they're not prepared to learn the language, join clubs, get out there and construct a whole new social circle, which can involve the bonfire of a lot of vanities. It's not easy to regress from Master of the Universe to 'Mike, who's going to give us a talk on greenfly this evening' (if we can understand him).

'You'll never get back on the property ladder.'

No, probably not. So don't sell your house in Dublin or Dundalk until you are absolutely sure you won't want it ever again. In fact, if the property ladder is of concern to you, you should stay on it.

'Lovely country, France. Shame about the French.'

Are the French as unfriendly as rumour has it? Or might they miraculously become friendlier once you can understand what they're saying?

'Oh, you'll forget us and all your friends.'

No you won't. But they may forget you.

'Well, maybe you can live on baguettes and tomatoes.'

No, you can't. Do not for one moment delude yourself into thinking otherwise. France is not going to come cheap. There looms the awful possibility that, sooner or later, you may have to work at something. And that, when you do, you may be resented for taking the bread out of natives' mouths.

'Well, you can always watch *Eastenders* on satellite.'

Indeed you can. But why go all the way to France to do something you can do at home?

'Ooh, the weather will be lovely.'

Yes, it will. When there isn't a hurricane or an avalanche or a killer heatwave or floods or six feet of snow.

'Don't forget the Barry's tea and Chivers marmalade! Sliced pan and baked beans!'

Actually, you won't need to remember them, since all these items have spread like measles across the face of France. But ideally, you should forget them immediately. They are a state of mind. Mental handcuffs. Importing your home comforts is a kind of security blanket, maybe reassuring for a little while, but ultimately it puts you in a position of isolation and denial. If you crave your gastronomic ghetto, forget France.

'Oh God, you're not going *rustic*, are you? This isn't going to be one of those things about vineyards or olive groves or chickens? About Pépé's log cabin halfway up the Pyrenees, knitting your own pasta, that kind of thing?'

No, it isn't. Not one grape is going to be crushed anywhere in this story, not a single olive will be pressed into service. No crumbling chateau is going to be restored to its former glory, no clattering 2CV is going to trundle up with a honking goose in the back.

Even the plumbers, who traditionally trek through my life, and every book about France too, are out of the picture. (In any case, despite all those fabulous fountains, France's baffling plumbing problem would need a book to itself.) This story is simply about waking up in the mornings feeling alive and well. Enabling your soul to sing in its shower. Getting to know and love a foreign country, and maybe even some of those chilly, incomprehensible, infuriating people who inhabit it.

Nonetheless, there are those who, even after living in France for years, insist that the French are unfriendly. Getting to know them is, they allege, like trying to thaw an iceberg with a match – feasible, but slow. And it must be conceded that yes, French people are reserved. Polite, but not exactly rushing round with welcoming cakes and invitations to drinks at, oh, let's say six this evening?

There are also those who accuse them of snobbery. Pride, even vanity, in their language, history and culture. Few seem to notice the insecurity under the polished veneer, the nibbling fear that France might be lagging behind in the headlong rush to globalisation, to a safe, bland world where everything is standardised, pasteurised and homogenised. In fact, they are anxious almost to the point of paranoia, convinced that nobody loves them and that the future is a dark, deeply unsettling place. They *need* foreigners, if only to cheer them up and add to the gaiety of the nation. Not that there are any pubs (outside the towns) to offer convivial evenings; most villages are comatose by 8 PM, and rural social life is extremely family-centred. If you love your Rover's Return, you are unlikely to love rural France.

And yet, there is wonderful quality of life to be had, an elusive aura, that mysterious whiff of magic. I couldn't think of anywhere else I'd rather live, although I did democratically consider the alternatives for at least ten minutes. But memories of Spain involved roaring motorbikes, chaos and criminals, a loud harsh country with too many burger bars, anglophone golf clubs and a dodgy attitude towards animals. America offered no mystique, and anyway you'd want to be desperate to battle through all the bureaucracy involved in emigrating there. Portugal seemed to live exclusively on sardines. As for Italy . . . ah, *bella Italia!* But who could handle all that drama on a daily basis? Holland? Belgium? Germany? Austria? Denmark? Each has its own merits of course, only nobody ever seems to articulate them very persuasively. I couldn't imagine falling passionately in love with Denmark, pining for Austria, yearning piteously for Germany . . .

No, it had to be France. After Serge, I was ruined for anywhere else. But where, exactly, in France?

This is a major decision. It will dictate your lifestyle and there is a huge difference between, say, a farmhouse in the Ardèche and an apartment in the suburbs of Paris, a townhouse in Bordeaux or a *manoir* in Montpellier. Inland, or near the coast? City or countryside? Hot climate or cool? France offers a vast choice, and each region has its distinct topography, architecture, atmosphere, food, customs, even language. Fluent French isn't much use in Perpignan, where you'd be better off with Spanish. Celts bond well with Brittany, while Londoners might find Picardy deathly dull.

My first choice was the Languedoc, a southern area of earthy charm with an unspoilt coastline, near Provence but much cheaper. The poor man's Provence, you might say. But a recce trip revealed two flaws. The first was the weather: spectacularly violent storms, frequent floods, stifling summers and freezing winters. The other was inaccessibility: at the time, Ryanair wasn't yet flying direct to Carcassonne, and somehow I couldn't see my eighty-year-old mother sprinting round Stansted for her connections. If you have elderly relatives – or very young ones – you will want to be close to airports with direct flights to Ireland. (Unless, of course, the idea is to escape your family, as may sometimes be the case.)

Paris? No sea, no beach unless you count Paris-Plage in August, and they're even talking about dropping that. Nice? Too expensive, and it might get exhausting trying to swim while wearing all one's diamonds. Toulouse? Great, if you work in aviation and enjoy discussing it 24/7. Bordeaux? Very pretty, only the Atlantic can get rough and all that wine might prove addictive.

Wherever I might end up, I wanted it to be somewhere *healthy*. An area with lots of walking, cycling, swimming, tennis and so forth, to make up for the gym I would no longer be able to afford and never had time to use anyway. I'd spent a year teaching in Cambrai many moons before, but northern France is neither the most scenic nor the most exciting of regions. The Sologne, perhaps? This little-known area, heavily forested, lies just south of Orléans and has undeniable allure. As a student, I spent a summer there playing au pair to two little girls, one of whom I nearly killed.

That trip got off to a thrilling start. Arriving at Le Bourget airport, I was met by Lionel, the Parisien businessman whose daughters were to be my charges. I was eighteen and I was dazzled, drop-dead delighted by the beauty of Paris as he drove me to the family apartment in the fourteenth arrondissement where – *voilà!* – there turned out to be no wife or children whatsoever. With growing horror, I realised that mother had been right: this Frenchman was a serial killer or worse, intent on doing terminal damage to the young innocent he'd lured into his clutches.

When he invited me to a drink from the fridge, I guessed what the fridge was about to reveal: the severed heads of his previous victims, neatly lined up in Ziplock bags, labelled and dated like frozen steaks. Perhaps the French actually ate their victims, as they apparently ate just about everything else?

'And now,' Lionel murmured, handing me a glass of a dark and presumably lethal substance (grape juice, as it turned out), 'perhaps you would care to follow me through to the bedroom?'

Waah! No mobile phones then, no way to call daddy or anyone else to inform them that I'd fallen prey to the fate worse than death. 'Er,' I gulped, 'why would I want to do that?'

'Because,' he said, smiling reassuringly, 'there is a little balcony, and evening is falling, and Paris is at her most beautiful at dusk. You must see the Eiffel Tower lighting up. As the sun sets, it will start to glow.'

Reluctantly I followed him – unmolested, but surely any moment now – through his bedroom and out to the balcony, and there below me lay Paris. Shimmering in the silken summer dusk, the Eiffel Tower was slowly blushing gold as the sky turned mauve, the dome of Sacré Coeur glowing ghostly white on its hill far across the Seine.

And that was that. Dhunk! At one irrevocable stroke, I was in love, locked in for life. I no longer cared what this view might cost, what horrors Lionel might be lining up for me when the grape juice took effect. Paris had stunned me, seized me, and I knew I would adore it for the rest of my life, even if that should turn out to constitute only the next three minutes.

But no. Next day, Lionel drove me down to the family estate in the Sologne, where a wife, children and even grandparents were duly produced, and I was given a sturdy black bicycle. On that bike, over the long hot learning curve of that distant summer, I discovered the French countryside, the poppies and the poplars, the massive white bulls and the eternally chiming church spires – and the French language – all but beaten into me by Mémé after I'd inadvertently fed eggs to her tiny granddaughter, not grasping what she was trying to tell me, which was that the infant was violently allergic to them. After the ambulance sirens died down and we all eventually regained our powers of speech, by way of punishment she made me read Voltaire aloud for an hour every day up in the attic, a slow, exquisite torture to us both. But after I left her chateau and her miraculously intact family, a surprising thing happened.

I found that I hadn't left at all. Somehow my heart had stayed behind, hiding out in that dusty attic, cycling through the forests, whispering hopefully to itself as it awaited the day when, at last, France would finally be mine.

It would take nearly thirty years, but it would be well worth the wait. I was going to get some of that *bien être* at last, no matter what it might cost. After all, the old cologne brand of that name was still available, affordable and an enduring bestseller, which I took to be somehow symbolic.

2.

Buyer Beware

Yes, à la Peter Mayle, of course it all began with lunch.

'*Santé!*' beamed Natalie the estate agent, clinking her glass of Martini to mine. Ruby-red Martini, speared with green olives which, this glittering morning, might have been emeralds. 'I hope you will be very happy in your new home.'

Yes. I hoped so too. Fervently prayed so, the way you do when you've chucked your job, sold your house and burned your bridges with the pyromanic splendour of a routed general. It wasn't a question of hoping to be happy any more: it was a question of *having* to be happy, whether I was or not. France, I prayed, don't let me down. I've put my shirt on you.

Natalie was a fresh, lovely girl on that fresh, lovely February day, bouncy in her blue jeans and blonde ponytail. I was someone Old Enough to Know Better, dizzily watching her home, family, friends and pension plan spinning down the drain. 'Bonkers,' everyone was muttering, 'Soon come to her senses.'

The thing was, I *had* come to them. Smacked into them the way a car smacks into a brick wall, crashing through with debris flying in all directions. My father had died at fifty-six and I remembered people commenting on his having been 'so young' and 'missing out on so much'. But I also remembered thinking that 'missing out' depended on the pace at which, and the intensity with which, you lived. In Ireland, I'd increasingly felt that there had been no going forward; now, in Normandy, there would be no going back.

'*Santé!*' I replied serenely, and we settled into our window seats to wait for our pizzas, gazing out over a flurry of English Channel which, that enchanted day, was as azure as the Greek Aegean. Bouncing off the white-frilled water, two multicoloured windsurfers soared like butterflies, swirling, twirling, swooping high into the wave-splashed sky.

Only a month earlier, I had been trundling in monoxide-choked traffic and dirty rain to my grubby desk to exchange disgruntled mumbles with my equally disgruntled colleagues in a scruffy office in the middle of a scruffy city.

'I will,' I suddenly heard a voice informing Natalie, 'be as happy as a pig in proverbial. I will be blissed out. I plan, actually, to wallow in ecstasy.'

Natalie suppressed a tiny frown. 'That's good. You must be resolute. Because, you know, not every foreigner is happy in France. I do not know why' – her frown deepened, as if she had been abruptly confronted with a page of Euclid – 'but the drop-out rate is somewhere around 60 percent.'

Yes. So rumour had it. Language problems. Misunderstandings with builders. Avalanches of paperwork. Frosty neighbours. Unexpected storms that ripped roofs off houses and washed cars down to Spain. Mysterious multiple taxes. And more language problems.

'Natalie,' I said as a shaft of sunlight lit her face, 'this isn't a whim. Moving to France isn't just for Christmas; it's for life. I can survive, I promise you. And' (cue Gloria Gaynor) 'I *will* survive.'

Our pizzas arrived and Natalie gazed speculatively into hers. Of course, that must be what all the foreigners said, grinning like demented kids waving from the top of a water chute. 'Hey, watch me, here I come, I can swim!' Not a clue about getting in over their heads, or having to be rescued, or sinking without trace.

'*Eh bien*,' she replied, raising her knife over the angel's-wing pizza, 'in that case, *bon appétit*! And congratulations on finding your lovely new house!'

Guilt settled in my throat like a clove of raw garlic. It wasn't a lovely house and it wasn't even in the Languedoc, in fact it was in Normandy, at precisely the other end of the country. But yes, by French standards it was new. A mere twenty years old, centuries removed from the thatched, beamed cottage of my dreams. Granted, Normandy had plenty of thatched, beamed cottages and I'd visited several of them – only to discover that every last one of them needed at least six months in intensive care, by which time I might be in it myself. So, biting the bullet, I was contemplating buying this mundane modern house in a tiny hamlet which had a church, a primary school, a cemetery next door to the *salle des fêtes*, and precious little else. Up on a windy plateau, it was half an hour's walk to the nearest town, down a corkscrew hill – no, no public transport, unless you were prepared to don knee-socks and prevail upon the school bus driver. No, no *pâtisserie* for those hot croissants. No bar, no tabac, no butcher, baker or candlestick maker. No swimming pool, no cobbled square, no anything whatsoever actually, bar a gritty tennis court and a bulging blackbird atop the church weathervane, warbling his Pavarotti repertoire from six sharp to eight every evening. Surrounded by miles of flat fields (through which I fondly envisioned Thomas Hardy characters trudging, trailing their shawls in the mud – Roman Polanski filmed *Tess* here), the hamlet was as obscure as they came. 'Just perfect,' purred Natalie, 'for someone like you, seeking *la France profonde*.'

Well, it certainly was *profonde*. Nonetheless, Normandy had several critical advantages: a coastline, a good train service to Paris, pretty scenery, a ferry to England, and Beauvais airport only two hours away. It couldn't be further from the Languedoc, but somehow I felt it was right for me. But . . . oh, God. How, after she'd spent days driving me all over Normandy and treated me to this lovely lunch, was I going to tell Natalie that I could not buy the house from *her*?

French law decrees that buyers must purchase their house from the first estate agent who shows it to them. You have to sign a bond swearing allegiance. Sadly, Natalie was not the first agent who had shown this house to me. And, for all my confidence, I was not prepared to start my new life in a French courtroom, jauntily sticking it to the judge.

'Uh,' I gurgled, 'I hope you'll come to the house-warming party.'

She nodded that she would. But it was not to be. The next time I went looking for Natalie, her boss sourly snarled that she had left his employment. A French estate agent, beaten to the draw, bears startling similarity to a cuckolded husband. For the first time, I glimpsed a furious Frenchman. It was not a pretty sight.

But nothing could mar the memory of that first crystalline day, the day we sat looking out over the sea caressed by a breeze vibrant with hope, optimism and potential. This obscure little pizzeria, I silently promised myself, would be my haven; this was where I would hole up on rainy days, reading Flaubert in my window corner, making a Martini last four hours, scribbling notes as I played at being Colette. Hell, I might even buy a fountain pen.

French buyers don't get surveyors. Irish ones do. Eyebrows shot up when I produced mine. A little bumble-bee of a man, he danced up and down on all the bedroom floors before racing out to the front lawn, where he stood buzzing furiously.

'*Ah, non.* I am desolate, madame, but it is completely out of the question. You cannot buy this house.'

What? But why not? What's wrong with it? Okay, I know it's not high-spec like an Irish house, it doesn't have a jacuzzi or a brushed-steel Aga or any of this month's other accessories, and whoever floored the hall seems to have had very short arms. But it's *safe*, surely?

'Ah' – despairing sigh – 'it is the attic floor, madame. You hear how it creaks. It will not hold. All will collapse.'

Will it? But the vendors say they only put it in two years ago. It looks okay to me.

Stroking his chin, he inspected me speculatively. 'Tell me, madame, have you considered building a new house?'

No. I wanted to buy, not build, and I wanted to do it now. A buyer was ready to move into my house in Ireland and neither she nor I had decades to spare while builders started brewing pots of tea. I knew people who'd gone that route – 'Ooh, lovely, let's restore this old wreck and put in a pool' – and most of them were now sucking their thumbs, gently crooning to themselves in some secure institution.

Furthermore, this surveyor happened to work for a building firm. Seeds of doubt were starting to blossom in my mind – not about the house, but about him.

'Well, thank you for your verdict. I'll think about it.'

'Certainly, madame. That will be €400, *s'il vous plaît.*' Pursing his lips, he gave me a paper-thin smile.

Handing over payment with the cordite whiff of rip-off in the air, I got back in my rented car and drove to the nearby lake, where the thinking process was speeded by the prospect of the departing plane which, four hours hence, was to whisk me back to Ireland. A hitch had arisen in Ireland: at work, the union was objecting to my redundancy application. If the application fell through, so would my plan of making a new life in France. I had to get back to do battle.

So, let's decide about this house then, fast! It seemed to make sense. Four bedrooms, a tiny kitchen (curiously, for a nation that cooks so much but is allegedly allergic to hygiene, French kitchens are minuscule whereas bathrooms are vast), a living room, TV room, study, laundry and garage. Plus some kind of kids' playroom in the basement, two bathrooms for the impending hordes, and a *wine cellar*. And – an important consideration, this – a small, manageable garden. (In Normandy, you're lucky *not* to get a couple of dozen acres thrown in – many foreigners end up mowing lawns the size of Lichtenstein.) When I first arrived to view 'the product', as estate agents so callously call prospective homes, other viewers were already leaving, and by the time I was leaving more were arriving. Clearly, this house was going to sell fast. Plain as a pikestaff, it was nothing to write home about, but its price was affordable, barely half what I would get for my Irish house. At a stroke, I could be free of the mortgage that strangles so many lives like a noose.

But what about that attic? Would it really collapse? Might some visiting child crash down into the simmering *coq au vin* on the kitchen stove below? And . . . it didn't have termites, did it? I'd heard how they were marching up from the Midi, invading Normandy as the Nazis had done before, destroying all in their path.

Or moles? Evidence of moles was everywhere: they were busily rotovating Normandy as if nostalgic for Passchendaele. Rumour had it that one day all their tunnels would merge and France would collapse into a crater somewhere in the core of planet earth.

Or dry rot? Oh, please, not that. I'd heard about the the havoc dry rot could wreak with people's heads . . . but no. The house wasn't old enough to even contemplate that . . . or surely the surveyor would have said if it was?

As for that community centre nearby . . . it wasn't *that* near, was it? The Saturday-night parties wouldn't be audible, would they? Of course not! The French are so quiet, their idea of a party would be the Irish idea of a nap.

Then, of course, there was that nuclear power station. Ten kilometres away, but, still, not exactly a selling point. I reminded myself firmly of a friend's comment: 'But if it blows, you won't know anything about it! You'll be gone. Normandy will be gone. Most of Kent, Sussex, Brittany, Picardy and probably all of Belgium will be gone – so, don't worry about it!'

All right, then. I wouldn't worry about it. Especially as I had yet to learn that Normandy *does* worry about it, issuing iodine pastilles to all the local residents so that they don't choke on their tongues when – er, *if* – it does finally implode.

Which only left the gas tank, buried in the back garden. This was definitely ringing alarm bells. Over the years, the news from France had been frequently punctuated by gas explosions. Boum! A Lille apartment block! Boum! A Burgundy bank! Boum! A Biarritz hospital! Whatever official was in charge of explosions seemed to rotate them democratically around the country, albeit sadly failing to achieve the one everyone actually longed for . . . boum! A Paris tax office!

Would the next one have my name on it? Boum! A tiny Normandy hamlet? Foolhardy Irish optimist meets maker? Oh well, whatever would be, would be. After all, 9/11 demonstrated the folly of thinking oneself safe anywhere, even in steel-and-chrome, state-of-the-art Manhattan.

Nibbling my knuckles, I thought and thought, staring over the lovely tranquil lake. The lovely *deserted* lake. Where was everybody? Did they know something I didn't? For a nation credited with such a high sex drive, the French are not exactly thick on the ground. Maybe they were all crouching down in their basements, glued to the sudden news about the nuclear station? Serenely, a flotilla of ducks glided by as I pondered the dilemma and I gazed at them, wondering if maybe they could, uh, quack it?

Eventually, through the silence, the sound of engines began to throb in my inner ear. I could all but hear the engines of that plane, revving for take-off, departing for Dublin without me. If I wasn't on it, I might never get my redundancy, my 'parole'. Buying a house is not normally something to be rushed, but it was crunch time. Taking a breath, taking the plunge, I dug out my mobile phone and punched the digits.

'Pierre Yves? It's me. Oh, you can tell? My accent? Well, I've reached a decision. I'm buying that house. Yes, now. I'll be round to your office with the deposit in ten minutes.'

Pierre Yves was the estate agent who'd shown me the house just before Natalie did. A stocky chap with fluent English and a rugby-player's build, he was friendly, candid and locally respected by all accounts. Sheer luck had led me to him, and I liked him.

He sounded puzzled. 'But what about the surveyor? The attic floor?'

'Pierre Yves, that surveyor was trying to do what so many men try to do to so many women – bamboozle me. He wanted me to build a house with the building company he works for. If there was really any problem with that attic, you'd know, wouldn't you? The current owners would know. You would tell me, wouldn't you, so that there would be no subsequent little legal problems?'

That'll flush him out, I thought, if he's withholding any vital information. (This was in the days before disclosure legislation.) But he laughed.

'Yes, I would! My good reputation is essential to my business. But I assure you, there is no need to worry. The attic conversion was done by a reputable local builder who guarantees it for ten years.'

'Right. Then we have a deal. See you *toot sweet*.'

⁂

At last, the search was over. I wafted into Pierre Yves's office expecting to find him singing *Douce France*, maybe even waving a congratulatory bouquet of roses and a chilled bottle of champagne. Instead, a stack of papers sat on his desk. Not excessive, by French standards, not more than a couple of hundred. Let's whizz through them then, before I miss that plane!

'*Alors, juste une petite signature.*' Beaming, he produced a pen and I got to work, swiftly grasping the situation. '*Une petite signature*' is French for 'This will take hours. This is designed to defeat foreigners, to send off all but the most resolutely masochistic, swearing never to darken French soil again'. Doggedly, I signed, and signed, and signed.

'And now, about the transfer.'

Transfer? As in a Wayne Rooney, Manchester United sort of thing?

'The money. The price of the house.'

Oh. Yes, well, here's a deposit. I'll zap the rest over from Ireland as soon as I sort my redundancy deal and make arrangements with the bank.

'Zap? Madame, are you sure you have entirely grasped the nature of this transaction?'

He gazed at me imploringly, and for a terrible moment I faltered. Actually, Donald Duck might have a firmer grasp than I had on this transaction. This transition, which would turn me from a solvent, salaried worker bee into . . . what? If all went well with my redundancy deal, I would have a small financial cushion; if it didn't, I would have a large problem. House sold in Ireland, house bought in France, no job, no money . . . uh, quite a problem, actually.

Airily, I capped his pen. 'Here we are. All signed, sealed and delivered. I'll be back in May to sign the other couple of thousand documents. With truckloads of money, of course.'

With a nonchalant grin, I was out the door and scorching away to the airport. Behind me, there followed some remark about how it was time to call in the *notaire*. I am ashamed to say that I had only the haziest idea of what a *notaire* might be. All I knew, with a rush of adrenalin, was that France was going to happen, and it was going to be terrific.

Or as the French say, *terrible*.

'The middle of French nowhere? Not Paris or Cannes or Biarritz? Just some godforsaken little hamlet? Are you *mad*?'

Apparently. But then, who is to define madness? Some people spend thousands on a suit or a home cinema and consider themselves perfectly sane. Some people blow themselves up for the sake of their god. Some people drape their dogs in diamonds (true story, Paris, March 2008) without attracting the attention of the chaps in white coats. Some little lad with a big ego decides to invade Russia or attack New York, and millions of his compatriots think, hey, yeah, great idea! Some parents punish their children for telling the truth. People do all sorts of crazy things, or things which appear crazy to onlookers. They have their reasons, and who has a map of their minds or hearts? Moving to France barely scores at all on the scale of insanity, and for me, it was simply the right move at the right time. Reminding myself of the many reasons why I was doing this, I calmed down back in demented Dublin.

No more office politics. No more budget cuts. No more gridlock. No more bikers' helmets through windscreens. No more senseless shopping for toys I already had. No more endless discussions of property prices. No more getting up on wet, dark mornings to do somebody else's often incomprehensible bidding. No more radio headlines announcing that a man was kneecapped in Belfast last night. No more tribunals trawling through the murky dealings of disgraced politicians, at vast expense to the taxpayer. No more priests up on paedophilia charges. No more women missing, presumed murdered. No more shuddering on icy beaches in July. No more tacky 'reality' TV. Or a lot less of all these things, at any rate.

Hurray! In Ireland, for me if not for everyone, there was an increasing feeling of being in the wrong place at the wrong time. The pace of life was hurtling forward way too fast: children as young as ten were being expelled from school for sexually harassing their teachers, while children even younger were being bullied into nervous breakdowns if their clothes or mobile phone bore a brand name not approved by their peers. Yet the motto seemed to be 'Don't rock the boat', as if Ireland were a raft cresting a tidal wave. Sometimes it felt almost like a conspiracy of silence, a tacit pact that 'Ireland is a great little country and we won't hear a word to the contrary, whether it's true or not'.

But the truth was that Ireland was becoming a suburb of Hollywood, shrieking for attention, cutting some very dodgy deals, living on a knife-edge and suffering, collectively, from massive sleep deficit. None of it bore any resemblance to the Ireland I'd grown up in, and the country's strident new incarnation left me feeling like a fish out of water. The pressure to admire the emperor's new clothes was enormous, but I just couldn't do it.

Would France be better? Calmer, saner? It, too, was in flux at the beginning of the century, its pretty face showing some slight signs of strain. But I'd always felt that it was more than just a pretty face. I wasn't naive: naturally, France had its problems, but they seemed less acute, its attitude more adult, than that of brash, born-again Ireland. Per capita, the crime rate was much lower. Moving there wasn't a whim: I spoke the language reasonably well, loved the culture, the climate, the strong sense of identity, the still-slow pace of life. In France, you could park on the street, leaving the car unlocked while you popped into the *pâtisserie* for your croissant – no meter, no ticket, no hassle.

No income, either. No friends, bar my old college friend Sheila, long married to a French dentist. No pension, no security, no shoulder to cry on if things went wrong. No public transport, should I break a leg and be unable to drive out in the sticks. No laughs or *craic*, none of the irreverence that still sometimes made Ireland fun to live in. If the French have a fault, it is that they are mostly polite, earnest and quiet, with a slightly anxious streak. (Apart from Parisiens, who, as any French farmer will tell you, are the spawn of Satan.)

Nations do not adapt to newcomers. Newcomers, if they wish to join in, must adapt to them. With something of a clang, it struck me that I was about to join an ethnic minority. Without even the support of the Irish community, because I didn't intend to live in a ghetto, harking back to 'the old country', referring to Ireland as 'home', pining for a place that no longer existed. What, *moi*? Ha! I would become more French than the French, slugging black coffee and red wine, humming Brel under my garlic-scented breath. After all, I wasn't being deported. I was *choosing* France, an oasis of civilisation, the favourite refuge of painters and philosophers and anyone else weary of the madding crowd.

Long before Ireland started becoming rich, getting into debt and into trouble, Yeats wrote that 'romantic Ireland's dead and gone/ It's with O'Leary in the grave'. Now, it was time to find out how France was holding up. Would it still be romantic? Would Serge still sing for me? I wasn't wearing rose-tinted glasses, wasn't chasing rainbows or any other chimera; all I wanted was peace and quiet, and some kind of authenticity. It was time to get a life – a real one, stripped of varnish.

Could that be possible, a mere six hundred kilometres away from the country formerly known as 'home'?

What do people wish they'd known when buying a house in France? As anywhere, it's a case of *caveat emptor*. Make a mistake and it can ruin your life. Employing a surveyor is vital, to the point of flying over a trusted one from home if necessary. My French surveyor never mentioned local soil subsistence, which so far has only cracked a few pavements but is rumoured to be a potentially significant long-term problem. Even after researching the project for a year on the internet, I didn't know about the two local taxes, *foncière* and *habitation* (the equivalent of rates and poll tax), which can add up to a pretty penny. If you're buying anywhere near water, think floods and mosquitoes. If you're buying anything that's more than ten years old, think insulating, rewiring and radical redecorating. When it comes to price, ask your *notaire* for the cost of the house per square metre: nobody sticks to the exact centime, but it will give you an idea of the going rate. And yes, haggle. All the locals do, and the 10 percent you stand to save could cover legal fees. My estate agent Pierre Yves was horrified to hear that I'd paid my vendors €500 for their ride-on lawnmower: 'You should have said! I'd have bartered it into the price of the house!'

If you're brave and are building a new house, bear in mind that you're not allowed put in windows overlooking anyone else's property. If you opt for an apartment complex, remember the substantial management charges. In all cases, draw up a list of the ten things you want most in your house and area, aiming to score at least eight of them. After you move in, allow a full year, experiencing all four seasons before making any further major decisions. France isn't a puppy, to be abandoned the moment it barks or misbehaves; you have to give it a chance, get to know it and learn to handle it.

But if you see a cute hand-carved sign saying *route du sucre*, run for your life.

There is such a sign near my house. How sweet, I thought, to live on the 'sugar road'. I had no idea that what it would actually mean was hundreds of sugar-beet lorries trundling to the refinery, bang-thump-clatter, whole convoys of them starting at four in the morning, every day from Hallowe'en to Christmas.

You get used to it, of course. But not overnight. Even for the most committed francophile, living in France is an acquired art. It takes time, determination, and something our instant-gratification society has all but forgotten: patience.

No, indeed. The surveyor never mentioned that.

3.

Breaking Up is Hard to Do

'No,' said the union rep firmly, 'we can't let you go. Sorry. Not unless management agrees to replace you, which they are refusing to do. It's our job to keep staff numbers up. So you'll have to cancel France and stay here. Shame, but *c'est la vie.*'

Whaaat!? Stay here in this job, in this city, in this country, against my will? All because a union which had fought so hard to keep me out of my job twenty years before was now locking me into it? With difficulty, I resisted the urge to seize the fire extinguisher and do terminal damage to all concerned. After all, I could still leave. Simply walk away, without a penny.

'Look. I am halfway through selling my Irish house and buying a French one. Deposits have been paid. If you don't negotiate this redundancy deal, I . . . I . . . will do something *irreparable!*'

Only at that moment did it sink in how very, very badly I wanted to move to France. How fed up I was of office politics, of wrangling over everything. Morale was miserable, and management was all but counting the paperclips. What had once been a fun, interesting job now felt like a prison sentence – a sentence with nearly twenty years to run.

'Sorry, but negotiations have hit a wall. Stalemate. No go. Forget it.'

Tottering home, I burst into floods of tears, ripped open a bottle of wine and drank the lot.

≈

Weeks of despair ensued, thumping of tables, kicking of walls, ranting and raving. And frantic, futile efforts to negotiate. All I wanted was whatever I was entitled to, but my entire future lay in the hands of people who weren't interested, weren't listening. It was like being held hostage. For the first time in my life, I found myself sobbing in a doctor's surgery, begging a prescription for something to help with stress. A good, kind doctor of long experience, he said he had never in his career seen so many people so anxious to leave their jobs. It was an epidemic. 'Some are having breakdowns. At least you don't have children to worry about.'

No, at least there was that. It's much harder to quit your job and move to France on a fiver when little Annabelle is the linchpin of the school dancing team or your husband doesn't feel he can commute from Normandy to Dublin every Monday.

'Hang in,' said the doctor. 'It's a long road that has no turning.'

≈

And then, one night a month later with France still suspended, a miracle happened. A colleague phoned.

'You'll never guess.'

'What? Al-Qaeda has dropped a bomb on union HQ?'

'Even better. Madame X has won her case.'

Oh, wonderful! Madame X was a colleague who'd sued for con-
structive dismissal, alleging all kinds of harassment.

'She's been awarded a fortune in damages. And word is that
management is now keen to get rid of any other mad cows – er,
staff – who might start plotting similar legal action.'

'You mean . . . ?'

'Yes!'

Next morning, the phone rang again. Abruptly, I was invited to
meet with the personnel manager. Brightly, he beamed.

'So you see, we've sorted things with the union. You're free to
go. Sign this paperwork and you can have your redundancy cheque
right away.'

Two hours later, the bank was wiring all the money to Pierre
Yves in Normandy. At last, the struggle was over.

When you achieve something of this magnitude, the relief is
indescribable. And yet, there is a bittersweet thread binding it all
up. For me, it marked the end of two decades spent in a busy,
dynamic, finally frustrating but frequently fascinating job. Most of
those years had been good, some had been wonderful, the last few
were wretched. There were friends and there were enemies; so many
shared experiences, memories, panics, laughs, scoops, deadlines,
midnight oil, ones-that-got-away . . . and now, finally, it was all
over, the ties were cut and I had that falling-off-the-edge-of-a-cliff
feeling, plunging into an entirely new life with no salary and no
safety net should things go wrong.

If you are thinking of quitting your job, do not discount this
moment. Like divorce, it can be liberating, exhilarating and exceed-
ingly traumatic.

In a flurry, the packing was done. Friends rallied from right and left, doing so much so fast that no thanks seemed adequate. Just when I was about to leave the country it seemed to be suddenly reverting to the good, kind place it used to be, warm, helpful and generous. My lovely cousin Mary, devoting three days of her time to the packing project, finally popped a bottle of champagne and poured it into plastic cups, the kitchen being stripped of glasses.

'Here's to France, and your great new life there!'

Yes. Uh, hopefully. *Would* it be wonderful? Or would it all be too much, too foreign, too difficult, too lonely? As a child who'd spent two years in hospital, I'd learned early to fend for myself, but . . . still. Suddenly France seemed very far away, almost menacingly foreign.

There was a wobbly moment. Oh-God-what-am-I-doing wobbly. Then Mary smiled resolutely. 'Listen! I have spent three whole days packing your stuff, so you are going to love France if it kills you! If it kills *me*! I will be over to visit next month, and you'd better be up and running by then, I will be expecting frogs' legs for my dinner!'

Yes, ma'am. Very good, ma'am. It hit me that I was going to miss Mary, miss all my lovely friends, very much. Why was it so difficult to explain why I felt I had to leave, to discuss it all in depth?

'I'm going to rent you a car until you can buy one. That'll be your house-warming present.'

Crikey. People were being so incredibly kind. Even my elderly mother had battled her way into town to forage out a book called *Living & Working in France*, a colossally brave gesture given that her only daughter was 'emigrating', as she saw it. While France was only a short flight away, to her it was a den of foreign iniquity, and she was baffled as to why I would want to live there. Does everyone feel last-minute guilt and confusion before moving abroad? I certainly did, in spades.

And then the removals lorry was arriving, and everything right down to the blender (well, French ones might blend *differently*), was being hefted into it. I might have wept had one of the cheery lads not distracted me with a query about insurance. Everything was insured, wasn't it?

'Yes. Why?'

'Oh, it's just we had a client once whose stuff wasn't. He was moving to Spain and decided not to bother with insurance because everything was packed so tightly he reckoned nothing could break. He was right there. Nothing did break. Only the ship was in a collision, unfortunately, and sank to the bottom of the Irish Sea. With all its contents perfectly intact.'

Oh, horror! Oh *no*!

'Oh yes. His car. His furniture. His computer. His documents. His entire life. He rang the harbourmaster to demand that Dublin Bay be dredged and everything retrieved. The harbourmaster said: "Certainly sir, only that'll cost you about twenty million."'

Reverently, I kissed my worldly goods *au revoir* and wished them bon voyage. In three days' time, I would – hopefully – be reunited with them. My friend Anne, who happens to be a nurse, was coming too for moral support. I prayed that her professional services wouldn't be required.

A line from a song by Jean Ferrat floated into my mind: '*qu'une vie entière puisse se tenir dans la main.*' 'That an entire life can be held in the palm of a hand.' Unless you're moving house, in which case it can just about be crammed into a huge lorry, and costs twelve thousand euro to tote to Normandy, France.

Yes, twelve thousand euro. And that was only the start: legal fees, agency fees and sundry other costs at both ends brought the final cost of moving to an eye-watering thirty thousand euro. Do not underestimate what a new life abroad can cost, because at prices like these you can hardly afford to get it wrong.

❧

'The tea bags, ma'am. Where are they? We can't start without tea.'

Fair point. It is eight in the morning and the lorry has arrived at my new house, filling the entire street of the hamlet in which I sense phones already ringing and tongues wagging. *Our new foreign neighbour has arrived with the contents of a dozen department stores!* Amongst which, somewhere, there are tea bags. But where?

The lorry crew, three friendly, hefty chappies, look at me in a way that says hey, no problem, if you can't produce the Barry's tea we'll just wait here while you fly back to Dublin to get some more. In Ireland I rarely drank tea, but in France, bizarrely, it is to become an institution.

In lieu of tea, a revolution threatens to brew, but then Anne finds the tea and plugs the kettle into one of the kitchen's few electrical sockets. For a country that manufactures so much electricity (even selling it abroad), France is incredibly parsimonious with power, and entirely disapproves of multiple sockets. Far-sightedly, heroically, my mother had given me a parting gift of fifty multi-plug adaptors.

And then, leaving Anne to direct operations, I headed off to sign Pierre Yves's stack of 7,985 (or was it 9,875?) documents, all duly witnessed by the *notaire*. Normally seller and buyer share a solicitor in France, but who'd trust that? I'd got my own *notaire* who, unknown to either of us at the time, was to handle the purchase of many more houses by Irish buyers. Ireland, cresting its boom and snapping up foreign property, was not going to quite be as far away as I thought.

The paperwork complete, an urgent task awaited. A phone had to be installed. The idea of doing this immediately was presenting some difficulty to France Télécom, who seemed to feel that next December might be more convenient. After a preliminary skirmish with a reluctant official, I'd been handed a piece of paper with a number on it – to be contacted, I was told without a trace of irony, as soon as I could find a phone from which to ring it. So, barmily, I rang from my Irish mobile, and a man answered.

'Hello? It's about my phone. The man in the office gave me your number and told me to call you.'

'Eh?'

'My *phone*! I need it right now, today!'

'I am sorry, madame, but I cannot help you.'

'Oh, for heaven's sake, not more bureacracy! I spent hours yesterday in your office and now you say you still can't help. What kind of outfit are you running here?'

'I do not know, madame. Perhaps my wife could enlighten you.'

'Your wife? I don't want your wife! I want a phone! What is so difficult about that? What kind of dimwit can't supply a phone?'

'All I can tell you, madame, is that I am Monsiour Dupont, the dimwit vet.'

The . . . what? Oh no. Stuttering apologies, I realised I'd rung a wrong number and was indeed speaking to the local vet. Thank God I didn't have a poodle that needed putting down.

Under the circumstances, he was remarkably helpful. 'What you must do is go to your local *mairie*. They should be able to help you with Télécom.'

'Oh, right. I see. Er, thanks very much.'

'Not at all. It is a pleasure to help a foreign lady.'

Mortified, I returned home to find, as if by magic, the village mayor standing on the doorstep.

Well, hello, how nice! Have a cuppa! And the vet says you might be able to explain how one extracts a telephone from Télécom?

Chummily, blissfully unaware of the hostilities later to develop, he invited me round to his *mairie* where Télécom, he promised, would be tackled and conquered.

Forty minutes later, after Télécom's singing menu had apparently directed him via Japan to an asylum in Brazil, he slammed down the receiver.

'Dolts! Idiots! This is absolutely *scandaleux*! Normally France is a most efficient country. I cannot understand . . . '

No, nobody can. Only much later, after an ill-fitting, badly designed phone finally arrived ('No, sorry, we can't put an extension upstairs. Too difficult.') did I discover the full extent of the company's mythical powers. France Télécom can reduce grown men to tears. It can drive people out of business, out of the country, out of their minds. It can leave normally peaceable people contemplating new careers as suicide bombers. Nonetheless, up against increasingly stiff competition from private operators, it did make an effort with my new account. It invited me to nominate a 'favourite country' to which calls could be made at a reduced rate. Naturally, I nominated Ireland.

Shortly thereafter, written confirmation arrived. Télécom hoped I would be making many happy calls to my favourite country, Iceland.

૨૬

No, the beds didn't fall through the attic floors – or if they did, we were too tired to notice. Moving house, combined with country air as pure as cocaine, knocked Anne and myself virtually into a coma. We might be in it yet had we not been wakened one morning by a loud, insistent noise.

'Somebody's breaking bottles! Next door, in the neighbours' garden! Dozens of them!'

Crash, bang, smash . . . agog, we listened. It sounded as if the neighbours had had a massive party last night, and were now, for reasons unknown, hurling the empties onto their back patio. Impressed, we listened. Crash, crash, *crash!*

'Wow. That's an awful lot of bottles. Why would they be breaking them, d'you reckon?'

I had no idea, but as the noise continued intermittently throughout the day, an inevitable conclusion began to loom. My new neighbours, on whom I'd yet to clap eyes, were raving alcoholics, as well as rampaging louts. By nightfall, at least a hundred bottles had been smashed. Torn between horror and a kind of awestruck admiration, we were amazed, impressed, baffled and . . .

And then, belatedly, enlightenment dawned. Discreetly tucked away behind the neighbours' hedge, smothered in roses and clematis on the public side, lurked a bottle bank. It was passing drivers, not the neighbours, who were chucking in their empties.

'Well,' said Anne, grinning, 'if you can't beat them, you'll just have to join them.'

Oh, no. No way. First rule of ex-pat life in France: three or four bottles of wine a week, no more. With meals only. Much later, I met a British chap who, with considerable regret, was returning to Britain.

'It's either that,' he said sadly, 'or cirrhosis. I've got to get back to where a nice bottle of wine is a treat, not an item of furniture. France is ruining my health.'

But so far, it wasn't ruining mine. *Au contraire*. The sun was blazing, the country air intoxicating, and down in the basement the bikes awaited their first outing. It was time to go exploring.

❧

Where, and what, is Normandy?

George W. Bush isn't the only one to ask this kind of question. If it weren't for its D-Day beaches, the paintings of Monet, the novels of Victor Hugo and the gloomy Gustave Flaubert, nobody might ever have heard of this quiet, modest region of France, even though it's the size of Ireland and has roughly the same population of four million. Divided into five *départements* – the Eure and the Seine Maritime in Upper Normandy, the Calvados, the Orne and the Manche in Lower Normandy – it lies flat as a crêpe a hundred kilometres north-west of Paris, tranquilly producing the nation's barley, apples, cream, cider, lamb and (completely uncontroversial) veal. Stretching from Le Tréport in the east to Cherbourg in the west, gently riffled with forests and streams, it is almost in sight of Kent (on clear days you can see Dover from Calais, a little further up the coast), but it is conservatively, profoundly French, peppered with points from which William the Conqueror allegedly set out to teach the *rosbifs* a thing or two. Despite the hordes of day-tripping Brits now merrily stocking up on cheese and wine – and holiday homes – Normandy doesn't do tourism the way Provence does: little Dieppe will never rival Nice or Cannes for glamour. Only once a year, for the film festival in Deauville, does Normandy pick up its skirts and shake its booty. But even as Johnny Depp or Brad Pitt is cutting the festival ribbon, tractors continue to chug barely a mile away, inexorably ploughing, sowing and reaping the crops that are the region's livelihood. And its beauty. In summer, the corn is almost literally as high as an elephant's eye. Cars are swallowed up in it, lost between rolling golden waves, and cycling the tracks that bisect the fields is sheer, perfect pleasure. An honest, God-fearing region, in winter Normandy is asleep by ten o'clock and anyone who likes pubs, clubs or nightlife should factor in this crucial information. Not only can you not find a bottle of beer at night, you can't even find a bottle of milk. Normandy doesn't do 24/7. In fact, France as a whole doesn't really do it.

What Normandy *does* do, in spades, is peace and quiet. At first I thought there must be something wrong with me – nobody could possibly need so much sleep – but after a few weeks the truth dawned. I was drugged, completely zapped, by a new rhythm of life devoid of urban stress, a new environment unpolluted by car alarms, burglar alarms, screaming sirens, crammed buses or toxic fumes. Instead, the scarlet sun slipped silently below the horizon each evening, an owl hooted in the night, a church bell chimed midnight and all the village lights were extinguished on its stroke. It was, and is, like a time warp. Moving from an Irish city to the French countryside is like moving back in time fifty years. Like moving into one of Flaubert's novels, or a northerly version of Pagnol. With the exception of Rouen, Le Havre and the other large towns, where you stand a very faint chance of finding a can of Coke or a loaf of bread after dark, Normandy is for farmers and fishermen, for those who believe that 'early to bed, early to rise, makes a man healthy, wealthy and wise'. (The natives, who have a reputation similar to that of the Scots when it comes to money, are particularly keen on the 'wealthy' aspect of that adage.)

Inland, thatched longhouses far outnumber modern housing, black and white and beamed longhouses surrounded by slowly, thoughtfully chewing cattle. Remarkably *big* cattle, bison with horns like motorbike handlebars, huge white bulls built like tanks. Flirty little Friesians too, fat fluffy sheep strewn everywhere like scatter cushions, and the goats whose job it is to furnish Irish and British delicatessens with stunningly expensive cheese. About six weeks after I moved in, my neighbours' goats gave birth to a fine crop of kids, which I was invited to see, to touch and even to feed: it took a while to digest that this was reality, not a theme park, that there would be no admission fee or souvenir shop or notices banning chewing gum. No guided tour, since the farmer was busy farming, and no CCTV security systems, since goats are just goats, *non*?

And wild boar are just wild boar. As I was driving to the supermarket for groceries one morning, a massive boar sauntered across the road, tossing its tusks as if debating whether to engage in hostilities. All I could do was slam on the brakes, suddenly grasping why people carry stout sticks when they go walking in the forests. You would not want to be on the kebab end of those tusks. Red-eyed, the boar stared at me challengingly, fleetingly reminiscent of the aggressive biker in Dublin, only it was better behaved, it didn't swear or throw any missiles.

Gradually, you start geting used to Normandy's abundant flora and fauna. A stag leaps over the bonnet of your car and you say: 'Hey, *bonjour*, have a nice day!' A fox chases a mole through your garden and you callously hope the fox wins, because the damn moles are a plague. (They dig up everything, including tennis courts, swimming pools and airstrip runways.) A kestrel hovers for hours over a haystack, a fleet of moorhens launches into the lake, two swans chivvy their cygnets up the river, an otter darts for cover, a goose tries to chew through your shoe . . . I'm no David Attenborough, but you can't help enjoying it all, watching trans-fixed, sometimes for hours.

In summer, everything changes, the beaches rev up and the action moves to the coast. But as yet it was only May and I found the inactivity captivating: the silence, the moon, the web of lilac in the woods, all those empty, shuttered chateaux. Being near Paris, Normandy is a favoured retreat of wealthy Parisiens whose pleasure it is to maintain a little chateau or manor house for use in August, for a week's shooting at Christmas and a week's cycling at Easter; for the rest of the year they lie dormant, dust-sheeted, deserted. Unlike the sexier, ditsier chateaux of the Loire with their Disneyesque twirls and turrets, Normandy's castles are sombre, restrained and – to those of us who'd love one if it weren't for the soaring property taxes – a sorry waste. Usually in excellent condition, immaculately maintained, they command all the best views but are rarely enjoyed. They're rarely burgled either, although there has been the odd little incident. An Irish friend who bought a holiday home near my Normandy house was annoyed one day to find his bikes and lawnmower stolen by youths who had also helped themselves to his cornflakes for supper. 'But mind you, they did wash the bowls and spoons before leaving.'

Indeed. Normandy is very house-proud.

In summer, the fields sing with sherbet-sharp yellow rapeseed. In winter, the ploughed earth is the colour of chocolate, the texture of herringbone tweed. In June, for four or five magical days, Normandy billows blue with flax, each field labelled by the fashion house for whom the linen will be woven (Hermès owns the most), the edges blazing red with poppies. At seven each morning and evening, the angelus rings: Normandy is studded with abbeys and churches, all of which are illuminated at night. After just a few

weeks an electricity conservation drive reduced the glow of the village church steeple to a haze, but by then I could already identify it
in the dark by its silhouette. Why does the bell ring at seven, not
six? Because this working angelus marks the beginning and the end
of the labouring day (plus noon for lunch, of course), even if it's not
quite accurate in August. On hot August nights, tractors chug up
and down the fields through to dawn, working by the light of
their headlights, their steady nocturnal thrum wafting in the open
windows on the warm breeze . . . when my first batch of Irish
friends came to visit, they slept so soundly that I feared they were
dead.

'Wake us at seven,' they said. 'We want to go to the market.'

So I did. I knocked on their bedroom door, turned on the
radio, made coffee, knocked again, turned on the television, loudly
whizzed smoothies in the blender, knocked again, started up the
lawnmower . . .

Finally, at a quarter to one, they emerged, furious. 'We've
missed the market! You never called us!'

Call them? I was nearly calling the undertaker!

But then, people do sometimes die in strange ways in
Normandy. One of the unluckiest was the lorry driver who, shortly
after my arrival, plunged off one of the three huge bridges that span
the River Seine. I wasn't supposed to hear about this (I have vertigo,
and talk of such incidents is banned), but I wasn't surprised. It's
bound to happen when you have rainbow-height bridges arcing
across the sky, coupled with sometimes violent winds. Such is the
tremendous drop from the biggest bridge, the Pont de Normandie,
that you'd have quite a while to contemplate your fate, rather like a
parachutist who, in freefall, realises he's forgotten his parachute. A
French friend of mine, who also suffers from vertigo, has a strategy
for driving over the Pont de Normandie, the Pont de Tancarville

and the Pont de Brotonne: 'I always try to arrange myself on the inside.'

Lane, we keep telling him. You mean on the inside *lane*. No, he replies enigmatically, I just mean on the inside.

Hmm. Personally, I had to have a little chat with myself, and accept that living in Normandy means sometimes driving over huge bridges. Gradually, I learned to simply grip the wheel, shut my eyes and shoot across. Or take one of the ferries which, miraculously, still survive.

Like the bridges, Normandy's cliffs are fairly impressive. Unlike Dover's, they are not white but rusty and streaky: the 'Alabaster coast' is a bit of a misnomer, though I suppose the tourist board might take it amiss if I suggested a good scrub with a bottle of Cif. Monet often painted these cliffs, as did Pissarro, Sisley and pals. Should you wish to see them, hurry up, because they are eroding at a spectacular rate (the cliffs, that is). Any day now, Normandy will be down in Provence.

❧

Eventually, after a decent settling-in interval, Irish friends started arriving to inspect my new French abode. All of them, without exception, gasped and clapped their hands to their mouths in horror as we drove up to the plateau on which I live. Admittedly, it does look somewhat bare, maybe even bleak if you're arriving from semi-detached suburbia. It has a wide sweep of unhedged fields, a belt of tall trees and . . . well, not much else.

'But good grief, it's so isolated! Aren't you *scared*?'

No. I'm not. My plateau isn't half as scary as downtown Dublin. It's quiet and peaceful, and people can walk from one village to the next unmolested. Since I arrived, there has been only one crime: two middle-aged ladies, armed with scissors, snuck out one night and brazenly helped themselves to dozens of the football-sized hydrangeas that line the lanes. In late summer, Normandy foams with hydrangeas – pale pink, deep rose, baby blue, indigo, cream and pale pistachio. It is overwhelmingly tempting to liberate a few for one's living room.

Only you wouldn't want to start your new life in France on the wrong side of the law, would you? So I didn't nick any hydrangeas. Instead, I found a much more interesting way to get arrested.

4.

Summertime

A summer's day, every day. Real, hot, high summer. As if in welcome, the sun shone non-stop that first summer – a hot, steady sun I'd never known before. Every morning sparkled and beckoned, every ditch danced with poppies, every wall hummed with bees foraging in the lavender. It must be a fluke, I thought. It can't possibly get as hot as this, can it? Thirty-five sizzling degrees?

Mais oui, it could and it did. Several neighbours installed inflatable pools (to which I was never invited, the locals were not proving to be very friendly), the birds whistled nonchalantly and the rustic silence was punctuated by the steady *thwack* of tennis balls on racquets. The village tennis court was barely two minutes' walk from my house and I couldn't believe my luck – tennis, instead of work!

French sports facilities are excellent. Every self-respecting little village has its own tennis court and every town has a swimming pool which, in my case, was five minutes' drive away. There were riding stables, a lake with canoes, water-skiing, roller ramps, mini-golf, a basketball court, a bowling alley, a cinema, a theatre, a sailing school . . . all this within a ten-minute radius of the middle of nowhere.

But, in summer, best of all is the beach. Having grown up in Dublin with its many lovely beaches, I'd chosen a coastal region because I couldn't bear to live far from the sea. While many Norman beaches are stony, not sandy, as the temperature headed for forty degrees I was very glad I hadn't chosen Paris, or even the sweltering south which was reportedly 'melting'. Some people spend weeks painting, gardening and decorating when they move house, but not me: I was savouring the sun, and spending a lot of time at the beach. All day, actually, *every* day. It was near, it was free and it was scorching.

In summer, a French beach is a culture all of its own. Each one has its row of little beach huts, striped pink or blue or yellow or just plain white, varying from tiny wooden sheds up to spanking clap-board cabins into which townies move for the season, resolutely hanging lace curtains and planting geraniums. While monsieur commutes to work in the city, madame and the children set up camp on the coast – a Brittas Bay-type arrangement that often offers welcome breathing space to all concerned. Sometimes madame is *très élégante*, dripping in diamonds (literally, when she swims in them), her white bikini by Chanel or Dior, her tan per-fected last winter in the Alpine sunshine. Sometimes she carries a tiny Yorkie, its blonde fringe matching her own, tied up in a fetch-ing silk ribbon. More often than not, she will know all her neigh-bours on the waterfront, because the same families have owned the same cabins for generations. Or the same manor houses, discreetly screened behind vast banks of hydrangeas, immaculately manicured like their owners. While the children disport themselves on the beach – with no screeching or swearing, whether the family is installed in a cabin or a manor house – madame will draw her deckchair into the circle alongside those of her friends, rather like cowboys circling the wagons. Slicking on her sunblock, adjusting her hat, taking out her knitting, she settles in for a nice gentle gossip to work up an appetite for lunch. It is a timeless tableau, often painted by Corot, Sisley and such lads.

Ah, lunch at the seaside! No, it's not a bag of crisps or a can of Coke. It is a milestone, a marker in the day's mellow progress, a retreat under a fluttering parasol while the sun is at its zenith. Dozens of little seafood bistros fringe the waterfront, and from mid-morning the air begins to suffuse with the aroma of chargrilled prawns, sea bass and sole. In Normandy, the classic dish is mussels steamed in cider or white wine, with just a soupçon of cream . . . but first, an aperitif perhaps?

Of course you can have a gin and tonic or whatever you like bar sherry, of which France has never heard. But trust me, what you want is a kir: a little dose of fruit liqueur, topped up with still or sparkling white wine. It didn't take long to discover that my favourites were lavender, *violette*, raspberry and cherry, and that I could knock them back like lemonade. With nibbles, of course – maybe a handful of nuts, olives or minuscule salt crackers. But you're only allowed your aperitif after you've had your swim, showered (all the beaches have showers) and run a kilometre in the sun to dry off. This is one of the many ways in which French women contrive to keep their *silhouette*. And the taste of that kir, out in the open sea air, is bliss.

And now – come along, *les enfants*! – we will stroll the length of the promenade, choosing our restaurant, which we can afford every day of the holidays because the set menu is only ten euro. We will leave our beach gear where it is, since nobody ever steals it, and we will embark en masse with our friends to study each menu in detail, inhaling the aroma of sizzling seafood before, finally, choosing the bistro that offers the best *rapport qualité/prix*. Yes, of course they can seat four mothers and six children, just push these tables together! Odile, put on your T-shirt, you know swimsuits are not allowed at table!

And thus summer's noon ritual begins. France is *à table*, eating fish brought in by the trawlers barely an hour ago, sold straight off the deck. Not, of course, that everyone goes to a bistro: for those who prefer to picnic, there is always a little stall selling hot dogs, pancakes and the most delicious ice creams (the saltwater toffee flavour should be illegal). And there are those who bring their own supplies: big cooler chests filled with baguettes, roast chicken, fruit and wine, all elaborately laid out on the sand or stones, shaded by a drunkenly angled parasol. Not that anyone ever gets drunk. A glass or two of wine – as much as is necessary to lubricate lunch – and no more. After all, madame wishes to be wide awake for her game of cards with her chums this afternoon, or her mini-golf, or perhaps monsieur will join her at one of the giant outdoor chess sets while the children have their windsurfing lesson.

As summer progressed, the regular beach bums started getting to know each other, and I gradually found myself becoming part of a group congregating at the east end of the beach. Mostly teachers with months of leisure time looming ahead of them, taking turns to mind each other's children while the others went in to swim, they seemed friendly. At first, we didn't know each other at all; then we began to recognise each other, to nod *bonjour* on arrival each morning, to exchange pleasantries, share sunblock, move our beach mats closer together – and, gradually, to bond. By the end of the summer, we even knew the restaurateurs, distinguishing the friendly from the fierce, the ones who put their prices up for the tourists from the ones who didn't. It was only sporadic, casual social contact, but still . . . I began to think that making friends might not be quite as difficult as I had been given to understand.

Back home, the house was strewn with half-unpacked suitcases, the cellar stacked sky-high with crates, everything shouting for attention. But what's the point of moving to a sunny climate if you're not going to enjoy it? If it was available on prescription, this spa treatment would cost a fortune. No deadlines, no traffic jams, no shrilling phones . . . all over the world, millions of stressed-out people would give anything for this simple, blissful freedom. To lie on the beach browsing a book, inhaling lungfuls of salt air, living at their own pace. Often, my mind drifted from my book, and I found myself simply staring out to sea, devoting hours to the study of passing clouds. Decompressing, deep breathing, shrugging off years of stress, without a single pang of guilt.

But, as anywhere, some people create their own stress. As summer wore on I began to meet some of my new neighbours, and noted a marked difference between those raring to get to the beach and those who would love to go if only they didn't have the kitchen to clean, the furniture to dust and all that ironing to do. 'Get a life', I sometimes wanted to shout, *carpe diem*! One glorious sunny day I found a neighbour closeted in her basement, ironing her bath towels, looking frazzled and shocked when I suggested going to the beach: ironing rates very high on France's list of priorities. No, of course monsieur couldn't go to the beach either, he had the lawn to mow, and the hedge to trim! Tweaking the garden into a mini-Versailles – often with the aid of a measuring tape – rates high too. Leaving them to it, I went back to the beautiful, sparkling blue sea.

In the late summer afternoons, after lunch, a little snooze and another swim, the beach takes on a different aspect. The soaring windsurfers, blithe and colourful as dragonflies, fold their wings and return to shore, leaving the rock pools at ebb tide to the shrimp-fishers silhouetted against the scarlet sky in their waders, trawling their huge nets through the shallows. Vast triangles on long sticks, the shrimp nets weigh a ton when full, requiring much skill in the handling if you are not to become unbalanced and be flung into the waves, inhaling half the English Channel as you vanish. Sometimes, as the sun was setting, I watched fathers taking their small sons by the hand, leading them into the water, teaching them how to hold their miniature nets at just the right angle. The boys scooping up their booty of shellfish with whoops of glee were a lovely sight, peaceful and timeless, and I never tired of it, thinking what a pleasure it was to see parents and children enjoying each other without any electronic hardware coming between them.

Meanwhile, one must make the most of *la saison*, which for the French means July and August only. A curious notion, when you come from a country that endlessly seeks new ways to prolong the tourist season, but France doesn't do golf tournaments or murder weekends or girlie jaunts or any other such spring or autumn events: everything opens up on 1 July and closes down on 31 August and that's that – even if 31 August falls on a blazing weekend with thousands of tourists around. Not only are parasols packed up and shops shuttered, entire restaurants are dismantled until there remains only a wooden deck where, you could have sworn, people were tucking into lobster only yesterday. In September, no matter how nice the weather, the only people to be found on the beaches are foreigners and pensioners, and too bad if they fancy a *barquette* of chips or a blackcurrant kir.

'Sorry, closed!' is one of France's favourite expressions. This is not a country to move to if you are a believer in Sunday shopping, in picking up a pizza at eleven o'clock at night or buying your Christmas decorations in April. France has seasons, and summer is summer, and *voilà*! After you get over the shock, you wouldn't have it any other way. It's reassuring to know where you stand, refreshing to see each season segueing into the next, changing not only weather and clothing but mood, menu and tempo.

Not that I was finished with summer just yet. It was bliss to be in shorts every day, to be swimming and tanning and feeling wildly healthy. My long-crocked ankle, swollen from a botched ligament problem years before, shrank back to its original size thanks to all the swimming and walking on pebbles. (They act, a physiotherapist told me, like a Japanese foot massage.) And besides, my new life as a layabout had lots more to offer.

∗

Sunday morning, a quarter to five. The sun is rising, a skein of mist evaporating off the . . . oh my God, look look look!

Overnight, the fields surrounding the house have morphed from green to blue. Miles and miles of the most perfect baby blue with the palest mauve undertone, gently undulating in the morning air. Stunned by the silent beauty of the spectacle, I gaze down from my bedroom window (on tiptoe, it's a dormer) at this miracle.

It's the flax. The future linen, destined to sashay down the cat-walks of Paris, signed Dior, Givenchy, Hermès or Chanel. I have never seen it in its raw state before, but here it is, growing literally under my nose, reaching the peak of perfection for just five brief, enchanting days. *Acres* of it, everywhere. The entire landscape is blue and the shade of blue changes depending on the sun and cloud and wind, deepening to steel, lightening to lilac, snuggling back to baby blue. Of course, everyone had been talking since late May about how 'it must come any day now', but it was still a shock when it did, and I was transfixed; it looked as if the sea had moved inland and was lapping at my garden gate.

The bike, I thought frantically. Let's get up and go cycling through the fields right now. It will be stunning. Let's take the camera and send everyone photos of this lovely morning. (Indeed, it was lucky for them that I didn't have a camera phone, or they would have been awakened to incoming photos at four in the morning – beep beep beep, look, the linen's in bloom!)

Moments later I was pedalling away, waved off by a hooting owl, greeted by an enormous hare flying through the fields, wrapped in silence until suddenly – whoosh! – I almost fell off the bike in shock as something shot past.

It was a team of cyclists. A very big team, a whole club out on a dawn run. Sheathed in multicoloured Lycra, they flew past like arrows, hundreds of them it seemed, green, red, yellow and purple, all grinning at my little old Raleigh.

'Bonjour madame' – b'jour – b'jour – b'jour.' Every last one of them said hello, fortunately not seeming to expect individual replies as I waved back, laughing as they streamed away into the distance. France loves cycling, especially on Sundays, but I'd had no idea they did it in such numbers at such an unearthly hour, sweating, helmeted, legs pumping like pistons.

Such muscles! And was it really possible to get that thin? They looked like a flurry of whippets as they receded into the distance. Pedalling on, savouring the pure air, I plunged deeper into the flax-filled landscape, bouncing along unmade tracks, realising for the first time that flax grows shoulder-high, that the petals are heart-shaped, that the undergrowth is a deep tangle of lime-green tendrils. Blue heaven, indeed . . . for a long while I met nobody, thought of nothing, simply enjoying the rhythm of the whirring wheels, picking up the distant sound of a church bell, then another, tolling across the fields as the sun hauled itself out of bed and high into the sky.

Dawn! I hadn't been up at dawn for years, except to totter out of a taxi from an occasional party or stagger to the airport for some red-eye flight. Dawn had certainly never been a voluntary option for getting up, much less going out . . . yet here I was, loving it. All alone, in the middle of nowhere, feeling more awake and alive than I had for years. Here and there, where the fields of flax gave way to dairy farming, cows lay folded on their forelegs, serenely chewing the cud, their fringes falling into their eyes, little black Friesian heifers and massive white Limousin bulls, all peacefully munching the meadow flowers. It was like cycling through a film by Jean-Luc Godard, only minus Gérard Dépardieu. (Dépardieu normally appears in every French film, there seems to be a law that says they can't make one without him.)

And then suddenly – oh my God! – two vast Doberman dogs, barking and slavering, galloping the length of a wooden fence, their fangs inches from my legs. Cycling in flat, pretty Normandy is a joy, but it's a joy much diluted by the guard dogs who have, apparently, all done assertiveness-training courses. Bengal tigers could hardly sound more savage or look more terrifying. Hastily, I pedalled on, my heart pounding as I hit Olympic speed.

Eventually, calm was restored and, a few miles on, I came to a chateau, grey and stately, surrounded by a sweeping lawn, turrets rising from its roof, fading wisteria swagging every window. Normandy is festooned with wisteria in early summer, swathed and scented in it, its flowers sometimes white but more often mauve, giving the landscape the blurred look of a palette on which an artist has been mixing colours. I'd plant some wisteria myself, I thought, if it weren't so very slow-growing: if you want a mature one, you need to plant it when you're five.

Curiously, I got off the bike and approached the chateau. Clearly it belonged, like so many others, to wealthy Parisiens, their 75-reg yellow Beetle parked in the drive (plus, probably, a couple of discreet black Mercedes in the garage.) The shutters were open, indicating early risers within, and a white canvas gazebo stood on the lawn, sheltering a table on which a white tablecloth was draped for breakfast. Slowing alongside the railings for a closer view, I could see every ingredient of a tourism brochure: the pot of jam (apricot, no doubt), the careless jug of pink roses, the silver coffee pot and – as I watched – madame emerging in a languid dressing gown, ruffled and trailing, baguette in hand. Transfixed, I waited for Gérard Dépardieu to appear behind her.

But it wasn't Dépardieu. It was another Doberman, rocketing straight towards me, snarling and drooling in such a frenzy that I seized the bike and fled, madame's voice carrying on the air behind me. 'Don't worry! He's only a pet. Perfectly harmless! Can't get over the railings!'

It was nice of her, considering that I'd been snooping, but the dog's snout was already level with the spikes as it flailed to get out. In a flash, I realised why French cyclists are all such boy racers. They need to be. No wonder the crime rate is so low.

⁂

Normandy is big-sky country and I intended to explore all five *départments* before venturing further afield: west to Brittany, east to Picardy, south to the Loire, 'where the sun starts'. But it couldn't have been any sunnier here, which left me somehow sidetracked, unable to get beyond the beach or, in the cooler evenings, as far as the bike would take me. Without the slightest effort, or even thought, I'd lost six kilos in six weeks, my skin was glowing and I was feeling ten years younger. In the heat, meals were minimal: melons scooped out and filled with raspberries, salads composed of whatever looked good at the market – curly lettuce, corn, radishes, chicken, cucumber, juicy tomatoes, it scarcely mattered what.

Nothing seemed to matter. Every evening, the air was pungent with the aroma of merguez sausages sizzling on barbecues, smoke curling through the trees of the neighbours' houses. Sometimes, missing my friends, I wondered if they might invite me in for a beer, but they never did. Never mind. Later, when I got round to it, I would throw a little house-warming party . . . vaguely, I was conscious that in the autumn I should start making a more serious effort to build a social circle, but for now I just couldn't seem to get up the energy. In fact, it was a challenge even to pick up the phone to the people I knew back in Ireland. I seemed to be turning into some kind of happy hermit.

Meanwhile, the bike beckoned. Because there are no hedges in upper Normandy, you can see for miles as you cycle along, the horizon is huge and the roads are virtually empty. Four times the size of Britain, with the same population, France considers itself underpopulated (the government constantly begging people to have more babies), and the sense of space is almost swamping. After about eight in the evening, not a soul stirs in the villages, the silence reverberates and you wonder, where do they all go?

Certainly not to the pub, which closes around seven. Nor to the shops: ditto. No kids hang out on the streets, no televisions blare, there is absolutely nothing of the Spanish *paseo* about it. In summer, the Normans simply sit out in their back gardens, tucked up leafy laneways out of sight, murmuring amongst themselves as they polish off the last of the rosé. Parents, children, friends, grandparents . . . the French love a good family gathering, but it's very rarely noisy. As I cycled along, weaving my way amidst the duck ponds, the sheep, the geese and the cows, it was almost like looking at a still life, a tableau frozen in time. Would it always be thus? Or would France, some day, wake up with a bang? I was reminded of the Ireland of my childhood, but look how that had changed . . .

despite its timeless aura, could France really stay suspended in aspic?

Selfishly, I wished it could, and would. It was utterly beautiful and, day by day, I was falling more and more in love with it. Out in the countryside, the stripy longhouses were drenched in apple blossom; in the snoozing hamlets, only the occasional chugging tractor broke the silence as the farmers harvested their hay all night long, the somnolent sound of it a veritable lullaby. In the fishing villages, things were livelier on summer nights, yachts and trawlers coming and going, tourists eating out around the harbours where you could, if you wanted, get a beer any time up to ten or eleven.

But France is not by nature nocturnal. Because of the shutters, house lights are not even visible, and much of the municipal lighting is switched off at midnight. The nights are very dark, netted with stars; after a while, I learned to identify Orion, the Dagger, the Plough, the diamond-bright planets of Mars and Venus, and many more (probably including a few satellites by mistake). Gazing up at it all, I felt that same falling-in-love feeling I'd had when I first heard the music of Serge Reggiani, and wondered whether France might be the one really rewarding, lasting love of my life.

When I stopped star-gazing I binged on the view of the church steeple at twilight, the hazy fields at dawn, and the daylong muffled *thwack* of tennis balls. I loved returning from a long cycle in the scarlet dregs of sunset, sunburnt, aching, ready to drop into the deepest sleep I'd ever experienced. (The country air was having a startlingly soporific effect on visiting friends, too, one of whom sat dreamily down one day on a non-existent chair.) I loved the growing feeling of owning my own life, of establishing a rhythm dictated not by deadlines but by nature. So far, France was doing exactly what it said on the tin.

But two small jobs had to be done. Every evening, I had to

phone at least one friend in Ireland, because it is vitally important to keep up your contacts. One of the first things any emigrant over the age of twenty-five learns is that the friends of a lifetime can never be replicated, and should be treasured. The calls were funny: apparently Irish weather had improved out of all recognition since I'd left. Instantly, everybody informed me what a 'glorious' day it was. Ireland and France seemed inexplicably locked in competition to see who had the hottest, sunniest, most fabulous weather, Ireland was winning hands down and I soon learned to keep Normandy's thirty-five degrees out of the conversation. After all, if it was hotter now, it might well be a lot colder come winter. People often enquired solicitously whether I was missing 'home', and it seemed so churlish to say 'no' that I dissimulated. But the truth was that I wasn't: there were simply too many new things clamouring for my attention. Despite their languor, the days seemed to zip by like bullets, even if I couldn't explain where they all went.

My other job was to watch the news on French television. No matter how remote reality seemed, no matter that my interest in bombs, tornadoes, crashes and crimes seemed to be flagging alarmingly: it had to be done, because television is a sure-fire way of learning, or improving, your French. Tons of vocabulary, clearly pronounced and illustrated – you can't go wrong. Doggedly, I listened to the newsreaders bleating on, picking up all kinds of useful new terms like 'armoured' and 'bankrupt' and 'up in smoke'. Much of southern France was indeed up in smoke that summer, razed by forest fires – something not to be overlooked if you are thinking of going to live in the south. (In winter, torrential floods take over – one Irish friend had to be winched from his rented house by helicopter.)

And so to bed. Oh my God, I forgot to put on the burglar alarm!

No you didn't. You don't have a burglar alarm.

But how can anyone live without one? In Ireland, I couldn't.

But you can here. Nobody has one. So just relax and go to sleep.

And so I did go to sleep, and did relax, and did gradually forget all about the burglar alarm, lulled instead by the hooting of an owl and the creaking of the upstairs floorboards, which despite the surveyor's dire predictions were still stoutly holding up.

Eh bien. So far, so good. The attic was proving resilient – unlike the one in the house bought by some Irish friends who came to visit, fell in love with the area, and promptly bought a house near Etretat. As monsieur was cooking supper one evening there was a crash overhead, and he looked up to see his wife's leg plunging like a dagger through the kitchen ceiling.

5.

Bag Lady

I have been very bad. I have disgraced my country. I have been nicked for shoplifting. Nicked for nicking a jerrycan. And nicked again for vagrancy. Nicked twice, in one day.

I didn't mean to do it, your honour. All I meant to do was go out and buy a car, because no matter how bohemian a life you think you're living in deepest France, certain practicalities remain. Obviously, one needs a car to go whizzing round France to have one's first wrangles with the 89,000 officials in charge of one's phone, water, electricity and so forth. So it was time to return the rental car and buy one: only that presented the problem of how to reach the car showroom to pick up one's spanking new Renault.

Luckily, my Irish friend Sheila, who's married to a Frenchman, was crucially helpful in volunteering to drive me to the car show-room. So we returned the rental car and, checking to see if I'd left anything in it, I found this big red plastic jerrycan in the boot. I'd bought it a few days earlier in a hypermarket, intending to fill it with petrol for the lawnmower, and then forgotten it. Unused, it was still tagged, barcode and all. So I took it out and tucked it under my arm, and we set off to collect the new car. Only the car wasn't ready, was it? Wouldn't be ready for another two hours, would it?

This presented a difficulty for Sheila, who had urgent business elsewhere. So, very kindly, she dropped me at a nearby shopping mall only five hundred metres away, where I could amuse myself until the lovely new car was ready.

So off she went and in I went to the vast hypermarket, the same one where I'd bought the jerrycan three days before. This time I didn't buy anything. I simply browsed for an hour or two – the place was the size of Laois – before leaving empty-handed.

Well, not quite empty-handed, because I was still carrying the bright red jerrycan, albeit without much thinking about it, as it had by now become part of the picture. Which was why a security man raced after me as I left the premises, roaring and bawling.

'Eh, you! Oi! Stop!'

Huh? Who, *moi*?

Yes, me. Next thing there were two of them, one growling into a walkie-talkie as if I'd tried to assassinate the president, the other suggesting I had failed to pay for my purchase. Oh no, I explained, I bought it three days ago, actually . . . but naturally he didn't believe me, since the wretched thing still had its price tag and bar code on. (I know, not smart.) Since people don't normally return to a shop with the same thing they bought last Tuesday, tote it round the store, and then carry it back out, this tale cut little ice with security.

Never mind, I said, I paid by credit card. Here, let me show you the receipt. But what with trying to juggle the jerrycan, my hand-bag, my wallet and a fistful of receipts, I dropped everything and all the bits of paper (including a few hundred euro, I might add) blew away on the unluckily stiff breeze. So, after something of a pantomime and a bit of a breakdown in *entente cordiale*, I was frogmarched back into the shop and up to the manager's office, feeling like some nitwit on *Candid Camera*.

It was a long and surprisingly gruelling interrogation. Not far off Gestapo standard, actually. Finally, I was let go on the basis of being Irish – an apparently mitigating factor although I'm not sure why – on condition I never nick another big red jerrycan. Feeling somewhat drained, I then set off for the car showroom . . . only to find a bridge in the way. A short bridge, but a very high one, with lots of traffic teeming miles below.

Well, I have vertigo, don't I? Really bad vertigo. It's not my fault and I can't help it. I just can't walk across bridges, is all. I did try to cross this one, but as soon as I set foot on it, it started to sway and I got all dizzy. Couldn't continue, even though I could see the car premises from where I stood.

So there I remained, immobilised, clutching my jerrycan, conscious of not looking my best in the howling gale and lashing rain. After a while, it dawned on me that the only way to get across this bridge was to hitch. To stick out my thumb and look pitiful (not difficult), in the hope that some kind soul might pick me up and ferry me across.

Eventually, someone did pick me up. Only it wasn't a kind soul, it was the cops. What was I doing? Where was I going? Didn't I know it was both dangerous and illegal to hitch here? Name, rank, serial number, please? Feeling an absolutely prize idiot, I explained my dilemma.

Next thing – I swear I'm not making this up – they bundled me into the back of their Black Maria (or 'salad basket', as the French call it), as if I'd been caught planting a sizzling stick of dynamite in the Élysée Palace. Very scary. And then they drove me across the bridge, to be sprung from captivity right outside the office of the salesman who was selling me the car. Unfortunately, its wall was glass, so he saw the cops, uh, helping me out. With my jerrycan. He did not look like a happy camper. He even stopped talking on the mobile phone to which he had been surgically attached since . . . well, since birth, I think. His jaw dropped and I could guess what was racing through his mind: 'My customer is a bag lady whose cheque has bounced . . . Interpol . . . long history of fraud, vagrancy, theft . . . '

Oh no, I hastened to reassure him, I could explain the red jerrycan. And the cops and the salad basket. Really. Finally, the police released me into his clutches, and I eagerly went to take possession of my new car. Ah, *mais non*, madame. Stop right there. There is a tiny problem.

Oh no, what *now*?

My paperwork. Alas, the 876 documents necessary to the purchase of a car in France had been turned down by the local gendarmerie. No, no reason had been given; perhaps because I'm Irish (a mitigating factor only minutes earlier)? Or perhaps the fact of simply not being French is now a crime in its own right? Yes, my application for a *carte grise* was accompanied by my passport, driving licence, residence permit, insurance certificate and deeds of the new house, but this has not been sufficient. I must have forgotten to include my late tortoise's death certificate.

So now what? Here I am a hundred kilometres from home, with no transport. What am I to do – move in and live here in the showroom?

Well. Hmm. The salesman thought about it. And then inspiration struck. Why not nip into a different town and present my documents at the *sous-préfecture* there, perhaps it would be more accommodating? If I hurried, that was, because the nearest alternative *sous-préfecture* would be closing in . . . oh, in fifteen minutes actually. I pointed out that – albeit motivated as I was – I might have some difficulty in walking eleven kilometres in fifteen minutes. Briefly, we gazed at each other, perplexed. And then, whipping out a set of keys, he said he would lend me a car to go there. Hurry, hurry!

So I put the boot down. I fairly blazed a track to that *sous-préfecture* and, when the guard on duty started to close the gates in my face, I said some regrettably unladylike things. Yes, in French. I hadn't realised I'd got so fluent so fast. But then, it hardly mattered, since everyone seemed to think I was a bag lady anyway.

Inside, the clerk looked at her watch and said oh, what a pity. Sorry, too late, just closing. Whereupon I explained that I was stranded and, if she did not process my paperwork *now*, I would unfortunately be obliged to torch France. Yes, set it alight and watch with glee while the whole wretched shambles burned to a cinder.

She said she could get me arrested for using threatening language. I said I'd already been arrested. She started to look anxious. I said I would sit down on the floor and stay the night. Stay as many nights as it might take. After all, I had nowhere else to go and no way of getting there.

Oh, very well then. She would let me in just this once, 'but don't make a habit of it, madame'.

No, I don't buy a car every day, actually, so I am unlikely to make a habit of visiting *sous-préfectures*. Finally, with that pained look every French clerk perfects over the years, the woman processed my papers and, at last, I got my car. Driving home in it, shattered, I felt cheated of the joy of a first drive in a new car, and had a kind of premonitory feeling: would every dealing of a bureaucratic nature prove as arduous as this one? (*Yes*, was to be the resounding answer.)

Next day, however, a happier prospect beckoned. I was invited to lunch by my estate agent Pierre Yves at his rustic home, the first French home to which I had been invited. He presented his charming family, adorable miniature macaroons and elegant Earl Grey tea, tablecloths billowed in the sunlight, infants gambolled and a delightful time was had by all – until I went to leave, got into the car, and found it wouldn't start. In all the flurry of the previous day, I hadn't registered a word the salesman had said about the immobiliser, or what you had to do to deactivate it. The engine was stone dead and the car sat on Pierre Yves's manicured lawn on strike, refusing to budge.

No, you don't want to hear the rest. Honestly. Trust me. I *am* to be trusted, actually – as I assured the next policeman to pull me in, barely a week later.

This time, the crime was unarguable. Driving without a seatbelt. The *flic* took out his notebook, and I took out my explanation. As I was reversing out of a parking space, you see, barely a hundred metres back, a motorbike scorched up behind the car and gave me such a fright I forgot to put on the seatbelt . . .

Pen poised, the cop considered. And then spotted a second crime. An 'IRL' sticker on the back window. French cars are not supposed to carry foreign stickers. Between that and the seatbelt, the fine was rocketing rapidly and yes, they do take credit cards.

'But,' I pleaded, 'I'm Irish' (uncertain by now whether this was an advantage or a handicap.)

Whereupon the cop looked hard at me and said something unexpected. 'Well, you'll be watching the match tonight then, will you?'

Eh? What match? Desperately, I nodded.

'Right,' he said. 'If France beats Ireland, I'll let you off. But if Ireland beats France, you'll have to come to the gendarmerie tomorrow morning with two hundred euro, madame.'

Which is how I treacherously came to pray for the defeat of my own country, and discovered that yes, prayer does work.

> ❦

Some time has now gone by. I've got a part-time job teaching English, which has been great for getting to know people locally. Everyone says they now recognise the little green Renault on sight, with its 'IRL' sticker merrily waving from the back window. (Why? I never thought I had a chauvinistic bone in my body, but there you go: moving abroad teaches you things about yourself you never suspected. Plus, the sticker is vital for identifying the car in those hypermarket car parks the size of Kerry which, as I have discovered, can contain thousands of identical Renaults.)

So the little green Renault zips around to and fro until – waahh! One day some man, who seems slightly detached from reality, drives into the back of it in the hypermarket car park. Big dent. He gazes at it.

'What dent? I don't see any dent. There is no dent.'

And he gets back into his own car and drives off. I have his reg number, so I pursue him, but to no avail. He simply ignores all contact, and the police say 'Ah, useless, forget it.' Eventually, I have to get the damage repaired myself, thereby losing my no-claims bonus, which teaches me a valuable lesson: if, as a foreigner, you are involved in a fracas in France, expect little justice, if any.

Scarcely is the dent repaired than – waahh! again – a speeding red sports car shoots through a crossroads, whirls my little green Renault away to the left, catapults me fifty metres down a road on which I had not planned to travel and slams to a standstill with a terrible thud. One of those resounding thuds that silences everyone in the recognition that we have missed death by a millimetre.

The driver and his three passengers get out. All British soldiers, they are en route back from the races at Le Mans to the ferry at Dieppe. The front of their car is badly crumpled, and so they whip out tool kits and get stuck in, apparently quite confident of fixing it. I sit on a ditch at the side of the road, gazing at the little green Renault, which looks as if it has gone ten rounds with a sumo wrestler. Eventually, two cops arrive, tutting about the nuisance of having to come out to an accident in which nobody has been killed.

The soldiers start chatting up the lady cop, who is young, blonde and good-looking. She smiles back. Soon they are all having a great old time. My services as interpreter are requested. Soon everyone is shouting in stereo. They are all extremely put out when, without warning or explanation, I burst into tears.

'Don't dramatise yourself,' admonishes the lady cop. 'Nobody died. It's only a question of panel-beating.'

I experience a very strong desire to panel-beat *her*.

The other cop whips out a notebook. Ignoring the English lads, he turns to me. 'You have committed an offence, madame. Here's your ticket. You have three days to pay the fine.'

Eh? I am being fined because a speeding car has crashed into mine?

'Yes. Priority to the right, you see. That's the rule in France.'

But how could I give priority to a speeding car, especially one rendered invisible by a field of ten-foot-high barley? I was doing barely thirty kilometres an hour and it was doing at least three times that . . .

'Save your breath, madame. Priority is *always* to the right.'

Never forget this when driving in France. If you're coming from the right, you're in the right. You can do anything you like. You can shoot out into mainstream traffic, killing everyone in your path, and you're still in the right. No matter how wrong you might be,

you're still right. Very handy, unless of course you're on the receiving end of the rule, which I reckon was specifically invented for the
frustration of foreigners.

Next day, I was black and blue. The car was in intensive care.
My bank balance was reeling from the impact of yet another claim,
plus the news that the insurance excess would now be doubled for
four years and the premiums would go stratospheric.

So, I may well end up a bag lady yet. Soon, I might not be
hitching over bridges but sleeping under them, with a red jerrycan
for a pillow.

6.

Meet the Folks

At twenty, you think you can save the world. At forty, somebody else will just have to save it while you save your own life. Sigh.

Mornings are best. Those pearly June mornings when, getting up at a time of your own choosing, you reach the beach sometime around ten, park your stuff on the *galets* (pebbles) and pick your way in jelly shoes to the water's edge. The colour of the water varies from milky turquoise through brilliant blue to steely grey, and its temperature rarely goes above twenty degrees, so that even on the hottest day you plunge in with a little gasp. But once you're in, it's very hard to get out. Uncrowded, unpolluted, the water becomes a cocoon, almost womb-like, and a lot of accumulated stress, mental and physical, was washed away as I swam and swam, serenely, my mind emptying of absolutely everything. If I wished, I could keep on swimming until sunset; there were absolutely no other demands on my time and I began to appreciate why France sets so much store on *la liberté*. To anyone debating leaping off a treadmill, I'd say yes, do it. Do it *now*. Run for your life! Leisure is one of life's most underrated luxuries. After so many hectic years, you have to learn to savour it, to let go of the instinct to fuss, to dash on to the next thing – but you can learn. You can simply empty your mind of all the junk, and relax. You can learn to say 'hey, no sweat'.

But even a beach bum has to earn her lunch. If she doesn't work it off, she might start having difficulty fitting into her little swim-suit. And so, in the afternoons, I got into the habit of walking for an hour, exactly as the health gurus say you should if only anyone ever had the time.

Walking, in the milky valleys of coastal Normandy, can be as energetic as you like, with plenty of cliffs to climb for those who enjoy slogging up cliffs. However, having vertigo, and also now being officially a layabout, I struck out on the flat, leafy tracks through the fields and salt marshes, slowly strolling amidst the roly-poly cows and sheep, often following the meandering path of some little river in which, every now and then, fish jumped for joy. I often felt like jumping for joy myself: never had I felt so fit and healthy, in body and in mind. Later, I was astonished to be asked whether I didn't feel vulnerable on these solitary walks. *Au con-traire*, the concept of danger never entered my head. Was this incredibly stupid of me? All I can say is that I *felt* safe, sensed no danger whatsoever. Invariably, the few other ramblers I met would nod and say *bonjour* and, out in the bright sunshine, it all felt absurdly innocent. Frequently I got lost, and worried not a jot: sooner or later there would be a ramshackle old farmhouse, with somebody out in the garden shelling peas or spraying roses, who would indicate the way back to the beach with a friendly smile.

Phew. Even if they weren't very fast walks, they were long ones, and by the time I reached the sea again it might be three or four o'clock, time to get back in the water. Glinting water, now, with the sun beating down, the children's sailing school in full flow as the dinghies ventured out like ducklings, roped together, their doll-size sails a joyous blur of pink and blue and green, the kiddies' whoops whirling away on the wind. (Mind you, the monitors are strict, shouting instructions through a megaphone, and woe betide the child that can't tell its sheets from its cleats.)

All this air and exercise was working wonders, and so was the battery-charging solitude. Sometimes it was even difficult to artic-ulate properly when friends rang to talk about what was happening in Dublin, London or New York: they seemed to be speaking about some other planet, one I definitely knew I'd visited but only distantly remembered. My tongue seemed somehow stapled to my tonsils, and conversations filled up with puzzling voids.

But of course it couldn't go on. Sooner or later, one must start meeting people and making friends. Not as easy in France as in some countries but, eventually, essential. So, how do you go about it, where do you start?

First and foremost, you seek out a *fête champetre*, the commu-nal outdoor meal hosted by most villages, on a weekend rota basis, in summer. Any fool can find one, and when you do you simply plough your way through the dust to the smouldering barbecue, buy your *frites*, and sit down on a battered old bench at a long wooden table. Amongst the forty or fifty people sitting around this table, there will almost certainly be somebody who speaks English. Somebody who, in fact, may well seize you by the lapels, burst into tears and start sobbing with gratitude: at last, a voice from home!

Not that you want to live in an English-speaking ghetto (because then you'd have stayed at home, *n'est-ce pas?*), but at least now you've got somebody to bitch to about the French, until you're suf-ficiently fluent to bitch to them face-to-face. Surprisingly, they won't take offence when you do, because there's nothing most French people enjoy more than running themselves into the ground. One week, the front cover of *L'Express* magazine posed the question: 'Should we be ashamed to be French?' Sad – tragic, actually – but despite their beautiful country, the French are congenitally convinced that every other country in Europe is passing them out like Ferraris at Le Mans. (If this is the case, long may it last.)

Another sure-fire social contact is the *brocante*, or flea market, also held on a weekend rota basis. Mooching amidst the stalls, dusting off old dolls and sepia photographs of *papa militaire*, you hear not just English but Dutch, Danish, German . . . take your pick, there's always someone dying to chat. Through the *brocante* I began to meet lots of people, hear gossip, develop contacts and gradually blend into a little cluster of people who liked to gather in various gardens for apéritifs on rose-tinted evenings.

And then, one day as summer was yielding to autumn, I saw an ad in the local newspaper. 'Come join our cookery class', it chirped. So I did. The group consisted of about a dozen women, mostly overweight – unusual in France – and strangely silent, plus one man with a cap and a cigarette permanently dangling from his lip. The dishes all seemed to be made with the cheapest of generic ingredients, and something about the atmosphere was oddly lugubrious. It took a couple of ponderous sessions before I realised I'd unwittingly strayed into a 'social rehabilitation' group for people with long-term problems, in obligatory pursuit of a new skill to qualify for their grants. The day the instructor asked what I did for a living, and I replied 'write', I saw horror etch itself all over her face, and knew without another word being exchanged that my relationship with this group was doomed. Still, at least I learned new ways with walnuts, blackberries and mushrooms, apples and pumpkins, all the hedgerow bounty we were encouraged to gather 'for free'. Unlike the Irish with their 'it-can't-cost-enough' attitude, the French love anything free and anything that grows wild: one Sunday, I was invited to lunch by French-Irish friends and the entrée was a huge aromatic dish of mushrooms, simmered in butter and garlic, richly redolent of the forest. They tasted as good as they smelled, and everyone purred in appreciation.

'I'm glad you like them,' said our host, beaming. 'I gathered them in the woods just this morning.'

Oh, really? There was a thoughtful pause, forks aloft as we, his guests, digested this, peering at the mushrooms to ascertain what kind they were. Are *trompettes de la mort* (trumpets of death) black, or yellow? We couldn't quite remember. Hmm . . . had he got the pharmacist to pick them over (the normal safeguard), in case any might be poisonous?

No, he hadn't. And it was too late to start fussing, since we'd all swallowed some by then. Happily, we lived to tell the tale. (Just don't try this at home.)

And then, one October evening when the sheep stood statue-still, shawled in mist, a leaflet arrived. The village festival committee was looking for new members. Normally I loathe committees, but I decided to join this one, if only for a short time, to find out more about the local community.

Next thing, at the end of the very first meeting in the village hall – a converted stable block – I found myself voted in charge of organising the caterer for a Spanish night. Like most French villages, ours has a *salle des fêtes* fully equipped for throwing parties, and the caterer was to do paella for a hundred people. 'There's a great caterer near Dieppe,' someone airily said, and this was how I discovered that French phone books are listed in a kind of geographic code: unless you know precisely which town or village someone lives in, you will find it almost impossible to find their number. Finding that caterer's number was like trying to find Osama bin Laden's.

But finally we ended up with delicious, albeit expensive, paella. My proposal of sangria to go with it was shot down: 'We will have kir,' the committee declared, and that was that. When it comes to food and drink, a foreigner is never going to win in France. Giving in gracefully – well, gritting my teeth but saying nothing – I got to know the other people in charge of music and assorted logistics over the several weeks it took to prepare the event. As always, there were some natural organisers, some of those people who love committees for the petty power, some old diehards as well as several blow-ins like myself, who simply wanted to get acquainted. For a tiny village, it was turning out to be surprisingly cosmopolitan: there was a shy couple from Madagascar, a laid-back Dutchman and his half-Finnish wife, a friendly Polish couple, a Parisien couple new to the area, a young goat farmer and a fervent National Front supporter. Between us, we spoke four languages, but worked together in French.

This wasn't school French or even college French. It was zippy, slangy, everyday French and I came home from those meetings exhausted, not by the agenda but by the sheer concentration required. Sometimes I misunderstood, failed to get a joke or had to have things repeated and – while everyone was cordial, especially over drinks at the end of each session – nobody was particularly patient. But why should they be? If every meeting was to be held up while each new word was painstakingly explained to me, we'd be there all night. It would be neither fair nor reasonable to expect the French to converse at my rusty pace, any more than an Irish committee would slow down for a French blow-in. So I battled on, catapulted from summer's silence to autumn's brisk agenda, and as paella night drew nigh, acquaintances slowly began to form.

Marian, the Polish woodworker, was especially likeable. Discovering a common interest in table tennis, we began to play regularly on the table that is part of the communal furniture in virtually every village. Natalie, the Parisienne, invited me to join an aqua-gym class on Saturday mornings at the local pool, where I met

Gabrielle the sculptor . . . and so, slowly but surely, a small circle began to blossom. Naturally, not everybody would turn out to be a bosom buddy, but the seeds of a social life were undoubtedly being sown.

Even if your French is fluent, making friends in France is not easy. My pal Sheila, long married to her Frenchman, confided that it took her several years to start making 'real, proper friends'. After a lot of effort, out-reaching and intensive work on her level of linguistic fluency, she finally cracked it the day her child was old enough to enrol in the local school. But even if you're lucky enough to have ice-breaking children, you still have to be prepared to take the initiative, to wade in no matter how horrible a hash you might make of things and to be less choosy about whom you befriend than you might be 'at home'.

'But,' Natalie unexpectedly said one day, 'you Irish have an advantage. You're extroverts. You'll talk to anyone about anything. The British are more reserved, and so they have a harder time. Some of them seem to be almost prisoners in their homes. They never mix with us.'

Later, as I began to meet the unsuspected hordes of Britons who quietly lurked in the area, I realised the truth of this. One Englishman could barely say 'Hello, my name is Joe' after a full decade in France. Another chap bellowed at all the local shopkeepers in English, terrifying them with his ferocity while his incredibly shy wife refused to join any of the local language classes, insisting that she'd never be any good. (Anyone who says this never will be.) Rather than socialise with the French, they mostly socialised with each other, unable to go to the cinema or theatre, to parties or barbecues or even to church, unable to read the newspapers or local advertisements or participate in community activities, missing out on the very fabric of French life. Some did try to learn French, and a few chirpy stalwarts managed to join in activities without it, but others spent much of their time watching the BBC, clinging to *The Antiques Roadshow* for dear life. One day, I was having a cup of tea with one of them when the phone rang and she gazed at it, visibly terrified. 'I can't answer! Can't talk to these people in French! They speak way too fast!'

Not true. The French don't talk faster than anyone else. They have not hatched a plot to defeat the anglophones. They simply have normal conversations at normal speed and, if you don't learn to keep up, you will find life in France quite maddening. Many of those who give up and sell up, returning 'home' with tales of how they hate France, hate it chiefly because they can't communicate.

Meanwhile, paella night was fast approaching. Tickets were selling well, musicians were engaged, and, the day before, a dozen of us set up the trestle tables, decorated the *salle des fêtes* and had a fun time dissing the local mayor, whom I was discovering to be unpopular. His plan to build social housing on the village's only green space, which was currently used by the children for football, would harden over the years into an out-and-out feud. In turn, nobody was discovering much about me, because the French are sanguine about the foreigners who fetch up on their doorstep, and not remotely interested in why you'd choose to live in their midst. Personally, I found this refreshing – constant explanation of your motives must get as tedious as does constantly having to spell your name – but if you're the kind of person who loves attention, be warned. In France, you will not be the star of the show.

And so paella night arrived, and was fun, and very hard work. No matter how local the event, no matter how cheap the tickets, the French expect value for money, high culinary standards and better service than is often the case in restaurants. We were run off our feet. Some of those who attended were gracious and pleasant, others were demanding to the point of rude, and I learned a lot from it. Once regularly waited upon in Irish restaurants, now it was my turn to do the waiting, and I felt like a CEO demoted to tea lady. But what mattered was the teamwork, the chance to take part in local life at last, to burrow another centimetre under France's skin. At the end of the night, when the dancing had finally died down at around two in the morning, somebody produced a bottle of calvados and we toasted our communal success.

'And now,' beamed Natalie, 'you must come to my birthday party next Saturday night. You must meet my boyfriend and all my friends.'

And so one party began to lead to another, and those first vital contacts were forged. The first time somebody recognised me at the market, said a cheery *bonjour* and had a brief chat about the rocketing price of vegetables, I felt elated out of all proportion. It was a milestone. Ditto, the first time the phone rang and the caller was French. Slowly, a door was creaking open.

However, the neighbours remained cool. In addition to the ones on the right, with whom there was growing hostility over matters horticultural, I'd had to implore the ones on the left to do something about their honking goose. The creature was huge, and trumpeted like a mating elephant from dusk to dawn. It had ended up in a casserole, and its *maman* and *papa* had been sulking ever since.

'And besides, didn't you know?' somebody finally explained one day, shedding light on what had been, until then, a murky mystery. 'Single people are viewed with immense suspicion by French spouses. They think you're out to steal their partners.'

Eh? Are they so easily stolen? By someone who's scarcely even noticed them, could barely tell one from the other? Amazed and amused to find myself cast in the role of femme fatale, I tried to explain that all I wanted was a circle of friends with whom I could hang out and have fun. But French men don't socialise with single women (Ireland is much more relaxed about this), and French women don't gossip or giggle like Irish women, don't go off on girly trips or shopping jaunts or enjoy nearly as much freedom: even after their children have grown up and gone, they devote a great deal of time to their homes and husbands. The idea of Thelma-and-Louise days out was received with baffled or anxious frowns, and it took far longer than I had anticipated to grow a circle of girlfriends. Years, in fact. By then, I'd been forced to eat my words and start socialising with other anglophones – who, it must be conceded, were less stiff and often a lot more fun.

However, if the French are slow to make friends, maybe that's because they're judicious, very loyal once solid relationships have been tested and forged. So, taking their time, they began to ask me to occasional drinks, between which we might not have any contact for months. That said, such evenings were always enjoyable, the cocktails invariably stylish and charming – and then six months might go by before we met again.

Between these encounters, I was starting to discover the many ways foreigners have of winkling each other out. Ex-pats often put up a notice on the board in the local supermarket to the effect that, at Café Sympa next Thursday evening, books will be swopped between those who like to read in English (or Italian, German, whatever). And, although nightlife is limited in rural France, there is always a class of some kind. Somehow, word of my existence had reached a nearby town, where I was asked to give English classes, and although I became friendly with only two of the twenty students in the group, they became delightful friends and introduced me to others. And then, one day in a local antique shop, the proprietor grinned at myself and Rita, the new Irish friend I'd recently made. (After thirteen years in Normandy, she was delighted to meet her first ever Irish neighbour and, incredibly, we discovered we'd grown up only three miles apart in Dublin, even knew some of the same people there.)

'Ah, the Irish ladies! You are no longer alone here, *mesdames*. Did you know that an Irishman has bought the little white house just up the road?'

No, we didn't. Dashing off to the house in question, we found it deserted, but we decided to drop a little note of welcome in the letterbox. Not that being Irish was any guarantee of empathy, but hey, let's at least get together for a cup of tea some day and say hello?

Next thing, a beaming chap from Malahide was standing on my front lawn, pumping my hand. 'Hello, I'm Ken! My wife is back at the house. It's our new holiday home. I've come to invite you to our house-warming barbecue.' And down he sat, to pour out his life story over the next two hilarious hours. As we laughed at his anecdotes, I was forced to admit the truth of experience over optimism: the Irish are definitely more spontaneous than the French. Warmer, wittier, and wonderfully anarchic. On first acquaintance, we chatted in a completely irreverent way that the French would consider appalling. Hurray! Now I could have Irish friends without actually having to live in the seething cauldron that was Ireland, where the Celtic Tiger was still roaring its head off.

But this didn't preclude enjoying French friends too, who have their own positive attributes: maturity, constancy, sometimes great erudition. They are arguably deeper and more philosophical. But it was only when I gave in and decided that a mixture of the two was permissible that life really started to rev up.

If you think you'd love to live in France, do a little self-survey. Are you gregarious? Do you like a game of pool over a pint in the evening? Do you enjoy a fun day out with the girls or guys? Do you pop in to your neighbours for a cuppa? If you're ill, will somebody call round to see how you're doing? Do you often drop in to the nearest Texaco at night for milk or cigarettes?

If your answers are mostly yes, then you are likely to find French society challenging. Fond visions of a romantic thatched wreck half a mile up a dirt track, with only a fistful of chickens for company, should promptly be revised. France isn't just a country, it's a state of mind. A state of mind reached by few before the age of forty, and even then only by those who genuinely enjoy their own company, since things sink into somnolence once the holiday homes have been locked up for winter.

If somnolence is not for you, maybe it's time to reconsider Marbella.

7.

Here is the Snooze

In *la France profonde*, winter separates the amateurs from the pros. Anyone can do summer, gambolling on beaches, playing tennis, eating cherries and drinking rosé, but winter takes a streak of steel. The beach cafés shut down and the sugar-beet trucks rev up, trundling through the night, keeping you wide awake until you become attuned to their rhythm, if you ever do. But there is an infallible French cure for insomnia: the evening news. Just switch it on at eight, snuggle down with Claire Chazal and . . . zzz.

Claire is the longest-running newsreader since her former lover Patrick Poivre d'Arvor (PPDA, as he's known) was suddenly sacked. An institution on TF1 – the French equivalent of Ken Hammond on RTÉ – PPDA made the headlines himself when he was slapped with a P45 and replaced overnight by a peppy young blonde, appropriately called Laurence Ferrari. But during my first winter in France he was still cosily ensconced, reading the news as if it were a bedtime story. The French loved his 'fireside' style of newsreading, but it came as a shock to me. I was bewildered. Nothing – explosions, tsunamis, riots, hurricanes – sounded in the least urgent. At weekends, Patrick was replaced by the mother of his child, the equally soporific Claire. Both of them looked and sounded as if they might be reciting recipes for apple pie. Frequently, I dozed off and missed the whole thing – although there are those who claim you can learn a language even in your sleep.

Of course, you can catch up with the news on BBC, Sky, or any of the English-language satellite channels. So sometimes I surreptitiously switched channels, to stare open-mouthed at whoever was reading the news in London, sounding by comparison as if they were being chased by a rabid Rottweiler. It was like swapping a Morris Minor for a Lexus. I could only assume that Patrick and Claire had been warned that foreigners were watching TF1 and that they'd better speak s-l-o-w-l-y, whereas Sky and the BBC expected foreigners to wake up and keep up, you layabouts!

When my French started getting zippier I switched to TF2, where the younger news anchor, David Pujadas, was undoubtedly livelier. David was notorious for the drama of his debut, which happened to be on 11 September 2001, a day that kept poor David shut into his new studio without so much as a coffee break for something like eighteen hours non-stop. His weekend colleagues, Béatrice Schönberg and the dazzlingly beautiful Carole Gaessler, were also lively – but, while they managed to stay awake, they didn't seem to be doing what journalists were supposed to do: grilling their prey for supper.

Coming from a country where it is the practice for journalists to give politicians a very tough time – preferably not allowing them to speak at all – I was mystified by the sheer politeness of David, Carole and Béatrice. David interviewed Jacques Chirac and actually listened to him. Let him *finish his sentences*, without interrupting. His style was thorough, but almost deferential. And then Béatrice interviewed Prince Albert of Monaco.

Until then, I'd only ever seen Béatrice from the neck up. Tonight, she was entirely visible, dressed in a frilly blouse, cutesy little skirt, sexy high heels and an, um, beatific smile. Simpering at 'Monsignor', as she respectfully addressed him, she gently fed Albert each question like a marshmallow, nodding sympathetically at his responses and looking as if she might at any minute pat his sweet little hand. But still 'Monsignor' prefaced almost every answer with '*Écoutez, madame . . .* ' – and that was exactly what Madame Schönberg obediently did. Packing all the punch of a budgie, she looked more like a flirty femme fatale than a senior journalist, and I was reminded of the time Jeremy Paxman interviewed Bill Gates for the BBC, lost his bottle in the face of such a big name and – in my opinion – blew the whole thing.

However, nobody else seemed to find fault with Béatrice's interview, which by French standards was perfectly *normale*. Why would Béatrice, or indeed anybody, want to give Prince Albert a hard time? Would he have been given a hard time on Irish television? Yes, I asserted, he would. If Miriam O'Callaghan had conducted that interview the way Béatrice Schönberg conducted it, *Prime Time* would be deluged with howls of protest. Did nobody think that Béatrice had flirted with the prince, or that he'd toyed with her?

Puzzled frowns. Scratching of heads. *Eh oui*, perhaps Béatrice had been *un peu coquette*, but why not? After all, she's an attractive woman and . . . well. Gallic shrugs and knowing grins all round.

And that was the point at which the penny dropped. In France, a pretty face excuses pretty well anything. Romance lurks everywhere. Subtle, sexy undertones, spicing up the news which would otherwise be so depressing, *non*? Viewers enjoy Béatrice's good looks (and David Pujadas's and Laurence Ferrari's) they savour the fact that PPDA had a doubtlessly delicious liaison with Claire Chazal and, if Claire is now dating a new hunk, hey, for many viewers *that's* the real news!

Officially, France proclaims itself to be above gossip about the private lives of public figures. Libel laws are tight and nobody admits to reading populist magazines such as *Gala* or *Hello!* But sales figures indicate that somebody's reading stacks of them, zillions. I've never seen any French journalist fillet an interviewee the way Adam Bolton or John Bowman could fillet them, but then they're not required to; their first duty is to look good, sound soothing, provoke nobody and, ideally, be photographed cavorting on the beaches of Nice or holding hands in Rome, hitting the headlines when they're not reading them.

In the face of such a soporific system, one can start to lose one's grip on world affairs. I found myself losing track of who had cheated, raped or assassinated whom and instead started foraging deeper into French cultural affairs. Despite increasing dumbing-down and large doses of American-style violence, there are still some fine programmes on French television. While *Bouillon de Culture* was axed (bring back Bernard!) *Thalassa* remains intact after thirty years. Every Friday night Georges Pernoud sets sail, taking his legions of viewers fishing in Senegal or factory-trawling in Russia, diving for sea urchins off Guadeloupe – anything and everything to do with the sea. Should cuddly Georges ever fail to wish his fans *bon vent* with that cheery salute of his, French civilisation might well collapse. A satirical song by Vincent Delerm even depicts the lengths to which a young Frenchman must go to win over his in-laws: 'Yes, all right, let's watch *Thalassa!*'

On the third channel, TF3, *Des Racines et des Ailes* (Roots and Wings) is a superb fortnightly documentary tracking anything from the Paris river police to a debs ball in Vienna, from painters to nightclubbers, from the aristocracy to artisans. Stumbling on it by chance one night, I was entranced by its exceptional quality, as well as by its originality (not a soap, not a cloned quiz, a real programme!), only belatedly realising that I'd fallen headlong into the French-TV trap: its presenter, Patrick de Carolis, was droolingly handsome. Charming, erudite, cosmopolitan, sexy, the works. Gazing hypnotised at him, I found myself concentrating with such ferocity that my French was rocketing in fluency. It's incredible how much you can learn when you are deeply, ardently motivated. But scarcely had I discovered Patrick than the delightful man departed off-screen to become director of France Télévision, a blow from which I never quite recovered. However, his replacement Louis Laforge is quite a looker too, and seems to understand that, in order to keep French viewers hooked, you need bundles of charisma. (A grasp of your subject helps as well, but let's get our priorities straight.) Strangely, it is very difficult to buy DVDs of *Des Racines et des Ailes*, or indeed of any French programmes, in the shops. You have to hunt them down in a brochure and send off for them with a naughty frisson as if they were pornography.

And then, one sorry night, it was Eurovision. Does anybody, anywhere, watch this idiotic pantomime? No. Nobody at all. Only phantoms, who flit through the ratings while real people go out to dinner, or maybe Latvians for whom it's a novelty, or . . . *zzz*.

However, it was my duty to watch it, at least this once, in France and in French. Two commentators, a man and a woman, were in charge of it and so, settling in with an anaesthesing glass of wine, I wondered whether this would mean double helpings of Terry Wogan-type wit. Terry was still the Beeb's commentator at the time and, traditionally, his wit *was* Eurovision, there seemed no other reason to hear or see the thing.

This pair were not Terry Wogan, nor Graham Norton either, not even between them. This pair gibbered and chattered, giggled and shrieked through every song, throughout the entire event, getting louder and louder, until finally – hurray! – the songs could barely be heard at all. It was like being locked in a beehive, the whole thing buzzing furiously until – suddenly, *ssshh!* – the French contestant came on.

Complete silence. Reverence. As it happened, the French song was sing-along good and its sartorially splendid singer compounded the felony by baring neither boobs nor bottom, which of course meant that France's chances were doomed. Deeply disappointed, the commentators resumed their shouting contest, the voting put France second last, and that was the end of that panoramic foray into European culture.

Next, there are the chat shows, excellent when it comes to learning slang. One of the most popular when I arrived was *On Ne Peut Pas Plaire à Tout le Monde* (You Can't Please Everyone), a fast-moving panel discussion of recent events hosted by the bright, brash (and again, handsome) Marc-Olivier Fogiel. At first, I couldn't get to grips with Marco at all. He and his guests seemed to speak on fast-forward, all sounding comically like Donald Duck. While the news offers the advantage of pictures to illustrate the words, chat shows don't, and all I had to go on was the wildly flailing hands and grinning faces of Marco's guests. And then one night, after months of baffled persistence, straining to catch even the vaguest drift, I thought I heard a word. Grasped it, quite distinctly. 'And,' said Marco. Or maybe it was *'yes'* or *'no'* or *'but'*. Whatever it was, it was a very tiny word. But I'd understood it, definitely. And so I owe Marco thanks: if it weren't for him, my French might still be creaking along at snail's pace. If you can understand him (he's now moved to radio, so no more helpful body language), and the smart, snappy, wrangling guests who enliven French chat shows, you've cracked it. You're fluent. It's like being able to understand Billy Connolly or Ian Hislop on *Have I Got News For You.* Waiter, champagne!

Lately there's been an innovation on chat shows such as *Vivement Dimanche* (France's equivalent of *The Late Late Show*). They've got a new simultaneous-translation system enabling anglophone guests to participate via little earpieces. On the plus side, this means that you can hear questions in French with answers in English, resulting in some great guests such as the Muslim writer Ayaan Hirsi Ali; on the minus side, it has produced loopers like Lordi, Finnish winners of the 2006 Eurovision. Walled into their monster make-up, Lordi made a virtually watertight case for dropping the new system, turning in a performance that set a new benchmark in inanity. For anglophones, it can also be confusing trying to follow two languages, but the new system is here to stay – even if it's unlikely to be adopted by the BBC, because after all, who would want to hear anything the French might have to say?

❦

Meanwhile, kindly friends were sending newspapers from Ireland, under the impression that I must be desperate to know the latest from Termonfeckin, Tallaght and Tourmakeady. Saving up these papers for rainy days, I'd start reading them and . . . *zzz*.

News that had been screamingly urgent on the day had become, by the time I got round to it, jaded to the point of irrelevance. It was like eating last week's cold tapioca. Worse, it seemed to be cloning itself. Almost everything seemed to boil down to just one word, over and over: disaster. The more I read, the more all the scandals and catastrophes began to resemble each other, varying only in detail – location, quantity, degree of management ineptitude, scale of political fallout. It was amazing to see how little still mattered, no matter how apocalyptic it had been on the day. How little difference any of it made to anyone other than those involved,

how little human nature ever changes. As time went by, I found
myself reading fewer newspapers, watching less news, callously
distancing myself from all the déjà-vu.

'But surely,' said a former colleague, 'you must still care?
Human lives are involved here! Tragedies! The planet!'

Yes, of course I still cared. Stories about child abuse, animal
cruelty, miscarriages of justice and wanton evil were as appalling as
ever. It was just that, for the first time in my life, I felt unable to
do, or even say, anything about them. It was like trying to swim
across a vast swamp, one that was too wide, too deep, too suck-in
squishy. The real world seemed to be rapidly receding, and when
friends in Dublin told me that they'd just installed their seventh
television, I thought they were gluttons for punishment. Unless the
programmes on the seventh set were somehow more appealing than
those on the first? Increasingly, my little house was filling with the
sound of music instead.

Serge Reggiani! Jean Ferrat! Isabelle Boulay! Sometimes their
world vision seemed to make more sense than any number of news
bulletins. One night I listened to Serge's song about his humble,
hopeless love for a woman too beautiful to notice an 'ugly' man like
him, and all but wept. And music had another advantage: I was so
keen to understand the lovely French lyrics that I listened to them
over and over, hitting the pause button to break each song into little
soundbites, until finally I understood every syllable and – eureka! –
could even sing along.

Which meant I was now ready for radio. Of all the media, radio
is the most difficult for a foreigner. Unlike television, it offers no
visual clues and, unlike a newspaper, it can't be perused at leisure.
There's no time to consult a dictionary, reread anything, hit the
pause or replay button. Miss it and, like a plane, it's gone forever.
One day, I thought they said the Queen was dead; in fact it was her

hundred-and-one-year-old mother. Words swooped by like paper darts: 'Japan has exploded!' turned out to be news of an explosion *in* Japan. For a while I was as lethal as a cruise missile, grasping garbled versions of important events, as likely as not to extrapolate the same nonsense as when, as a child having just learned to read, I spotted the headline on my grandfather's newspaper: 'A spoonful of poison for each little child.' It was a story about some father who'd poisoned his family, but at five I was hysterical, convinced it meant that all of us children were to be poisoned.

Eventually, I found my level on local radio France Bleu, which is similar in scale to 98FM. Gerard Farcy explaining how to keep your roses bug-free (though not mole-free), some man from the chamber of commerce announcing a film festival, a chef from Dieppe giving a yummy recipe for rabbit casserole with honey and mustard . . . at last, I didn't need pictures, no longer yearned to yell 'Stop, wait, you're going too fast!' Of course, everyone was shocked by this choice of station, because true French *intellos* listen to France Inter, not France Bleu. But hey, it worked. Drunk on success, I started aiming for ever-greater heights, to the point where I might even some day participate in a phone-in to give my views on . . . well, no, perhaps not foreign policy. On the moles, maybe, or that divine recipe for carrot soup.

And then, after a year or more in Normandy, I discovered that RTÉ television could now be had. For many migrants to France, it is the answer to a prayer, ever-advancing technology bringing not only RTÉ but four BBC channels, plus ITN, CNN, and dedicated wine, travel, arts, fashion, cartoon and shopping channels, as well as hundreds of radio channels. In English! Hurray! *EastEnders*, *Coronation Street*, Ryan Tubridy . . . at last, we're saved!

'Ah,' said Irish friends who'd given up on France and sold their houses, 'if only we'd known about this, how different it might all have been.'

No, it wouldn't have been. Digiboxes, Canal+ and the like are a luxury, nothing more. They do not change any aspect of real life in France. But, in context, they're great, and at first it was nice – occasionally – to see Gráinne Seoige reading the news on Sky Ireland and to follow the continuing adventures of her hairstyle. Gráinne has since departed to pastures greener, but I still get a kick out of listening to Pat Kenny and posting comments on Facebook within seconds of hearing what he has to say. I even enjoy hearing the angelus ring simultaneously in Dublin and in my little Norman village. But the drawback to digiboxes is that people tend to become dependent on them. Extremely dependent, in some cases, watching *Masterchef*, *Flog It*, *The X Factor* and *Strictly Come Dancing* all day every day.

France isn't about *Strictly Come Dancing*, or *Ros na Rún* or any other fix from 'home'. It is – supposedly – about *France*. Unless you watch at least as many French programmes as English or Irish ones, you might as well stay in Kerry or Kent or wherever you were in the first place. Until you can understand France Bleu telling you about this Saturday's tea dance in Douai or Dijon, you will remain a prisoner of virtual events in cyberspace. Housebound, completely out of touch with local life.

Besides, Louis Laforge is *waaay* prettier than Bruce Forsyth.

❧

As time went by, other cultural keys to France gradually began to fit into previously locked doors. The *Frustré* cartoons of Claire Bretecher, with their hilariously cynical mothers, exasperated fathers and scheming children. The satirical newspapers *Charlie Hebdo* and *Le Canard Enchaîné* (similar to *Phoenix* magazine), essential for lightening up life on days when the world just seems a hopeless mess. And the supermarket bulletin board, arguably more important than any TV news bulletin – this is where you'll find someone to fix your lawnmower. Little local magazines announcing houses, cars and canaries for sale, man-with-van, gardener €20 an hour . . . simple as they seem, these little contacts take you deeper into the heart of France (or anywhere), easing the way, opening up new vistas, until one fine morning you wake up not feeling like a foreigner any more.

One fine morning, you're walking down the village street and a voice suddenly shrieks over the tannoy: *'Allez allez allez! Tirage au sort! Clio à gagner! Tickets trois euro chacun ou dix euros le lot de cinq! Venez vite et nombreux à la mairie!'*

Yes, it's urgent news, but no, France hasn't been invaded. The medium is the public-address system, and the message is a raffle. Quick, you could win a Clio!

Or did they say 'Quick, the nuclear station has exploded, gas masks available at the *mairie*'?

❦

There has been a terrible tragedy. An eighty-year-old woman, Léonie Cravel, has been brought to trial for the murder of her forty-two-year-old daughter, who was paraplegic, epileptic and '100 percent' handicapped. One night, after four decades of utterly devoted care, Léonie could bear her daughter's mute suffering no more. So she 'released' her, by strangulation with a length of string. When arrested, she freely admitted what she had done, but could express no remorse for her 'crime of compassion'.

Now, after vigorous debate on its ethical implications, the case has come to court and France is on the edge of its sofa, a nation divided, watching the evening news on tenterhooks. As a rule, the French don't have a sensationalist streak, events of an O. J. Simpson nature are viewed as decidedly downmarket and interest only the most sanguinary amongst them. But Léonie is exceptional. Will her plea for clemency be accepted, as most people volubly wish, or will she be imprisoned for the rest of her tragic life? So frail that her lawyer, Maître Jean-François Titus, has to all but carry her up the steps of the courthouse (on which she totters and nearly falls), Madame Cravel cuts a most pathetic figure as she arrives to explain her desperate action. A weary, feeble figure that would melt the heart of a stone.

'Nonetheless, she did do it,' argues state counsel. 'She did kill her defenceless daughter.'

Yes, she did, she admits it. This has already provoked heated debate about euthanasia in all the media, but it is on television that the judge's cards are unexpectedly marked for him as he retires to consider his verdict.

'In such circumstances,' says newsreader David Pujadas, 'suspended sentences are the norm.'

Across France, there is an almost audible gasp. Almost everybody wants a suspended sentence, but is this going too far? Are news bulletins supposed to . . . well . . . sort of . . . nudge the course of justice like this? Might the remark drive the judge in the other direction, might he feel coerced? Of course, nobody knows whether the judge has even seen the news, or what his views might be, but in any event state counsel has demanded a minimum five-year prison sentence for Madame Cravel because, no matter what the reason, people can't be allowed to kill their daughters or anyone else. Justice must be seen to be done.

And, mercifully, it is done. Next morning, Madame Cravel receives a two-year suspended sentence. She is free to go home, if she can ever face the scene of her 'crime' again. Out on the steps of the courthouse, wearing a woolly hat and clutching Maître Titus by the hand, she croaks her thanks into a battery of microphones, bursts into tears and sobs all over her lawyer's burly, kindly shoulder. Watching this, I am tearful myself and can almost feel *la toute France* quivering with emotion. With relief, too: this has been an important moment in the course of social justice.

But we will never know whether that televised remark about legal precedent swayed the decision, or had any effect at all – or indeed if it was intended to. All that's clear is that yes, France does have a heart, and that Madame Cravel is perhaps lucky she doesn't live in a country where she might have risked a death sentence.

'Not,' she murmurs, 'that it would have mattered.' Her life is ruined anyway. The only good thing about this trial-by-television is its demonstration of France as a humane, compassionate nation.

Mind you, if she'd forgotten to pay her *taxe foncière*, she'd probably have been guillotined.

8.

The Edge

Punctually on 1 April, the neighbours, who have apparently been hibernating all winter, appear. No, not to say hello, or how are you, or to introduce me to the divine Frenchman who would be the icing on the *gâteau*. Not to issue invitations for the first barbecue, or to say anything cheerful at all. Their mission is to air their grievance. The hedge between our houses has begun to sprout, and a faint greenish fuzz, like a teenager's first beard, is beginning to spread across its surface.

'You own it – so, when will you be getting it trimmed?' they anxiously enquire.

Why, I reply, I will be getting it trimmed at just about the same time you will be getting your trees trimmed – yes, those forty-foot silver birches whose leaves clog my drains in winter and whose branches block all the summer sunlight from my patio. Sunlit patios are, after all, one of the chief reasons for living in France.

There is a long, thoughtful silence. 'Well,' they say at length, 'that would be very expensive.' Oh, hardly much more than trimming my hedge? After all, the hedge is causing no grief, it is blocking no light, it is minding its own business. Their trees are actually a far bigger problem.

'Hmph. We'll have to discuss it.'

No more is heard about either hedge or trees until, one sunny day a few weeks later, I am out mowing the lawn when *monsieur le maire* appears. Every village in France, no matter how tiny, has its own mayor, and ours has held office for longer than anyone can remember. Looking agitated, chain-smoking, he marches purposefully up the drive.

'*Bonjour, madame.*'

'*Bonjour, monsieur.* To what do I owe this pleasure?'

'Ah. Well. You see. It is about your 'edge.'

My hedge? Why? What has it done? Been naughty, has it, out carousing with the lads? Accosting old ladies, tripping up small children?

M. le maire is not renowned for his sense of humour. Unsmiling, he stalks over to the hedge, kneels under it and starts plucking at small, shiny new leaves.

'Look.' Triumphantly, he holds a leaf aloft. 'You see. Untidy. New growth all over it.'

Indeed. Somehow, he makes the new growth sound like a crime, one of which he strongly disapproves, as if hedges have no business growing. But spring growth is not in fact illegal. Indeed, it is in the nature of hedges to grow – and in the nature of my neighbours to whine, evidently. To go snivelling to him and send him in to fight their battle for them. I have to smile. Badly briefed, he is kneeling under the wrong hedge, the one that belongs to my other, much nicer, neighbours.

'I see. Well, what a pity. There's nothing I can do about the bits growing out of it, I'm afraid.'

'What? But why not? Surely . . . ?' He looks aghast, as if he has never before encountered such insubordination. Of course, this is what comes of letting foreigners move in.

'Because it's not my hedge, don'tcha see. Belongs to Benoit and Blandine next door. They usually trim it every summer. Until they do, it's not bothering me. Or anyone else.'

Belatedly, his mistake dawns on him. He looks ridiculous, and would only compound his idiocy by making a second fuss about the other hedge, the one he's been sent in about. The one that does not conform to France's first rule of gardening: everything must be geometric. Symmetrical. Precise to the millimetre. All anarchy nipped in the bud.

'Well, madame, I am glad to see you are at least mowing your lawn. That is a start. Good day to you.'

Off he marches, leaving me fizzing with rage. So, the neighbours are hauling in the heavy guns, are they? Won't cut their trees, but conniving with the mayor to make me cut my hedge? Sending round Mr Medallions to do their dirty work for them?

Right, so. If they are really fretting over this hedge, let's grant their wish. Let's get it cut. Stamping indoors, I seize the Yellow Pages and find a hedge-trimming outfit. Yes, they can come next week. Yes, a thousand euro should cover the scope and nature of the job.

A week later, the team arrives at 8 AM. By sundown, they have reduced the two-metre hedge to one metre. It is now so low that I can peer over it and wave to the neighbours as they cook their barbecues, entertain their guests, sun themselves . . . hey, we'll be seeing lots of each other this summer! The hedge is also sufficiently low that it no longer offers any noise protection from the road behind: they will be able to hear every passing car, every thundering lorry, every school bus picking up *les enfants* at dawn. The thousand-euro investment has cost me a proposed trip to Greece, and greatly upset the friend who was going to come with me, but at least it has paid other dividends.

Curiously, the neighbours do not pop in to thank me for complying with their wishes, for spending so much money on such comprehensive cutting. Nor do they acknowledge their half of the bargain, i.e. the felling of those giant birches. They do not respond when I wave gaily to them over the hedge, over which I now have an unimpaired view of their kitchen and can even see what they're cooking for dinner.

They seem to be both skulking and sulking. Until one day, weeks later, they emerge like moles in their garden. There are voices, the clink of glasses, barbecue smoke, frolicking children in their new pool, every indication that they are entertaining guests. It is that most sacrosanct of French moments, Sunday lunchtime. Their charcoal-grilled lamb brochettes smell herby, and garlicky, and divine.

I am alone. I have no guests. I have no brochettes. I have no friendly wave from them, no invitation to come join them, not even for a glass of wine. All I have is a radio, on which RTÉ is playing. In English, *bien entendu*. I look over the expensively trimmed hedge into their sunny garden, I look at my own garden shaded by their birches, and I see red.

I take the radio outside. I turn up the volume. To max. Bryan Dobson bawls the news at deafening decibels, as if relaying it to Australia. Startled, the neighbours gape over the hedge. I wave cheerily back to them. Isn't it great, now we can see and hear each other? Yes, *hear*! Their raucously frolicking children will learn lots of English from Bryan, from this impending entire afternoon of RTÉ. The first of many over the coming summer, now that there's no longer a hedge to muffle the noise.

I think the April Fool's Day tradition of enquiring about hedge-trimming might be suspended next year.

Meanwhile, the silver birches, now in full leaf, continue to block my sunlight. But there is some small compensation: last night, the neighbours' cat escaped over the hedge, which used to be too tall and thick for it to climb. It ran out onto the road, and was, alas, flattened by a lorry. *Les enfants* are distraught. I am about to write a little condolence card and pop it in their letterbox.

Back at the *mairie*, *monsieur le maire* has run up against a small difficulty. His lovely new ride-on lawnmower has, apparently, attracted some attention. Rumour has it that it may have been a little incentive from an optimistic entrepreneur, to whom the awarding of a contract is within his gift. Pure speculation, of course, no proof at all; only what the French call the 'Arab pipes'.

Eh bien. He hasn't been round lately, seems to have forgotten all about my 'edge. I must invite him to come see it, and discuss those silver birches. After all, pruning them would constitute a nice little contract.

⁂

Towards the end of the summer, when the hedgerows are heavy with blackberries and the hydrangeas are ready for hanging, my friend Jim rings one evening. He lives in Derry and is, he announces, feeling depressed.

Well, Jim, you know, Derry . . .

'No, no. It isn't that. It's . . . um . . . the therapy.'

What therapy? Reluctantly, he confesses all. His work, which he used to love, has taken a turn for the worse. The bank has been taken over by a new conglomerate and 'practices' have changed. He has been shunted into a vast, noisy, open-plan office where paperwork flies off his desk every time someone rushes by, his new boss is the anti-Christ, and he is spending all his time fobbing off angry customers shouting down the phone about their newly muddled accounts. The word 'redundancies' echoes everywhere, and formerly friendly colleagues are turning on each other in all manner of Machiavellian intrigue. In a moment of black despair, he confided to his ex-wife that it was all very depressing, and she sent him off to see a 'therapist'.

What? A shrink? But Jim, this situation *is* depressing! For everyone! It's not of your making. You're not imagining it. Anyone would be depressed. In fact, everyone probably is. You didn't cause it, you don't need therapy . . .

'So the shrink,' he continues, 'recommended scream therapy.'

Eh? What's that?

'He regresses you back to your infancy and gets you to lie on the floor and scream. Let out all your anger. You know, against your parents and everything.'

What? Your parents took over the bank and introduced these new work practices?

'Oh, look, I was ready to try anything . . . but the screaming doesn't seem to be working. If anything, I feel even worse.'

Well, no wonder. You are an idiot, Jim, but never mind. Why not hop on a plane – now, first thing tomorrow – and come over here for a bit of a break? It's not very exciting, and nothing ever happens, but it's peaceful and sunny and restful. And after all, the French are usually depressed, so you could all sort of cosy up and be depressed together. As a banker, you might appreciate such economies of scale?

Worryingly, he doesn't laugh. Instead, he wrestles with his conscience about taking time off at short notice. Eventually, under duress, he agrees that maybe yes, he does need some 'sick leave'. He *is* sick, and tired, of all the pointless pressure. Exhausted, actually. A week in France can't do any harm, and it might do some good. Okay, he'll hop on his motorbike and take the ferry.

So he does, and when he arrives I'm aghast: the bike is big and burly but Jim, once out of his leathers, looks awful. The absolute incarnation of a stressed-out man with a lot on his mind. Is he actually going out of his mind, seeing this nutty shrink? Is he on the, um, edge of sanity?

'Well, I was ready to try anything. But it's not really helping . . . it's just costing a hundred euro a session.'

What? You're shelling out a hundred euro to lie on some quack's floor and scream? Jim, you're mad. You should see a shrink!

Reluctantly, he laughs. And says 'everyone' is seeing a shrink these days.

Are they? Not in France, they're not. I've only ever heard one person mention one.

'So what do the French do, then, when they're stressed out?'

Hmm. Well, they complain loudly and at length, of course, to anyone who'll listen without charging them a hundred euro. Family, friends, customers, the postman, the man on the phone trying to sell them a new kitchen. They're really quite democratic about it. And then they go for a long, moody walk on the beach. You know, like in a Jean-Luc Godard movie. There's usually a dense mist on the horizon and a lone seagull squawking mournfully. And then, well, they go out to lunch.

'I don't feel like going out. I'm not very hungry.'

This turns out to be a blatant lie. Several hours later, after an extremely long, brisk, exhausting walk – it felt like Normandy to Provence and back – Jim is ensconced in a little *auberge*, nursing his grievances and a *kir normand*, studying the menu beside a crackling log fire. (Well, a smoking log fire – the French don't believe in piling on more than one log at a time, and worry if a flame takes hold.)

'Foie gras with chestnuts and bacon? That sounds good. No,

wait, maybe the oysters from Cancale? I love oysters. Oh look, they have *tabouleh*. It always reminds me of that great holiday in Morocco. No, actually I think I'll have the cream of salmon and fennel soup to start. And then the . . . um, let's see . . . maybe the veal with wild mushrooms and truffle juice. Or the roast chicken stuffed with sage and apricots. Well anyway, I'm definitely having the hazelnut and raspberry mousse for dessert. Or the white chocolate with cherry sauce. After the cheese, of course. They do cheese before dessert, don't they? What about wine? Would we manage a bottle of Chablis as well as a bottle of Médoc, d'you think?'

We do our best. In fact he turns in a sterling performance, eating as if for Olympic medals, dispatching plate after plate before, three splendid hours later, snuggling up to a cognac. Musing, he gazes into the fire. 'What *is* it about French food? What do they *do* to it? I feel . . . I feel *nurtured*.'

A week later, after several more long walks on beaches, in forests, across muddy fields swept by larks and starlings, there is no further talk of not feeling hungry, nor of work – possibly because his mouth has been too full of omelettes, mussels, gratins, prawns, casseroles, salads, roasts, breads, cheeses, wines, pies, mousses, fruit, chocolates and *digéstifs*. He has even cooked some of these repasts himself, wrapped in an apron, tea towel over one shoulder, leafing through *The Joy of Cooking* with sticky fingers. In Derry, his idea of cooking is beans on toast, but here, 'Well, it's just a pleasure, isn't it? All these markets, all these gorgeous ingredients . . . you can hardly come to France and *not* cook.' All mention of the bank, and the shrink, and the screaming has petered out. In fact, he seems to have forgotten all about them.

And then one day he gets back into his leathers, onto his bike and zooms away: 'I might as well see a bit more of France since I'm here, eh? Call you when I get down south! Bye!' Blowing a kiss, he

vanishes into the crisp September morning, apparently forgetting
that the bank is expecting him back on Monday.

❧

A month goes by. Bar the occasional enigmatic text message, nothing more is heard from Jim, nor from the neighbours, who have
said no more about the hedge. It is *la rentrée*: summer's over, everyone's back at work or school, and gardens have taken something of
a back seat for the autumn. But finally, one evening the phone
rings.

Having biked slowly down the length of France, Jim still isn't
back in Derry. He's in the Pyrenées Atlantiques, near Bayonne.
Where he has, he says, found a house.

To rent? For the winter?

'No. To buy. I'm staying for good. I rang the bank and quit.'

But Jim, people who quit don't get any redundancy packages!
What are you going to live on?

'I'm going to do more or less what I did before. Manage
people's money for them.'

But you hardly speak any French—?

'Won't need to. I'm going to put an ad in *French Property News*
and on the Anglo France website, advertise to handle people's
accounts and international transactions . . . you know, foreigners
who run businesses here and need an accountant who speaks
English. Well, that's me. So, when are you coming down to see the
house? It's just a small cottage but it has a great garden, really sunny
. . . this is a beautiful area, and the food is fabulous. I think I might
do a cookery course when I get settled in, maybe grow a few
veggies . . . '

Not long after this conversation, there is a knock at the door one morning. My neighbour – the female half of the couple – is standing there, smiling the smile of a person who wants something. A smile that puts my teeth on, um, edge.

'*Bonjour!* I just thought I'd drop in because, well . . . my son wants to do some work-study experience in English next summer. At first he thought of going to England, but now he hears he might learn better English in Ireland. So . . . uh . . . maybe you would know some companies where he could apply?'

Yes, as it happens, I do. There's a vacancy at a lovely bank in Derry.

9.

Don't Mention the War

'What's missing?' I asked a visiting child one day. 'What do you not see on French streets?'

Fair play to her, she cracked it almost immediately. 'Litter! No litter!'

For a long time, this continued to be true. The French don't muck up their environment. Public spaces and buildings are well kept (apart from the dog dirt), filled with flowers, a joy to behold.

But one day I noticed a plastic bottle chucked into a ploughed field. Hardly earth-shattering, but still, new.

And then there was another. And another. Within the space of a few weeks, bottles seemed to be mushrooming everywhere, swiftly followed by graffiti. Graffiti, formerly confined to urban slums and railway stations, suddenly seemed to be appearing on the sides of old sheds, school walls, town halls, all sorts of places it had never been before. Incidents started happening in schools – not as heavy as the stabbings in British schools, but confrontational, aggressive.

With regret, all this was noted in village gossip at the cafés. 'It's the kids,' people started muttering, as if their own kids had absolutely nothing to do with it. 'They're losing respect. For their parents, their teachers, the government. For everyone and every-thing.'

Mild surprise was registered, along with a classic shrug. 'But there you are, what can you do?' I was surprised myself, in this tra-ditional bastion of civilisation where most children are at home in the evenings doing their homework, not nearly as addicted to tele-vised trash or tequila slammers as in many other countries. Up to now, French parents had seemed to be generally in control of their children. The undercurrent of tension was new.

And then one night – *wham!* – riots suddenly break out. Juvenile riots, first in Paris and then all over France, led by eight-een-year-olds, enthusiastically joined by boys as young as twelve, protesting about unemployment and conditions in their HLM (subsidised housing). Every night for three weeks, cars are torched, more than twenty thousand in all. Bins are set on fire, and when a man tries to point out the danger of this to two of the young arson-ists, they kill him. Molotov cocktails are hurled at a hospital; a kindergarten and a sports centre are burnt down; a handicapped woman is trapped in a burning bus. Shops, schools and, bizarrely, car-rental agencies are razed, throwing hundreds of employees onto the dole. Armed guards are put on public transport. Following a sorrowful address to the nation, lamenting it all, a pale president authorises curfews 'where necessary' and declares a state of national emergency. Suddenly, we are living in a very different France, one stripped of its parasols and billowing tablecloths.

The catalyst for the riots? Two immigrant youths who were electrocuted after breaking into a power station, allegedly while being chased by security guards. Nobody is sure exactly what hap-pened, and no clarification is forthcoming.

Watching all the chaos erupt on television, I'm astonished. Simply cannot imagine a situation in Ireland whereby violent riots, all over the country every night for weeks on end, would be greeted by the Taoiseach with such a sad sigh, such hand-wringing despair. If thousands of disgruntled young hooligans were systematically wrecking Tralee, Drogheda, Naas, Galway or Buncrana, would he simply send in a few extra police and hope for the best? Would the government not impose order?

I'd say it would. But here in France, the right to riot is sacrosanct. Remembering the exacerbating effect of the hard line taken against rioters in 1968, France is holding its fire, tiptoeing around the disaffected youths and throwing its hands up in despair.

'Where did we go wrong?' the nation laments. 'What have we failed to give these boys? What is it they want?' A reasonable question from a nation that gives housing, education, financial aid and masses of sports facilities to natives and immigrants alike – and one that draws a response from a young riot leader.

'We want work!' he yells. 'Our slums are disgusting. It's not enough to just repaint them!'

Indeed. Unemployment is rising and lots of people want work. Lots are actively looking for it. Lots have qualifications or experience or both. Many immigrants living in slums want to clamber out of them, and are doing their best to improve their lot. Not all are out burning the place to the ground. And not all of the rioters are even genuine, as it turns out.

'We're enjoying this,' a teenager admits on radio. 'We're tanking up on whisky, pulling up our hoods, going out and having fun.'

This is when I first learn the word *casseur*, or professional hooligan.

Meanwhile, the benevolent burghers of the brutalised towns and villages are attempting to clear up, scratching their heads in bewilderment as they survey the millions of euro worth of damage. It's going to take a lot of taxes to repair all this. The prime minister

offers the rioters an olive branch: henceforth, they will be allowed
to leave school at fourteen (the minimum leaving age was formerly
sixteen) to take up trade apprenticeships. Since they claim they
want work – well, now they can train for it earlier.

A baker appears on the news. 'Dolt! Dimwit! Is this how he
tackles a national crisis? France is on the brink of civil war! And
anyway, what makes him think that employers want to hire babies?
We want apprentices of sixteen or seventeen – old enough to have
a bit of sense.'

At the market next morning, a clothes seller concurs. 'France,'
he says darkly, 'is being bullied. We have a tradition of letting ourselves be. But I for one will never employ bullies, nor deal with
them.'

This response is, however, out of tune with the general view,
which seems to be that 'the young' must be humoured. If they want
to leave school at fourteen, then so be it. If their parents can't control them, pity the poor parents. If the immigrants' native countries
can't entice them to stay, then France must entice them. Social
workers spring up all over the media, deploring the plight of the
school-burning 'poor children'.

A town councillor erupts on the news. 'But this is ridiculous!
Grown adults are being intimidated by infants! Our sanctuary, and
our hospitality, are being abused by kids trying to bully the entire
country! Has the government no strength, no resolution, no
authority?'

Apparently not. The riots continue. Perhaps it is government
policy to let this safety valve blow off steam? After all, the rioters
are doing more damage in their own neighbourhoods than
anywhere else. Nonetheless, the international business community
starts cancelling meetings. Tourists cancel holidays, investors start
pulling out. As Northern Ireland can testify to its cost, nobody

wants to put their money where there's mayhem.

Heavily, France sighs. 'Terrible. Appalling. But there we are, what can you do?'

Abruptly, something clicks in my mind. The memory of a dinner party down in the Midi, where I once got my knuckles rapped for asking how France feels about Germany, nearly seventy years after the war. This question wasn't random: it was triggered by the sight of a war memorial in the village square. A memorial to the men of the village, all of whom had been shot one morning by the Nazis, from the youngest lad of nine to the eldest *pépé* of ninety-two. On the day I saw the memorial, the square was buzzing with German tourists, sunnily shopping. A German friend had told me that some Germans like to spend money in France as a kind of apology 'for what our grandparents did to their grandparents'.

But my query fell on stony French soil. 'The war,' I was frostily informed, 'is over.'

Well yes, of course it is. I just wondered whether any of the shopkeepers ever look at all these German tourists and wonder—?

'Germany is our friend now. We work together for European integration.'

Good for you! But is it ever difficult?

'We know Germans who come to France every year to donate blood. This is how sincere Germany is about *entente cordiale*.'

Giving blood sounded like a nice gesture and I was happy to hear that, even if France was determined to forget the war, Germany evidently still remembered, and regretted. But I couldn't say this, because around the table everyone seemed to be shrinking back. I sensed a distinct frisson of . . . what? If intuition was to be trusted, something that felt suspiciously like fear. Certainly unease. They declined to discuss the subject further, leaving me wondering why. But the message was clear: today, political correctness reigns, we are all polite to each other, how rude of a foreigner to mention the war!

Sorry. It's just that I'm Irish. I come from a country where we express our political views with considerable candour, intensity, and often humour. We've never forgiven 'the bloody Brits' for the Famine of 1847, and maybe never will. We know that's rancorous, but at least we can laugh at our rancour. In all but the dourest of bars, people can say what they feel, and nobody clams up when asked a straightforward question.

Which leads me to wonder if France is still, just a little, very slightly, afraid of Germany? Anxiety seems to creep into the atmosphere at the very mention of the war. One day I innocently had a drink in a local brasserie, where somebody must have spotted me, because I was thereafter given to understand that 'locals' do not patronise this bar 'where the grandparents were collabos'. Then the subject was swiftly changed.

And is France also afraid, now, of upsetting its immigrants? And the countries, perhaps of future importance, that they come from? It certainly seemed to be taking a very muted approach to these riots, which were now in their thirteenth night. The cities were all knee-deep in broken glass.

I couldn't help getting the impression that yes, France is fearful. French people don't have feisty political discussions of the kind I'm used to. If I want one of those, I have to look to my Polish or English neighbours, and it usually ends in hoots of irreverent laughter. We're used to giving each other a hard time, and giving our politicians one too: whereas, when French journalists interview politicians, they nod and smile and never heckle. French politicians don't get a real roasting, and if they want to dissemble, they can. Red herrings? *Eh oui*, with a nice sauce!

Back to the riots. Good news. Only six hundred cars were

torched last night, as opposed to twelve hundred the night before. Only one school was destroyed, and only 'a handful' of firemen were injured. I remark on this excellent progress to François the bartender as he serves up my *café crème*. Furtively, he glances round, visibly wondering whether to risk a candid comment. We've known and liked each other for quite a while now.

'D'you really want to know what I think?'

Yes, please. A bit of straight talk would make a refreshing change. Besides, what's that bit in the constitution about *liberté*?

'I think the prime minister's mad. Letting kids leave school at fourteen is criminal.'

I agree. But what's his angle on it?

'It's deceiving them. It's letting them think their rocks and riots are achieving something, whereas rocks and riots aren't real weapons at all. Education is their only real weapon. And now they'll get less of it than ever. They won't realise until it's far too late that, the day they wrecked their schools, or left them, they wrecked their only hope. The government is literally making fools of them.'

A father of two children, he goes on to expound further on how education is the only key to progress. How very young apprentices are 'bound to be exploited', and lowering the school-leaving age will thrust them into a workforce which is way beyond them. 'Next thing,' he says, 'we'll be sending eight-year-olds up chimneys, like in *Oliver Twist*. And the eight-year-olds will be delighted with the fun of it, the freedom of not going to school . . . until they realise what's been stolen from them. Then we'll see real riots.'

Unfortunately, some new customers come in at this point, so the conversation is hastily terminated, as if it were illegal. But as I leave, I get a smile and a wink.

'*Au revoir, madame.* It has been a pleasure talking to you.'

Decamping, I get the feeling that my foreignness has freed him up to say, for once, what he thinks. Not that it's anything radical, but at least it's sincere.

And sincerity is rare in a country that still seems to think the walls have ears.

※

Even as the young immigrant rioters start running out of steam – it's November and the nights are getting chilly – the natives are getting restless. In Rouen, EDF workers take to the streets to protest against privatisation. In Paris, a lightning strike is called by SNCF ticket-sellers, whose jobs are under threat. As ever, France's motto is 'a protest a day helps you work, rest and play'.

Along with cooking, protesting is something France does well and thoroughly enjoys. Hardly a day goes by without some new complaint. Agricultural agitator José Bovey goes to jail for burning GM crops. Languedoc *vignerons* smash up supermarkets by way of objecting to foreign wines. Commuters are resigned to Métro trains squealing to a stop, planes are grounded, *autoroutes* are blocked. If individuals are afraid to speak out at private dinner parties, if barmen are reduced to whispering, the mobs, on the contrary, have no qualms whatsoever about shouting aloud in the streets. Safety in numbers and all that.

Frequently, of course, the protests are justified. Even successful. But success isn't always the point. One day, I asked a friend how her anti-globalisation march had gone.

'Great,' she grinned. 'The cops arrested lots of us!'

No, she wasn't naive enough to think that Americanisation, or capitalism, or homogenisation could really be halted. But she'd had her day out, it had been fun, had attracted attention, had made the regional news. And hey, guess what, she'd met a lovely man amongst the marchers, and they were going out on a date next week! This happy news made me wonder: should I take up protesting too, as a hobby? If it yielded dates, I'd be delighted. On the other hand, what if I got arrested (again) and deported? It was tempting, but in the end discretion won out for once.

Unlike America, France doesn't seek psychiatric counselling for trivia. It doesn't seek compensation when stung by a bee. It doesn't demand trauma intervention if somebody nicks its bike. Instead . . . one out, all out! And off they go, picnics in rucksacks, banners aloft, to protest. Today's rioters can hardly be blamed for picking up on the role model that first saw the light of day in 1789, when the revolutionary hordes seized their pitchforks – a role model later reinforced when, in 1968, students stripped Paris's streets of their cobblestones (some allegedly making very nice patios in private gardens). Protests and riots seem to be the therapy of choice, arguably saving the state a fortune in shrinks, and if you get interviewed on telly, even better. As my local newsagent remarks, 'These young rioters are getting way too much media attention. Starve them of publicity and they'll soon get bored.'

But as it turns out, the (then) interior minister, Nicolas Sarkozy, comes up with another solution to the riots. France, he announces, has decided to 'withdraw its hospitality' to its foreign guests.

Whaat? Coffee in hand, I freeze beside the radio. Am I to be deported after all?

'Henceforth, any foreign national convicted of damage to French property, or injury to a French citizen, will be repatriated. After serving his prison term.'

Uproar. The Assemblée Nationale collapses in schism over 'the injustice of this double penalty', civil rights organisations go mad, radio phones are hopping.

Only bartender François stands back, pulling a pint with a grin. 'So the hooligans are to be sent home, huh? What makes me think there won't be any riots tonight?'

But there are. Not as fierce, but still fiery. One of the arsonists, aged twelve, has his say on television. Asked why he took to burning buses, he beams into the camera.

'Because of the b . . . the bour . . . the . . . ' He's having a little difficulty remembering the new word he's apparently just learned. I wonder if he means bourbon? But then it comes. 'The bourgeoisie.'

The bourgeoisie, eh? The middle classes? And what have they done to you, sonny?

'They . . . they . . . they don't take us to the cinema! Well, sometimes they do, but not often enough!'

Even as I explode in laughter, I can hardly believe it: is this really what has cost France millions, forced it to declare a national emergency? Is this why thousands of extra police have been deployed? Is this what thousands of journalists and millions of readers, viewers and listeners have been so earnestly discussing for weeks, often in tones of hushed respect for 'the underpriviliged'? Kiddies wanting to go to the *movies*?!

I'm half sorry for the child, who clearly needs urgent parenting. But in that flash, France looks a fool. Frankly imbecilic. As François says next day: 'We *are* fools. Taking naughty children seriously. All this political correctness . . . look where it's got us. We are an international laughing stock.'

And then he hesitates, looks furtively around, and mutters into my ear. 'I'll tell you something else, too. These riots have paved the way for [right-wing leader] Le Pen. Come the next elections, you'll see, the National Front will make huge gains. The government and the immigrants have both shot themselves in the foot.'

Sure enough, in 2010 the National Front does very well

(although there is also a strange counter-swing to the left). Not that I, or the rioters, or any other foreigners, have any say in it, since we can only vote for mayors or European representatives. In order to be allowed to vote in village and European elections, I had to sign a form agreeing to be 'voluntarily' struck off the electoral register for national elections.

Radiation volontaire, it's called. *Volontaire*, my eye. Foreigners are allowed to pay tax but not allowed to vote. Perhaps we should band together – Irish, Algerians, Americans and Iranians alike? Go out on strike, burn down a few dozen schools, set fire to a couple of thousand cars?

Opinion varies. Karl Lagerfeld, the German-born, Paris-based fashion designer, firmly asserts that 'I never meddle in the politics of a country which is not my own'. (A pity his compatriot Adolf didn't share his sentiments.) But other immigrants, including many British, feel strongly that, as EU members, they should be allowed to vote.

France is, after all, a democracy. Everyone is allowed their voice, even if that means trashing the country and burning it to a cinder. Just so long as nobody mentions the war.

❧

More riots. 'I'd turn a pressure hose on them,' says Nicolas Sarkozy, before announcing more sanctions, this time on the rioters' parents. Those whose children are convicted of damage risk losing their food and housing grants, as well as the subsidised holidays the children enjoy in summer.

The total cost of the damage is now estimated at €250 million, not counting the loss of revenue. As it happens, the EU is about to fork out €103 million to France, which was destined for 'urban revitalisation'. Instead, the money will now go to 'urban repair'.

'Sweeping up glass and rebuilding schools,' snorts a furious François. 'As if we didn't do enough of that after the Nazis.'

Instantly, silence descends. A hasty switching of subject, as his customers all beam nonchalantly: goodness, what a lovely day it is! Draining their beers and coffees, they melt away on urgent business. François has done the unpardonable. He has mentioned the war. But he doesn't care, because he is moving anyway: his son has asthma and the climate is better down south. Six months later, the café is sold and, sadly, our friendly barman is gone.

But one reassuring little incident indicates that there is still hope for freedom of speech. The satirical magazine *Charlie Hebdo* has bravely published some cartoons linking the prophet Muhammad with violence, which have caused outrage in their native Denmark and beyond. Fundamentalist Islamists are threatening to kill the cartoonist, bomb Europe and so forth, and so as a writer I feel honour-bound to buy a copy of *Charlie Hebdo*. Freedom of the press is, after all, a key element of democracy.

But when I reach the newsagent's, *Charlie Hebdo* is nowhere to be found. '*Ah non*,' says the assistant, 'they're all gone. Sold out.'

It transpires that half a million copies have been bought before lunchtime, and the magazine is having to reprint. Somewhere, somebody seems to be not only standing up to bullying, but putting their money where their mouth is. *Vive la résistance.*

Six months later, despite his remarks about power-hosing protestors, Nicolas Sarkozy is elected president of the Fifth Republic. Or is it *because* of them?

'Nicolas,' asserts one of my English-language students, 'articulated what everybody thought, but was afraid to say.'

So now I've cracked it. In Ireland, you speak out; in France, you vote for somebody to do it for you. If you're allowed to vote.

10.

Vive La Révolution

Zut alors. Pierre the mayor is in trouble again. And all because he wants to improve the village, as is the mission of mayors, to make it bigger and better for all of us. Having successfully resurfaced the tennis court, he is now resolved to build his little *cité*, or housing estate. Just a small scheme, with fourteen *foyers* (homes) for a mixed new populace of young and elderly couples.

Our Normandy village needs new blood. The school must have fresh supplies of children if it is to continue to exist. If this new housing estate was built, Pierre wonders aloud, what joys might follow? Someday, we might even have a bakery or – *bon dieu!* – a corner shop. And so Pierre engages an architect, draws up plans, and sets his sights on a plot of land. With his dream taking shape, he changes tense: 'if' becomes 'when', and the project begins to sound more and more like a fait accompli.

Unfortunately, this plot of land is dear to the hearts of the villagers. It is where their children play football. It is where the midsummer bonfire is held every 21 June, complete with blazing barbecue, dancing, much music and merriment. It is rustic and pretty, adjacent to the picturesque, historic little church. On the minus side, it is small and rather cramped for Pierre's projected fourteen houses. Mixed little houses, he says, for young and old alike, cheap and affordable; although how the elderly half of the new residents are to contribute to the school is not entirely clear. Free Viagra, maybe, or HRT with every key?

Unfortunately, Pierre's houses won't be quite as cheap as he thought, because the county architect takes one look at the plans and says: *ah non*, these roofs are not traditional. They must be redesigned. Must be built of better, much dearer materials. Back to *le drawing board*. And then there's a bit of a tizz about the access road, which would – *will* – run alongside the presbytery, turning it from the peaceful home of the Sandret family into a humming traffic junction, endangering the Sandret children. Unfortunately, the unveiling of Pierre's plans exactly coincides with the birth of yet another Sandret child.

So, teething problems. But Pierre remains undaunted. He – uh, *we* – will have our new *cité* come hell or high water. We will grow, we will march into the twenty-first century with our school intact, our heads held high. Rumour has it that, in due course, there might even be a bust of Pierre outside the *mairie*, honouring his vision and resolve. Maligned today, he could be a hero tomorrow.

Only then, the Canadians move in. Dynamic Canadians intent on opening a B&B, they are horrified to hear of Pierre's master plan and vocally oppose the blueprints for it, which are on display at the *mairie*.

Mayor for nearly thirty years, Pierre is used to getting his own way. Unchallenged. After all, he hosts a charming little drinks party every new year in his *mairie*, he dishes out flowers to all the *mamans* on Mother's Day, is he not entitled to a scintilla of loyalty?

Alas, no. Not any more. The Canadians are rearing up on him. Turning on him, accusing him of trying not to revive but to *wreck* the village, to sell its soul and turn it into a faceless suburb.

Next thing, writs are flying. A survey reveals that 90 percent of the villagers feel that the scheme would destroy the rural environment. Should they wish to live in suburbia, they threaten, they will move out to Le Havre or Dieppe or Rouen. Not only will the village not expand, it won't even survive in its present form. Anguish abounds, and a summit meeting is hastily called.

The meeting, held in the village hall – ironically, restored by poor Pierre some years ago – is heated. First up is *le Canadien* Laurent, to deliver an impassioned speech worthy of the Senate. This field, he thunders, is our *patrimoine*, our heritage, our community asset. It is to be preserved, not plundered!

'Ah,' retorts Pierre rather unwisely, 'you're only a blow-in, what would you know?'

Whereupon an old codger totters to his feet. *Eh oui*, perhaps this young Laurent is only a blow-in. But what a breath of fresh air! For years, *monsieur le maire* has enjoyed a reign of terror, but now it is over. Now, people will follow this lively Laurent's example and stand up to him! He, for one, is *delighted* to welcome the vigorous new resident amongst our fold. Well done, laddie!

'But,' splutters Pierre, 'but, but . . . I'm only trying to do my best here. We need to up our numbers. I only chose that site because no other was available.'

A snoozing farmer leaps to life. Rubbish, nonsense! He will happily sell his own ten-hectare field to the community, on condition that the houses built on it be nice traditional cottages, causing no hassle to the Sandret or any other family. Would Pierre care to name a price here and now?

Curiously, Pierre fails to seize the offer. He must, he mutters, think it over, discuss it with his . . . 'Henchmen!' bawls a voice. 'You and your henchmen! You think you have this village stitched up, think you can ride roughshod over us, bribe the women with

flowers, treat us like your peasant playthings! Well, you can't any
more. Your reign of terror is over!'

Understandably, Pierre pales, perhaps mindful of *La
Révolution*. Consulting his paperwork, he guardedly remarks that
the *cité* project is as yet merely embryonic. Nothing is set in stone.
Further research might be required.

'Further research,' yelps a voice, 'has already been done! The
regional council has looked into it, and declared itself opposed. On
environmental grounds! Social grounds! Infrastructural grounds! It
is a non-runner, *monsieur le maire!*'

And so, during a somewhat pregnant pause, the project stalls.
And continues to stall, for a very long time . . . weeks go by,
months, years. The Sandret infant survives into kindergarten without being catapulted from its pram by any speeding vehicle. The
presbytery remains unswallowed by any spaghetti junction. The
B&B is open for business, billing itself as a 'tranquil rustic haven in
open countryside', and full to bursting. Bleakly, Pierre continues to
plead for 'progress', but his entreaties fall on stony ground. After all,
Pierre doesn't actually live here: his house is a comfortable three
kilometres away from the fief over which he presides and plans to
'develop'.

As yet, no shotguns have been loaded, nothing more provoca-
tive has transpired than an ill-researched newspaper article heavily
weighted in Pierre's favour, and his own headline comments about
'the bad atmosphere' of his own making. But, under our little
village's somnolent aura, there now lurks humming tension, as if a
distantly rumbling thunderstorm might at any moment turn into
a tornado. In the nature of French feuds, this one looks set to run
until the Sandret infant staggers up on his Zimmer frame to collect
his old-age pension . . . until the morning of the bulldozer.

Bright yellow, assisted by a tractor, it appeared as if by magic, trundling into the disputed field at first light, catching the village unawares. Most people had left for work, but those who remained rallied, virtually in their pyjamas, to Laurent's battle cry. *'Allez, allez, vite, vite, le maire va nous écraser!'* ('The mayor is going to flatten us!')

And so it proved. The driver of the bulldozer announced that his employer's instructions were to keep driving, regardless of who might throw themselves in the mud under his tyres. The villagers called the police. Pierre, arriving in person, took one look at the protest and ordered the police to remove all demonstrators. The police retorted that they would give any orders to be given, and demanded to see his building permit. Words were exchanged, names were taken, and finally the bulldozer was halted in its tracks.

But not for long. Pierre sought, and got, derogation from Bâtiments de France (the government's architecture protection agency) to build within the normal five-hundred-metre exclusion range beside the historic church. A concrete mixer turned up, only to be blocked by a quick-thinking farmer who parked his tractor across its path, leaving the cement to set fast in its belly. And then, bloody but unbowed, Pierre revealed the full extent of his master plan.

Not just fourteen little houses, at all. Scores of them, hundreds, ringing the entire village, turning it into a town. The playground to be tarmacked, a concrete 'health track' plonked in the middle of the cornfields and – horror – a brand new industrial zone to be created in the field where, in winter, wax-jacketed locals currently hunt rabbits and shoot pheasant. A *second* industrial zone – there's already one barely a kilometre away – plus a new tax to pay for all this, to be extracted from all residents whether they approve of his urban jungle or not. A tax to be levied on every resident, every year for the next *fifty years*.

Collectively, the shocked village appeals to Bâtiments de France, to the regional council and to numerous other bodies, two of whom send *enquêteurs* (inquisitors) to investigate and hear the howls of protest. One evening, we all line up like schoolchildren to be summoned one by one to say our piece to these bored-looking chaps, the atmosphere reminiscent of old-style confession in a Catholic church. As I'm the last to be heard by the second *enquêteur*, who is wearily packing his briefcase and stifling a yawn, I ask him whether, realistically, he reckons the protest stands a snowball's chance in hell.

'Realistically,' he replies, 'no. In France, the system always wins. Hands down, sooner or later, every time. You can't beat it. Waste of time even trying.'

When I relay this to my neighbours, many – incredibly – nod in recognition, in resignation, almost in defeat. Personally, I'm levitating with outrage and have to be all but talked down from the church steeple; perhaps prophetically, the church bell happens to toll at the very moment the man snaps his briefcase shut.

But if protests go unheard, if the system always wins, then France isn't a democracy at all! It is totalitarian, Nazi, Stalinist!

Further enquiry into statistics reveals *monsieur l'enquêteur* to be wrong. One percent of planning protests are in fact upheld.

One percent. Just so nobody can accuse the state of not listening to its people. Those are the odds you face if you try to change anything in France: one in a hundred. It is a long time since 1968, and many of the rioting students of that year now occupy plush jobs in the civil service, where they can buff their nails to their hearts' content, chucking today's protests into some dusty bin before they go out to their two-hour, civil-service lunch.

And so, at the time of writing, it remains: the mayor versus his village, a vendetta shaping up to endure into eternity. Whatever about *liberté* and *égalité, fraternité* has gone out the window, and the next municipal elections are awaited with unprecedented eagerness.

But will they be in time to get rid of Pierre? Rush matters, and the civil servants might have a nervous breakdown. Let this mayor build what he likes, is their attitude, and if a few mouthy foreigners get flattened in the process . . . *eh bien*, all the better!

This slow-mo strategy seems to be working. The foreigners are talking about selling up and moving to more congenial villages with less tyrannical mayors. So are some of the natives. Far from seducing new settlers, *monsieur le maire* is driving people out instead, breaking up the community just as all the 'blow-ins' have started to integrate into it, blighting the landscape and sowing dissent. And then one day, he does something else: he hits a four-year-old child a clip round the ear. The little fella wandered into the grounds of the *mairie* and allegedly damaged a shrub, plucked a flower or somesuch offence right under Pierre's nose, and Pierre rushed out to 'put manners' on him.

This has turned out to be a grave tactical error, because now the child's dad – a hefty fisherman – is gunning for Pierre, promising to 'sort him out' when he 'catches hold of him'. Overnight, Pierre vanishes from view and sends his deputy to present this year's fuchsias at the Mother's Day drinks party – which, without its traditional host, turns into the merriest in recent memory.

Minus the mayor, everyone gets on famously, and it's hugely heartening: maybe all is not yet lost? Especially since word has just reached us of pending matters judicial, which may distract Pierre for years to come . . . in fact, into his dotage. It is not inconceivable that he may yet find himself a resident in the old-folks section of his own lovely new housing scheme.

11.

Let's Eat Out

It is a gilded spring day. In the village square, the weekly market is in progress, the stalls overflowing with cheeky scarlet tomatoes, muddy ochre carrots, emerald cucumbers, black logs of freshly baked bread, mauve-tipped artichokes in from Brittany, golden football-size melons up from Cavaillon . . . amidst it all, an American lady stands transfixed, clutching her husband.

'George! Look! Just look at this!' Embedding her nails in his forearm, she gapes squeaking, at the scenario, which is indeed picturesque. 'My God, it's so, so . . . '

Lost for words, she gazes around her as if somebody might furnish the words she can't seem to find. So gorgeous? So fresh? So natural, so colourful, so healthy, so brimful of nature's bounty? Indeed it is, madam, indeed it—

'So *unhygienic*! Look, nothing's wrapped! *Nothing!* All this food, out in the open air. Anyone could *touch* it . . . '

They could, and they do. Have done, for centuries. Pummelled the potatoes, pinched the peppers, prodded the pumpkins . . . And yet, thus far, there have been no reports of death by contamination. Not a single incident of poisoning by peasant's finger. Apparently, the French have made the great mental leap from market to tap, have latched on to the concept of washing their food before they cook it. Not that they wash the pig's trotters, or the sausages or tripes; they just don't pinch or prod those – although the cooking process will kill all bugs anyway. Their confidence is cast-iron, as befits the country that wrote the culinary equivalent of the Kama Sutra.

Nearby, two English women are debating whether to buy a baguette. One is recklessly keen, but the other holds her back: 'No, they're no good, don't last at all. You have to buy a new one every day!' But, aghast, the Americans are now confronting an even worse affront. Something far worse than food straight from the farm, with no shrink-wrapping in sight.

'Live chickens! My Lord, haven't they heard of bird flu?'

Why yes, they have. Indeed, there was a dodgy moment there a while back, when all the village mayors ordered everyone to confine their free-range poultry indoors. Everyone did. For a couple of weeks. Until they sort of . . . well, forgot. While the incarceration order was never officially revoked, the chickens eventually just somehow wandered back outdoors, clucking and scratching as if they'd never heard of H5N1. Now, a clutch of them has been rounded up to squawk in their cages this morning, until someone buys them for eggs or, if they're unlucky wee chickens, for lunch.

The American lady is literally clutching her bosom, horrified by the spontaneity of it all, the unruly freedom, the apparent muddle. In fact, there is no muddle whatsoever: *au contraire*, food production is vigilantly monitored and you would be a long time trying to finger the cow that isn't wearing its Department of Agriculture earrings, neatly numbered, dated and annotated. Sometimes the cows even make a personal appearance at the far end of the marketplace, on the hoof, for sale to the highest bidder provided the vendor can supply their name, rank and serial number.

But no, the farmers have not thought to shrink-wrap them. No doubt the quantities of plastic required would up their overheads, and to a French farmer a sou is a sou. (No matter that sous are now centimes, and francs became euros years ago: most French farmers are too busy burning down supermarkets to read all this bumf from Brussels.)

Twittering in horror, the American lady is led away by George, who seats her at the corner café and orders two Cokes, complete with sugar, caffeine, stabilisers, E-numbers and all those other comforting chemicals. Clearly, the pair are in culture shock, and it's hard not to smile. Because whatever a French chef might be accused of, abusing his or her ingredients with chemicals will never top the list of crimes. The nearer they are to nature, the better; many of the best restaurateurs grow their own, planting, sowing, digging, pruning, plucking, knocking off the worst of the mud with their elbow before popping them straight in the pot. France must be the only country in the world that can make even a parsnip palatable.

The country is, as we know, peppered with restaurants. If you joined up all the dots from one to the next, you'd have a virtually solid canvas. However, all that glitters is not necessarily gold, and if there is one glitch in the fabric of French food, it is – not invariably, but alas often – the restaurant in which it is displayed, served and eaten.

❧

Naturally, French restaurateurs mean well. Take their business most seriously. Indeed, one of their number, the star-festooned Bernard L'Oiseau in Burgundy, went so far as to shoot himself when he suspected that Michelin might be about to strip him of an *étoile*. They hadn't actually done it, you understand: the poor man merely feared that they *might*. (His widow Dominique, evidently of a more pragmatic disposition, rallied rapidly: her biography, *Bernard, Mon Mari*, was for sale in the restaurant window almost before the organ music had faded away.)

And they make great efforts to please their anglophone visitors. All are legally obliged to display their menus outside their premises, and they make heroic attempts to translate them. Thus you find such delights as 'chicken roasted in spit', 'squabbles', 'beef with warships', 'puréed shuttles' and – my favourite – 'shoddyffed to the cream of her capers'. Since moving to France, my cooking has, without the slightest effort, improved immeasurably, but I have yet to find out exactly what 'shoddyffed' might be – perhaps a Welshman might know? – or what capers it has been up to. But in any language, it is virtually impossible not to eat well, and healthily, all in the same melting mouthful. Cookery books beckon like beacons, and even endives acquire allure. (Mind you, I would ban tripes. And Brussels sprouts should be illegal in any language.)

One day, the comedian Jamel Debbouze confessed that he sometimes signs comment books in French restaurants thus: 'I detest this restaurant. Nicolas Sarkozy'. A cruel, um, caper, since many are magnificent, true temples of gastronomy, especially the ones where reverent silence reigns and you find yourself wondering whether you're expected to genuflect as the waiters lift the silver lids in concert. A singularly focused race where food is concerned, the French can sometimes be seen demolishing the most fabulous meals with the look of anxious concentration one might normally reserve for, say, one's tax returns or one's application for permission to operate an electric toothbrush. All is dutiful hush, and should any minor glitch occur, the restaurateur will be the last to know, since the French firmly believe in complaining only to their friends, never to the *patron*. An oddity this, since they rarely hesitate to complain about anything and everything else to all and sundry, but there we are. Head waiters just seem to affect them the same way as school principals.

Food-wise, there is indeed little to complain about. I have been known to clutch my companions in astonishment, we have actually *blessed* ourselves on tasting certain dishes – I particularly recall a fig-stuffed caramelised pear – so fabulous have they been. As a result, one can easily forgive the dog in the corner of many a local bistro, scratching behind its left ear for fleas; one can forgive the decorator's inexplicable plunge into 1940s nostalgia, using original materials; one can even forgive the unisex toilets, where, if you're not quick enough, you are plunged (perhaps mercifully) into Stygian darkness after ninety seconds when the light cuts out automatically. You can even forgive them for not knowing that no, Irish coffee doesn't work with *crème fraiche*, only with Chantilly.

The one thing you really do have to work at forgiving is the service. That puzzled look when you arrive and say: 'Hi, here we are, name's Murphy, we've booked a table for six at eight?' That long subsequent powwow, in agitated whispers, with the receptionist or maître d' or whoever failed to note the booking. The eventual seating at a table for four, by the kitchen, with extra chairs tacked on. And of course the fifteen-minute wait for the menu . . . which, if you look at it constructively, is good practice for the impending twenty-five-minute wait for the starters, and later the thirty-five-minute wait for the bill, followed by the forty-five-minute wait for the machine to accept your foreign credit card. After all, there's only so much any one waiter can do in an evening, when he's in sole charge of a dozen tables and has the hoovering to do too, while waiting for Visa to respond. It's at moments like this that one ponders France's acute unemployment problem, because clearly some vacancies remain to be filled in the catering sector. Maybe it's because each extra employee means the boss having to fill in an extra twenty-seven hours' worth of paperwork every week, in triplicate.

Over the years, my research into French restaurants, while never reaching the dizzy heights of La Tour d'Argent, has been diligent. Of course, menus change and staff come and go, but there have been memorably wonderful experiences at La Fermette Marbeuf and Casa Olympe in Paris, at Les Hêtres in Normandy, Le Pelican near Pézenas, La Garaudière near Beaune, Les Crayères in Reims, and in the back of a tumbledown little shop near Saintes, where *la patronne* kept us prisoner for hours with course after course of a stupendous meal we didn't even know we were going to have. The chairs were rickety, the mood was jolly, and the food was phenomenal. More than in any other country, it pays in France to peer into dark doorways and forget all about trendy décor – indeed, one of the worst meals I ever had, in London, was in the most exquisitely designed of trendy restaurants, over whose name we will draw a veil.

All but the most elegant of French restaurants accept children. Usually this is not a problem because, as an Irish friend notes in amazement: 'They sit up straight, eat their spinach and behave impeccably.' Only once, at the lovely L'Absinthe in Honfleur, did a shrieking toddler ruin our Sunday lunch as it raced between the tables, tripping up waiters, stampeding like a bull while its parents argued over whose bright idea it was to bring it. I yearned to capture it and carry it, roaring and writhing, into the kitchen for the chef to do with as he would. Don't get me wrong: I do like children, even if I can rarely eat a whole one. But between us, we would have dispatched that one, filleted and flambéed.

In Paris, waiters are notoriously snappy, in more ways than one. Waiting is regarded as a noble profession, they do it efficiently and are paid well in the busy bars, cafés and restaurants. In the provinces, however, things move more slowly. I once watched in awe while a waitress cleared our table plate by plate, glass by glass, ferrying two items at a time across the street from the waterfront to the kitchen in her fists. She was just a summer youngster, nobody had suggested she use a tray and, well . . . French schools put more emphasis on philosophy than initiative. A tray simply hadn't dawned on her.

We tipped her anyway, because she meant well, but it comes as a shock to many tourists, especially Americans, to discover that tipping is not expected. At most, a euro or two for really brisk, friendly service, a fiver in a ritzy restaurant, but service is already built into the bill and anything else is entirely voluntary. 'Voluntary' means (a) the waiter has really made a difference to your enjoyment or (b) you're a big group who've made major demands. Being rowdy, changing your mind or requesting translation all count as being demanding, and you should reward accordingly. But you'll never find a line left open on your credit-card slip for a tip (which amazes my Irish friends, accustomed to meekly paying for service twice), and you'll never have the experience I once did in New York, where a waitress chased me down the street shrieking that I'd forgotten her tip – for serving one coffee that cost one dollar. In France, you don't tip unless you've spent at least twenty euro, and, far from being ingratiating, over-tipping is embarrassing.

However, the one thing that no money seems able to buy is a smile. Is it that all the waiters' feet are killing them? Is it that famous French reserve, often interpreted as frostiness? Is it the entire industry's exasperation with the thirty-five-hour week, which restaurateurs say is ruining them? Or do they really regard eating as the religious ritual it sometimes seems to be? Probably it's a combination of the whole lot. But don't despair. The food is usually so good it'll put a smile on *your* face if not theirs, and as yet there's no law against that. (Though the government seems to be working on it.)

One night, a local restaurateur brought a tray of *digéstifs* to our table, unbidden, before we left. What, we wondered, had we done to deserve this delightful gesture?

'You talked,' he said, 'out loud. You smiled and laughed and brightened up the atmosphere of the entire evening. Everyone enjoyed it more because you were here. I love it when you Irish come in – you always seem to have fun, and so everyone else does too.'

So, don't be intimidated if things are subdued when you arrive. Just create your own atmosphere. The French don't mind at all – in fact, they love to see people enjoying themselves, even if they're genetically programmed not to show it.

※

Meanwhile, back to basics. It is a rainy Sunday in late October, and the last apples have been pressed for cider; now we're into mushrooms. The leaves are falling on a landscape that reflects the colours of the mushrooms themselves: ivory, rain grey, straw yellow, cinnamon and slate. Huge heaps of cloud fill the low, broad sky, and tiny, booted figures clump across the treacle-textured fields, sweeping methodically from side to side in green waxed jackets, leather gloves, feathered hats and green wellies, carrying broken guns over their forearms. Sometimes they stop, sit down on folding stools, take a slug of something warming from their hip flasks and wait intently, peering into the mud, their red-collared retrievers alert and panting, ears pricked for orders, alongside them. Mainly – but not exclusively – male, these are the local hunters, out shooting partridge. Their hunt has none of the drama of the once-resplen-dent English hunt, with its scarlet jackets and halloo'ing horns: it is low-key, vernacular, smudged and muffled behind the curtain of rain. And yet, it is beautiful. A tableau, a vestige of country life as nature intended, richly organic. One of the hunters is a neighbour, and I stop to say hello; a profoundly traditional farmer, he shakes hands, or rather fingers, as is the custom when your hands are dirty, while his companion reins in the dog, a fine muscular Labrador full of energy, looking as if he knows he is exactly where he is meant to be.

Just last night, there was a programme on English television about 'problem dogs', sent off to learn manners at a 'dog borstal' with their no-less-problematic owners, most of whom simply didn't seem to understand their dogs' canine nature. One of the dogs, a big buster called George, had become unruly because, at ten months old, he was cooped up indoors all day with no more than a short urban walk for exercise. Looking at this other dog now – they resemble each other like cousins – I can't help thinking how lucky he is by comparison, loving every moment of this busy, chal-lenging day out in the open Norman countryside, with a master who knows why he owns him.

Evening is falling. My mud-spattered neighbour and his friends have bagged twenty partridge. Shouldering their guns and bulging sacks, they head home, bandoliers of ammunition looped across their chests as they wade through the black drills of ploughed earth, looking like . . . well, looking like men. Not old men, but not new ones either. Looking like men of the region and of the land, which is exactly what they are.

No doubt the partridge are peppered with shot. No doubt one of the hunters, eating dinner tonight, will spit out a few splinters of ammo or, if he's hardy enough, blithely wash them down with some

Burgundy or Bordeaux. The meal, literally fallen from the sky, will be whisked from muddy field to scrubbed table in a matter of hours, and it will taste like a gift from the gods to those who have spent their day in search of it.

And no, madam, sorry, it won't be shrink-wrapped.

❦

Fast-forward two months, and once again Christmas is approaching. I have been to visit my neighbour with a crate of empty bottles, and his fat sheep, scattered like toys around the orchard, have paused in their munching to watch him fill them with the fiery calvados he makes from his own apples, to sell on the side to one or two friends. He siphons it from a keg into a funnel, and thence into the bottle, with the practised hand of decades, and not a trickle, not one drop of the apple brandy is lost. Yes, of course you can buy official calvados in the supermarket, properly bottled and labelled, and it's very good; it just doesn't have quite that tang of autumn mist mixed with apple pips and blades of grass and stray leaves, that heady hint of wood and wool. It doesn't carve quite the same dramatic canyon in your tummy midway through a ten-course meal, which is what calvados is designed to do. The *trou normand*, knocked back in one gulp, works on the scorched-earth principle, clearing everything in its path, leaving the committed gourmet ready and raring to tackle the second half of his or her humungous Christmas meal (often eaten on Christmas Eve) with revived gusto.

However, before we get that far, the meal must start somewhere. Traditionally, it starts with plump tangy oysters from Cancale, Arcachon or St Vaast – lemon juice or shallot vinaigrette being the only desirable dressings, ask for Tabasco and you might well be asked for your papers – but we have decided to blaze a new trail. With radical daring, we foreigners are going to start with scallops.

And so I pack up my crate of moonshine calvados (apart from flaming the pud, it makes an ideal Christmas gift), get in the car and drive on to the home of *m'sieu le pêcheur*. Very possibly, he has some other real name – surely it can't actually be Mr Fisher – but I have never been able to ask him, because whenever I come to collect my scallops he is, logically enough, away at sea. I first heard of Mr Fisher from a neighbour who works on the cross-channel ferry, who told me, scandalised, about tonnes of scallops being dumped into the English Channel because nobody wanted them. Whereupon I leaped up, hand in air, shouting that *I* wanted them, I would take them all! Well then, he said, go see Mr Fisher, he will procure you some straight off his boat, fresh out of the ocean. And . out of their shells too, he even does all the preparation for his little circle of cash-paying customers.

Terrific. *Terrible.* And so I have since visited the Fisher home many times, as again today, to pick up my sack of cushiony scallops and pat the heads of the five little Fishers, who line up to say '*allo m'dame*' in chorus, each one a head taller than the next. (I suspect they sleep Russian doll-style at night, the smaller ones tucked into the larger.) Despite his perpetual absence, Mr Fisher must get home now and again, because the eldest of these steps-of-stairs is only six, while the baby is barely teething, and madame is pregnant, *eh oui!*, once more.

After due banter about impending baby Fisher, and an appreciative nod at the scarlet sunset behind farmer Marcel's *pigeonnier* (dovecote) in the nearby field, the booty is duly produced. Two kilos of silvery scallops are slipped to me (I feel as if I'm buying cocaine), and even in the dusk I can see that many have their sacs of orange coral still attached . . . which may explain why scallops taste so good with a certain orange sauce that is, alas, particularly difficult to make. My own method, less dramatic but nonetheless delicious, involves Noilly Prat and crème fraiche. But not yet. Not yet.

First, the glistening scallops are to be chilled and rested overnight. 'Shake them,' advises the perpetually harassed, albeit kindly, Mrs Fisher, 'in a drop of milk. They keep better and they fill out, plus the flavour is enhanced.'

How they could possibly fill out much further without bursting, or how flavour can be much better than ocean-fresh, I do not know, but I take her word for it. The scallops will be cuddled and cossetted and given every possible care en route from this world to the next. After all, they do cost 60 percent of the price of the ones in the supermarket; even in France, there's no such thing as a free lunch.

And now it's almost dark, and it's time to meet up with my English neighbour Tim, who has requested my assistance on a little mission. While his wife is away in England working for a week or two – somebody's got to earn a crust somewhere – he has been issued with instructions to procure a turkey. Like the calvados, turkeys are available in the supermarket, packed and prepared, but he and his wife have decided that they will have a proper local beast, fresh from the farm, and we have already sourced it at a farmer's stall in our local market earlier in the week. Now, it is ready for collection; the only stumbling block might be the directions to the farmhouse, because he's not quite sure he understood Mrs Farmer's crunchy accent. Something about a crucifix, apparently, something in patois that entirely defeats his sat-nav.

So, armed with our mobile phones, we drive off into the Stygian night, only to discover that it's rush hour in farmland. There is not only a car coming at us, but a tractor a few hundred metres behind as well. Good Lord, don't things get busy round here at Christmas, next thing it'll be road rage!

No matter. Soon we shake off all this traffic and slew up a road – well, muddy track – to the left. We know it isn't far to the farm, but there's still no sign of it . . . on and on we drive, only to eventually arrive, baffled, at the crossroads of a main road. No, definitely not. We must have passed the turn somewhere without realising it – not a difficult feat in this comprehensive, all-enveloping darkness. At night in Normandy, all is pitch black, and the sky is shimmering with stars.

'Ring madame,' Tim finally concedes, 'or we could be going round in circles till Christmas.'

So I ring her, and she says what did I tell you, you turn left at the *calvaire*, it's in a grotto, you can't miss it (you fools) . . . while I relate this to Tim, he reverses and hey presto, yes, there's the crucifix! Now we're motoring. A few hundred metres on up a dirt boreen, we spot the battered old car which is our next landmark, and we're home and dry on turkey turf, madame's husband waiting to meet us at the door with a hefty child in his arms, nodding sleepily off over his shoulder.

No. On closer inspection, it's not a child, actually. It's the newly deceased turkey. The biggest, sturdiest turkey imaginable, its paws dangling down the farmer's chest and its wrung neck dangling down the farmer's back, its beak agape in shock, a beady eye fixing us reproachfully as if to say: 'I was running round this farm only five minutes ago, you know, until you ordered my execution. How can you have done this to me?'

Naturally, credit cards don't work for this kind of transaction. A rumpled wad of cash is fetched up from the depths of a grimy pocket, and Tim staggers as the turkey is transferred to his grasp. It is *enormous*, and its very integrity is a problem for him. Briefly he wrestles with the prospect of trying to say something in French, but then he chickens out and turns to me. 'Would you ask *m'sieu* here if there's any chance he might chop off its head for me? I, uh, don't like to be the one to do it . . . '

So I ask Mr Farmer, who rather unexpectedly says no, no chance. He doesn't like to be the one to do it either, he adds with a touch of asperity. After all, this creature was a friend of the family up to five minutes ago. Here's your bird, thanks for your custom, and now goodnight. Goodbye. Firmly, the door closes.

So we clump to the car, Tim heaves the bird into the boot and wrestles the lid down over its boulder-size chest, and we head for home, wondering how exactly you brace yourself to chop a . . . uh, maybe a little shot of that calvados might help?

Scarcely is he home when his wife rings from London to find out whether the proper, authentic, corn-fed, free-range organic turkey has been got?

'Yes,' affirms Tim, a little crisply after his somewhat traumatic odyssey to turkey Mecca, 'it has. It's out in the garden. I've tied it up on a long rope and it seems quite happy. When you get back, dear, you'll only need to sharpen the axe and kill it.'

Yes, well, this kind of Christmas shopping makes a refreshing change from Tesco. Now all that's left is the monks, who should have our cheese ready and waiting for us over at the moonlit abbey, its rind washed by their very own gnarled hands. Rumour has it that they give it a good flaying with their rosary beads at Christmas, to get the bumps out and maintain the religious aspect of things . . . and then there's the lady who hand-stuffs her squawking geese to make the foie gras, but maybe you don't want to hear about that. Not unless George is standing by with a stretcher.

12.

Santé!

It is two days after Christmas. Christmas can be tricky in a new country; but then Christmas can be tricky in the old country too. Hearteningly, this one turns out to be delightful, thanks to lifelong French-Irish friends who invite me to participate in the oysters, foie gras, presents and general merriment. There is even smoked salmon from Ireland, plus a Christmas pud somehow smuggled through security, and the craic is every bit as good as ever it was 'at home'.

However, I now have a minor injury which needs ointment from the pharmacy. It is a whistlingly cold day, and on arrival in the village I am surprised to find throngs of people milling around. What can be going on? The atmosphere is restive, almost as if some kind of riot is brewing. Perhaps one of the shops is having a particularly exciting sale, like Harrods, and people have been camping on the pavement overnight in their sleeping bags?

Mais non. The village has three pharmacies, and as I approach the first of them I realise that it, along with the other two, are the focus of the excitement. All three pharmacies are crammed to bursting, and long queues are snaking out onto the pavement. Oh no! A leak at the nuclear power plant! They're here for urgent iodine supplies!

But no. Nothing has leaked or exploded, except for a highly contagious outburst of post-festive hypochondria. After a long wait in the queue, during which everyone is excitedly discussing their *grippe*, their *crise de foie*, their *mal de tête*, and various other cherished ailments, I finally near the counter. The pharmacist has whittled down the seething hordes until only one woman remains in front of me. She is brandishing four prescriptions.

Four? Even the pharmacist, standing as he does to make his third million of the morning, looks somewhat dazed by this. Frowning, he peers at her over his spectacles. *Four*, madame?

Eh oui. She has *la grippe*, she explains, as have her husband, her son and her daughter. *Toute la famille.* The doctor has made a house call and issued an identical prescription for each of them. She is here to pick up the resulting twenty or thirty medicaments. Taking the paperwork, the pharmacist sets about filling a bag – a veritable sack – with industrial quantities of lotions and potions.

And another. And another. And another. Each bag is stuffed to bursting with identical quantities of identical medication – no, not generic, brand names only, *merci beaucoup* – and, by the time the lady leaves, she is all but swaying under the weight of the taxpayer's purchases, festooned like a Christmas tree, lumbering as if emerging from the hypermarket with a week's shopping.

Fascinated, I ask the pharmacist if it's always this busy at this time of year. After all, his shop has only been closed for two days over the Christmas break.

'Oh yes,' he nods, not entirely displeased (his children will be going to the Sorbonne, possibly Harvard), 'everyone has eaten too much, has a headache or sick stomach, then there's the cold weather . . .' Handing over my tiny tube of ointment, he eyes me with pity. By comparison with all the others, my two-euro purchase looks pathetic. And I paid for it myself: both euros!

I couldn't believe it. Everyone eats and drinks too much over Christmas in most countries, gets a touch of winter flu, but France must be the only place where – in the secure knowledge of reimbursement by social security – everyone buys such vast quantities of medication. If an entire family had flu, it seemed logical to me that they should share one prescription, and then get another if necessary?

'Not at all,' says Philippe, my friendly physio, when I relate this story. 'They'd feel deprived if they didn't get one each. France has a famously excellent health care system, but it is being destroyed by abuse. Soon, it will collapse. *Pooff!* All gone.'

Apparently the government shares this viewpoint, because it has started to run ads encouraging people to opt for generic medicines, which are 30 percent cheaper than branded ones, to visit the doctor rather than call him out and to economise in numerous little ways. But when it comes to health, the French don't believe in economising. *Au contraire*, they feel they are getting value for their taxes. They are *entitled* to waste as much as they want. Anyone leaving a pharmacy without at least five or six tubes, packets and bottles feels cheated. The ever-spiralling cost of it all simply doesn't concern them.

And besides, what would one talk about then? The French love, absolutely adore, discussing their health. Ask someone how they are, and they will tell you, in detail. Blow by blow, every nut and bolt, for a full hour. The phrase 'Oh, mustn't grumble' is unknown. Grumbling is part of the fabric of France, and to be in full health is as disappointing as holding a losing lottery ticket. Sometimes when people ask me how I am and I say 'Grand, thanks', I feel I'm disappointing them, letting the side down in some vague yet definite way. Perhaps I should invent an affliction, to be trotted out on festive occasions?

At the weekly market, there is a herbalist's stall. Every Monday, it is thronged with local farmers' and fishermen's wives eagerly comparing ailments. Their aches, pains, bunions and migraines; their husbands' aches, pains, bunions and migraines; their poorly grandchildren and (the bit they love best) 'heavy legs'.

'Heavy legs' is an affliction unknown in Ireland, where legs weigh roughly the same as in most other countries. As is a 'liver crisis'. If you feel off, you take an aspirin or a bit of Bisodol, and that's pretty well that. In France, you can get a whole week or more out of either legs or liver: buckets of sympathy, buckets of advice and buckets of nearly 'free' medication. Amidst a veritable litany of ailments, hypochondria is by far the most virulent. Recently, some of the more obscure afflictions have been removed from the list of things you can claim for, and the government has begun to plead with the populace to shape up and cut down . . . A deeply unpopular attitude, this is decried and denounced by the legions of women waiting their turn at the herbalist's stall. In retaliation against the government's demand that everyone nominate just one family doctor (many had several), the nation staged a protest by nominating then-minister for health Dr Douste-Blazy, with the result that the doc-turned-politician ended up with over four million patients.

Ironically – touch wood – I have never felt healthier in my life. The pure air, fresh food, exercise and deep sleep seem to be all the medication I need. But one day, later when the weather warms up, I take my visiting elderly mother to the beach, where her hat blows away and she subsequently gets a little touch of sunstroke. Sinking onto a bench, she confesses to feeling unwell.

Mere metres away, there is a lifeguard's hut. I run to it, and there, incredibly, is a fully qualified nurse. Within seconds, she is kneeling at my mother's side with a rucksack full of medical equipment, taking her blood pressure, at once soothing and extremely efficient. Later, a doctor confirms the very simple remedy: a lie-down in a dark, cool room, and lots of water. No, no truckfuls of pills, madame, just a quiet little rest. My mother is astonished.

'They were so helpful! So nice, so kind! I can't believe that nurse was available immediately. And the doctor only charged half what he'd charge in Ireland!'

Other foreigners, both resident and visiting, confirm this. The medical service is startlingly good. A nurse even visits the home of one English lady to take regular blood tests, and visits another to dress a finger wound, whereas 'in England you'd have to go to her, whether you were able to or not'. Some doctors still make house calls, and take great pride in the quality of care they offer. An English acquaintance, terrified of having to go into a French hospital for the removal of a troublesome bunion lest 'they might experiment' on him (well, he is English, and the French do have the upper hand here, and they will eat pretty much anything), emerges ecstatic. Wonderful, fabulous, a four-star holiday camp! When I tell some French friends the story of an Irish man who, at the age of ninety-four, spent three days on a trolley in the corridor of a Dublin hospital waiting for a bed (before dying), they literally clutch their chests, aghast. But is Hireland not in Europe? What is this tale of primitive horror? Is Hireland not very rich? (It was at the time.) Such a zing would never 'appen 'ere in France, they indignantly assert: *ah non*. Nevair, evair.

Except, that is, on the night of the fright.

It is now a warm summer's evening, and I am reading in bed. Suddenly, my right leg begins to itch. To throb. To swell. To turn traffic-light red. Within minutes, it resembles a giant salami, puffing up like a balloon as if about to burst. Perturbed, I seize the phone and ring my doctor cousin Mary in Ireland.

Instantly her voice goes into professional keep-calm mode, the languidly casual tone that disguises certainty of imminent death. Oh, she says, probably nothing to worry about . . . maybe just a teeny, weeny little blood clot, the tiniest touch of thrombosis, most unlikely, but better call a doctor to be on the safe side . . . an ambulance, perhaps?

Now, screeches the subtext, quick before you're unconscious! Alarmed, I dial the emergency service (whose number is not in the phone book – you have to crack the Da Vinci code to get it). After a long interval, a voice answers. The voice listens to my story, and sighs. An exploding leg? Oh, dear. What a shame. The nearest hospital doesn't have the staff to deal with exploding legs at this hour of night. Instead, the voice will put me on to a doctor who, over the phone, will advise.

His advice is to 'Put an ice-pack on the leg. Frozen peas, if you have some. Take an aspirin, go to sleep and, in the morning, see your GP.'

Whaat? But there will *be* no morning! An embolism is rushing to my brain! I will be dead before dawn! I need to be helicoptered to hospital right away!

Ah, well. You see, madame, the thing is, there is no hospital.

Whaat? But France *is* one big hospital!

Alas, *non*. Not tonight, Josephine. There is no hospital in the entire area capable of doing the necessary tests at this hour.

But my leg is the size and shape of Italy! It is about to erupt like Vesuvius!

'Oh,' he says, stifling a yawn, 'most unlikely. Embolisms take time. Travel very slowly. An aspirin will probably break it up. But see your GP tomorrow anyway, just to be sure. *Bonne nuit, madame.*'

Bonne nuit? Is he mad? I am now practically levitating with pain, shuddering with shock. Desperately, I grab the phone again and ring my nearest friendly neighbour. Moments later he is, to his eternal credit, standing in my living room in his pyjamas under an anorak, gazing at my vast twitching leg, incredulous.

'You can't be serious. They can't have said that. You must have misunderstood. Let me call them.'

So he does and, *eh oui*, the emergency service is desolate. No ambulance, because no hospital is available. The same doctor repeats the same advice: aspirin, and get her to her doc tomorrow. Bye now.

I am frantic. But nothing can be done. No help is available, in this fabled land of fabulous health care. Not one of its three thousand hospitals can help.

And so my neighbour departs, wringing his hands, while I take an aspirin and hobble back to bed with my purple, palpitating leg wrapped in a sack of peas. There I prepare to meet my maker. *C'est la vie*. And now, apparently, *c'est la fin*.

Mary calls back. Why am I still at home? Has the ambulance not arrived yet?

I relate the news. She goes soprano. *But this can't be! Even in Ireland you'd get an ambulance for a bloody thrombosis! My God, this is unbelievable, you must get treatment, you must!*

But I can't. There is none to be had. Long live France – a lot longer than I am about to, apparently.

Six hours later, after an extremely detailed examination of the bedroom ceiling, I sit up again, astonished to find that I can. Minutes later, I am panting outside the doctor's surgery as he arrives for work. Examining the leg, he whistles.

'*Ooh, là là!*' Indeed. Sadly, shaking his head, he informs me that I have been the victim of a very naughty, very nasty insect.

Whatever it was, it has given me a vicious bite. Yes, the results certainly do resemble all the symptoms of embolism. But not to worry, it isn't one. I will be well, all will be well. Panic over.

It took days for me to recover. Not from the bite, which responded to treatment immediately, but from the fright. Such was the residual shock, I considered selling the house and moving next door to the Salpetrière, or whatever might be the biggest, busiest, 24/7 casualty department in Paris.

Okay, luckily it wasn't an embolism. But what if it had been?

Brilliant medical system? Hah! Clearly all the money for staffing overnight emergency departments has been used up by the battalions of mothers with their fifty zillion prescriptions for flu remedies.

Or maybe you just have to be French? Recently, a speeding biker came off his bike on the corkscrew hill that spirals down into our village. Very nasty injuries. Arriving instantly, the police stopped traffic for nearly ten minutes until not one but two ambulances came screeching up, amidst enough blue lights to illuminate Versailles, and whipped him off to hospital. I wouldn't have been in the least surprised to see an army helicopter hovering into view.

Mind you, it happened in the early evening. Good thing it wasn't midday, or he might have had to wait until the emergency crews had finished their lunch.

❧

A local lady has just died, aged a hundred and four. To the very end, she was in the best of shape, cheery and chatty, mentally alert, scarcely even needing spectacles. Was it her famously positive attitude that kept her so well? Or the fabulous food? Clean air? Superb health care? Daily glass of red wine?

Idly speculating, I'm mulling on this with a friend on the Irish end of the phone. A friend whose view it is that 'France doesn't pull its weight in Europe. Thirty-five-hour week, ha! The French are a bunch of incompetent layabouts.' Hearing about the centenagarian lady, he snorts. 'You have to bear in mind that the French use up hardly any mental or physical energy at all. Being a hundred and four in France is equivalent to being thirty-four anywhere else.'

Oh, so cruel! But if there is a grain of truth in it, maybe the French are right? While keeling over from a stress-induced heart attack might impress your boss, there's not much else to be gained from it. And besides, if it happened at night, you could be a long time waiting for your defibrillator. Keep a packet of aspirin handy, just in case, plus a bag of frozen peas.

And brace yourself for the imminent arrival of your eighty-eight-year-old mother, who's recently heard of Jeanne Calment, a Frenchwoman who famously lived to be a hundred and twenty-two, and decided on the strength of this information that France is the perfect place in which to live out one's old age. No, really, there is no point in ever bothering to go home again!

13.

Party Time

Okay, it's not the Irish idea of a party. Nobody goes to the pub first, nobody knocks back a dozen tequila slammers, nobody throws up, swings a punch or burns down the barn. Nobody even arrives late. But a French party can be a riot, if you hang in long enough. Or if you're let in: how was I to know, arriving at my very first party with a beautiful bouquet of golden chrysanthemums, that in France these flowers are reserved for 1 November, to be placed on the graves of the dearly departed? Presenting them to your hostess is akin to saying you wish her dead – not the ideal kick-off to festivities.

However, I didn't know this. I just knew that I wanted to have some fun. So I got dressed up to kill (which in Normandy often just means clean dungarees), and arrived at the party all willing and ready to rave, tragically clutching my doomed chrysanthemums.

First, however, prior to any fun, there are the kisses of greeting to negotiate. Stereotyped cartoons of these are not in the least exaggerated. Every new arrival at every gathering must kiss everyone already in the room – which can make it an exquisitely long night. Beginners should know that starting on the left cheek eliminates that gruesome *danse macabre* whereby one or both noses get broken, but even after years of taking aim, it remains a challenge, kind of like Olympic-level archery.

Next, the delicate question of quantity. It's not true that French kisses are unbridled. The number allocated increases according to how well you know the kissee; one too few subtly suggests your loathing of him or her, while one too many can convey your intention of bedding him or her before the night is out – rather a startling prospect if you've never even met before (unless, of course, you're an Irish teenager). Two kisses are good – unless you're family or close friends, in which case two will indicate that the kissee is, after all, to be struck out of your will. Two are the minimum, and four is the limit – but to be judiciously bestowed, lest you be mistaken for the town bike. Ideally, no body parts should touch: your aim is merely to brush the air beside the proffered cheek. In mixed company, it is the woman who proffers, and the man who kisses.

Next, what do you call the person you're kissing? French formality is such that many in-laws call each other 'monsieur' or 'madame' for years, for decades, beyond the grave. In very swish circles, *spouses* even do. It's a tricky conundrum, especially when addressing women. Married or single, a French 'mademoiselle' generally becomes 'madame' after the age of twenty-five, but guessing her age can be a minefield for amateurs. Get it wrong and . . . well, you won't actually be deported, but you won't be going to many more parties either. Annoyingly, it's not difficult for the French themselves, who are born with some kind of radar that can read every woman's date of birth on her forehead, as accurately as a laser scanning a barcode.

So far, so good. You have apologised for the chrysanthemums, bestowed the correct number of kisses on each of the twenty or thirty people in the room, and negotiated their titles. But now the nightmare really kicks in. To call them *vous*, or *tu*? Both mean 'you', but *vous* is formal and *tu* is for friends. As a teenaged au pair, I once inadvertently addressed the kids' grandmother as *tu*: the reaction could hardly have been more explosive had I embedded a machete in her head. Now I always say *vous* when in doubt, waiting to hear what they call me. ('That sad immigrant ignoramus', I suspect, although it's never audible.) Rumour has it that Jacques Chirac never dared call his formidable wife Bernadette anything other than *vous*, and most Frenchmen reckon that his discretion was the better part of valour.

Okay, you've got the hang of it. Nobody seems to be ringing the embassy to request your removal? Great. Proceed to the next stage: aperitifs and canapés. Do not expect to be offered a pint. Do not expect Tayto. Do not say 'Jaysus, I could murder a single of chips.' Do not, under *any* circumstances, express sympathy for an American president or a British prime minister. If your small talk seems to be eliciting no reaction, don't panic: the French are quite capable of gazing silently over your shoulder at the wall for ten minutes without meaning any offence. Most of them simply resent the fate that has inexplicably cast them in the role of bank clerks or sales reps, when clearly they were meant to be film directors. Silence actually indicates profound reflection on what you have just said, even if it happens to be 'our postman's goldfish died yesterday'. In France, death is no matter for mirth.

After a brief interval – no more than two or three hours – the party will start to warm up. People may utter two or even three consecutive sentences. Not, of course, that any of these sentences will concern you, since the French are not remotely interested in the foreigners who flit through their lives. Nobody will ask why you're in France, what you do, how's it going, or is it true about Biffo getting Taoiseached? Nobody's really sure whether Ireland sort of runs into Iceland, or Holland. At most, you might be politely asked how your dear queen is doing – as if you knew David Norris, or cared!

And now – now, *à table!* Dinner is served, let us all sit down. The word 'dinner' is the most electric in the French language. Within seconds, every guest will be eagerly seated, nakedly inspecting the arriving trays of wonderful food. Yes, it *is* wonderful. It is not only ceremonial but an ongoing contest, and God help the hostess whose paper-fine *rosbif* is not perfectly pink. This is where the fun part of the evening starts. You will be just tucking into your divine prawns or palm hearts or . . . oh really, it's time to get up again? The French watch their figures like hawks, and so at a party each course is worked off with a hectic spate of dancing before the next. Fabulous dancers all, they will not tolerate or even believe your mumblings about not knowing how to waltz, rumba or fox-trot, and you will curse your parents for not having sent you to Billie Barry when you were five. Or curse yourself, for having clung to the bedpost and threatened matricide if you were made to go.

Three or four hours later, the meal is over and everyone's having a grand old time. That man in the corner, the one you thought was in a coma, may actually have attempted a joke. Young Yvette may have stopped counting the calories in her Perrier. And – a sign of real acceptance, this – Madame may have tipped you off as to where to find the skin cream that will give you a complexion like hers. Well, *almost* like hers. One must try, *chérie.*

Eh oui, despite their surface gloom – or perhaps because of it – the French love to party. They put weeks of organisation into it, and it shows. Not for them the sausage sticks, the cans from the off-licence and the casual 'Hey, let's all go round to Fred's flat'. Dare to throw a party of your own, and not only will they all turn up toting beautifully wrapped gifts, they will turn up on time, with game plans, on the *dot*. This is a terrifying experience for the unwary and, especially, for the Irish. On the plus side, they'll all leave on the dot too, with no danger of you excavating a snoring Sebastien from your hydrangeas three days later. Three days later, the thank-you cards will be rolling in: *Merci, merci bien*, it was *magnifique*! And now, you must come to us . . .

You will come. Just as soon as you've sorted your *tu*s from your *vous* and learned how to dance a killer tango. On my first St Patrick's Day, a Sunday, I bravely hosted *un petit* drinks party. Amongst the guests was a local florist. Arriving in a suit buttoned up to the neck, she gazed in horror as a drink was offered. 'What? At four o'clock? In the *daytime*?'

Nothing would induce her to taste the punch. Which was a pity, because everyone else loved it, never suspecting that alcohol lurked amidst the fruit juices. It simply never crossed their minds that, on a Sunday afternoon, 'drinks' might actually mean drinks.

But it did. Oh yes, oh ho, it certainly did. Not that I set out to sabotage anyone: it simply never occurred to me to make punch without alcohol, and it never occurred to them that I'd put some in. But it worked wonders. At ten that night, I was obliged to tactfully suggest to the stragglers that perhaps nine renditions of 'Whiskey in the Jar' was enough. That nine whiskeys was perhaps also enough. Yes, I would perfect their pronunciation of all the songs and throw another party soon . . . one of them was so drunk he completely forgot his list of medical problems in mid-sentence, and another actually called me *tu* by mistake.

Which just goes to show how lethal *tu* much drink can be.

14.

Home Is Where the Heart Is

'So,' said my Irish pal on the phone, 'how's it working out? You've been in France for over two years now.'

Have I? Good grief. It feels more like two months. 'Yes, it's good,' I truthfully tell him. 'It's great.'

And so it is. While I still haven't met 'Monsieur Hulot' (the stereotypical Frenchman who'd so enhance France) the experiment is definitely working. Life is now filled with air and exercise, freedom, interest and stimulus and lovely landscapes, and it has a healthy, happy rhythm. Naturally, quitting one's job means some belt-tightening (exotic holidays are out the window, and there won't be a new car for years), but it is, so far, worth it. Living in France is proving rejuvenating, and even on a budget it's possible to have excellent quality provided you get your priorities straight. No frills, no impulse buys, we won't be getting a new fitted kitchen . . . but champagne is affordable and a lot of fun activities are free.

'So when are you coming back?'

'What?'

'For a visit? You must be bored rigid all the same.'

Eh? Must I?

'Yes. Out there on your windswept plateau with nothing only cows and crops . . . when are you coming home for a dose of civilisation?'

Well, yes. Although the promised homesickness had yet to strike, I was now into another winter. Icy, crackling, *brrr*. French seasons are crystal clear: you know exactly where you stand – or attempt to stand. On my daily walks, I was bowling along in fast-forward, chivvied by the freezing, violent wind which was hurling up huge plumes of surf at the cliffs, pebble-dashing the windscreens of unsuspecting spectators who parked too close to the harbour wall. Once or twice I was almost airborne, heading for Hastings, speechless with the needle-like intensity of the cold. One day, *indoors* with the heating on, I'd had to wear gloves, a hat, a huge woolly scarf, leggings under trousers and three sweaters, the whole glamorous apparition wrapped in a rug. Maybe, if the planes weren't all grounded by fog or snow, and French air traffic control wasn't on its weekly strike, now might be a good moment to visit . . . home?

'But I *am* home. Sitting here in my living room talking to you, at home.'

'Duh! You know what I mean! It's time you came to visit Ireland. Friends and family. We miss you, you know. Hey, did you hear the latest about . . . ?'

And my pal embarked on the latest Irish gossip, which, like a good beef *marmite* (not to be confused with Marmite), had been simmering nicely, and was now ready for serving up with a glass of wine. There's something comforting about well-aged gossip, news that no longer really matters: it illustrates how little of it was ever really important in the first place. You enjoy each tasty morsel, chew it over, have a laugh, and then forget all about it. So we did laugh, and it was heart-warming to hear that I was missed – a possibility that had never crossed my mind when I'd left Ireland. These long chats were getting ever more affordable, thanks to new internet bundles, and plane fares were cheap, too: I could fly to Dublin and back for less than the price of parking at the airport. Sometimes Ryanair even did free tickets, which even after taxes still weighed in at under a hundred euro (although I did notice a sorry decrease in flights to my favourite airport, Shannon). To assuage my assumed *mal de pays*, friends were still stalwartly sending comfort supplies from Ireland: newspapers, Rolo chocolates, Dubliner cheese (yes, really, to France), fruit gums, rashers, Barry's tea (mountains of it – I now had, almost literally, all the tea in China). I had a choice of four Irish radio stations, internet access to every Irish website . . . how could anyone be homesick, in this global village? Nonetheless, I was coming to realise that emigrating further afield – to Oz or New Zealand, say – would have been a very bad idea. I wanted – surprisingly, *needed* – regular fixes of Ireland. I needed to feel that it was near and sort of on standby, even if nobody there seemed to believe that I was in France by choice, cheerfully enjoying life *chez les frogs*. Now, invited to visit, I had better be grateful – and be glad I hadn't gone somewhere too far away to casually pop on a plane to get back, which might have been psychologically disastrous. Unless you're very young, there's a lot to be said for only emigrating down the road.

'I'll come over next week,' I promised, humbly.

'Great. I'll pick you up at the airport.'

Even if in some respects it's like going back to visit the bloke who used to beat you up, visits home are good. Not even visual Skype calls are enough: eventually you want to physically *see* your friends, embrace them, hang out and have fun with them. Not that they will be lined up where you left them, like dolls in a playhouse, unchanged since you last met. In your absence, life goes on, people move on, things will be different.

Booking my ticket online that night, I wondered whether Ireland itself would have changed much since I'd last seen it. Such was its rapid rate of development – motorways, shopping malls, housing – I'd almost needed a map to find my way around on my last visit. A short, frenzied trip, it had been gobbled up with flying visits to all and sundry as I made the classic mistake of trying to pack everyone into too short a space of time. Of expecting too much of them, too, because Ireland works a full forty-hour week. Nobody has time for much more than a quick coffee with visiting layabouts from thirty-five-hours-a-week France. This time, I wouldn't expect anyone's undivided attention. *Au contraire*, I'd be grateful if they made time to see me at all. I'd make a real effort not to annoy them by calling jeans 'a jean', to stop saying '*ah bon?*' whenever they said something interesting, and above all not to kiss them on both cheeks, which made their eyes cartwheel with terror. I wouldn't mention the weather, and I would take the advice of my friend Seán, who'd long lived in Paris.

'Don't say anything about enjoying France.'

But . . . ?

'Just don't! People who move abroad voluntarily are seen as deserters. Traitors. Some people resent us for doing what many of them would love to do but never will do. So when you get there, just say that France is fine. Nothing more. Above all, don't criticise any aspect of Ireland. Zip the lip and pretend it's perfect. Otherwise people get upset and don't want us coming back any more. They'd probably take our passports off us if they could.'

This sounded barmy, almost paranoid. But in the time I'd been in France, I'd realised he was right. I'd learned never to say I was loving France, merely to shrug that it was okay. If there had been any recent disaster that could be mentioned – a gas explosion, a rugby defeat, an avalanche – all the better. Anything that clearly illustrated that France wasn't perfect. Which, of course, it isn't.

'And,' Seán added by way of final warning, 'remember to get all weepy if anyone sings "Galway Bay". Fake the most awful nostalgia, and you'll be fine.'

And so, thus armed, I embarked for the mother ship. Who knew? Maybe the nostalgia would turn out to be real. Maybe I'd have to be dragged back to Dublin airport at the end of a week and returned to France at gunpoint, with a note around my neck telling it that it was welcome to me.

⁂

After an hour outside arrivals, I gave up. The promised friend hadn't arrived, and we couldn't seem to contact each other on our mobiles. No matter: people not turning up was simply part of the Irish lifestyle. Instead, a bus conveniently stood waiting. Boarding it, I rummaged through fistfuls of coins for the exact fare required. Patiently, the driver grinned.

'Ah, Girl Guide, were you? Always prepared?'

His laugh, and that of the other passengers, was lyrical, lovely. French bus passengers, far from laughing, all look as if they are being transported to a labour camp in darkest Siberia. And they're not even required to produce exact change. Laughing back, I hauled my suitcase aboard, whereupon some kindly man said 'Here, missus, let me help you with that.' Setting off, the driver turned on his radio, where Joe Duffy was doggedly hammering away at some wretched politician. Roasting him, flaying him in best Irish tradition. Hurray! Although *Liveline* sometimes brings me out in what the French quaintly call 'buttons', in that illogical flash I felt at home.

The drive into Dublin, it must be said, does not present the city at its best. Miles of roadworks to raise the Port Tunnel, whose roof had recently been discovered to be too low for the intended lorries . . . Dorset Street, scruffier than ever . . . O'Connell Street, where two cops were trying to break up a brawl. ('Yet another street fight,' reported Geraldine Lynagh on the news that night, 'the gardaí say they can't cope any more.') And then there was the Spike, variously viewed as 'beautiful' or 'a monument to Dublin's junkies'. Resolutely, I pushed the Eiffel Tower from my mind: after all, Parisiens initially hated that too. Once, O'Connell Street was lined with trees, but now they were gone, as was 'The Floozie in the Jacuzzi' fountain, which had been (ab)used as a rubbish bin. Instead, the stark street was lined with burger joints – a bleak vista in this land of much-vaunted prosperity.

Getting off the bus, I found myself in front of the building where I'd worked for twenty years. Sold since I left, it now stood deserted, awaiting integration into Arnott's department store next door. Maybe it should have evoked a flood of nostalgia . . . but I felt nothing. It was part of the past. As the Chinese say: 'You can't stand in the same river twice.' Inexorably, the river flows on.

❦

A few friends, a few *stunningly* expensive bottles of wine, a chow mein from the takeaway, and we were all picking up where we'd left off, having fun, catching up on all the chat and *craic*. Was it my imagination, or were the Irish now talking way faster than the French? Conversations seemed to leap like lightning in every direction: everyone was lively, laughing, no sentence ever seemed to get finished, nobody had the slightest hesitation in interrupting anyone else and everyone was united on just one subject, the *thunderingly* scandalous state of the health service, bewildering in so prosperous a country. It was France turned inside out – exactly the opposite of that country's economic torpor and allegedly marvellous health care. And it was a huge relief not to have to decide whether to address anyone as *tu* or *vous*. Even in formal institutions such as hospitals or banks, Ireland is on first-name terms with everyone. In France, I was *madame*; in Ireland, I was just me – a nuance I'd never really noticed before, but now rather liked.

The conversation was, at this moment, about a new film we'd all been to see. For a dangerous moment, the atmosphere teetered; how could it possibly have screened six weeks earlier in France than in Ireland? After all, France wasn't in any respect *ahead* of Ireland, was it? Feeling somehow responsible for this time lapse, hastily explaining that sometimes movies screen the other way round, I was relieved when somebody asked my opinion of what we'd seen.

'Terrific,' I said, wallowing in the luxury of speaking English. Whereupon half of the gathering vehemently concurred, and the other half vehemently argued that no, it was dreadful! Rubbish!

The film's merits didn't matter. What mattered was the robust response to it. In France, a film is either 'excellent' or 'interesting'. 'Excellent' is rare and high praise, while 'interesting' is polite code for 'fell asleep'. Nobody would ever say 'crap' or 'bloody great' or raise their voice in heated discussion, as we were now doing. Nobody would thump the table or help themselves to yet another glass of wine, as we were now also doing. Nobody would ring their babysitter to say hang on, I'll be late home, can you hold the fort? It was nearly midnight and the French would be long since in bed, snoring all the way from Cannes to Cherbourg. (As a friend remarked during the ghetto riots of 2005: 'France doesn't need to impose any curfew. A voluntary one has been in operation for centuries.')

Eventually, offhandedly, someone looks at me curiously. 'So, what do you do all day in this French outpost of yours? It must be getting pretty dull by now.'

Fleetingly, the outpost sprang to mind, with its miles of walks, cycles, skating lanes, beaches. The tennis court, sports complex, bowling alley, cinema, theatre, library. The Italian class, the table tennis I play in the village hall with my pal Marian. And then I remembered Seán's advice.

'Yeah. It's pretty dull. I just do a bit of walking and reading.'

This seemed to be the right answer. 'Mmm. Of course, this French lark is just a whim. It'll wear off.'

Maybe it will. Who knows? Maybe next year will bring an ungovernable urge to take up flamenco dancing in Andalucia or tulip farming in Amsterdam.

'We hear on the news that things are pretty bad over there. Riots, high unemployment . . . and all that famous red tape of theirs. It must drive you mad.'

Eh oui. There are days I could cheerfully slay the mayor, the chief executive and the entire staff of several French monoliths, plus Nicolas Sarkozy, the strutting little politician who adores America and would love to see France turn, like Ireland, into an offshore American state.

'And is it true, do they really eat horse meat?'

Yes, it is. They do. I wish the French would stop doing that, I really do. But there you go. Everywhere has its incomprehensible little foibles. At that moment, Ireland's little foible was the merry borrowing of buckets of money. 'Credit's so cheap,' I was told, 'and the banks are lending as much as we like. You don't even need the deposit for a house any more, you can borrow the whole lot.'

Really? For once, I decided to do as I'd been told and say nothing. But, in a city-centre pharmacy one day with two friends, I did pipe up to protest when the requested price of a packet of aspirin was twenty (yes, twenty!) times the supermarket price. Instantly, my friends forked over the money, grabbed my arms and marched me out for a good talking-to.

'Look, Liz. You're out of touch. You've got to realise that we don't query prices in Ireland. We've got lots of money, and it doesn't matter what aspirin or anything else costs. You just pay it without even reading the price tag.'

Of course, nobody knew then what was to come. But I did hear the economist David McWilliams on radio, warning that the property bubble could burst and tough times might lie ahead – whereupon the interviewer roundly castigated him for being a pessimistic misery. A pessimistic *mistaken* misery.

The sales are on, and spending is epic. Ireland's shopping centres (or 'malls', as they now seem to be called) look like something out of the last days of the Roman empire. The restaurants are crammed, traffic is at a standstill, all the current-reg Mercedes hum bumper to bumper, and as I drive around in my mother's antique little Toyota (later to become a stolen victim of recession), I feel like a very poor relation. A Third World peasant. A visitor from some other, sadly deprived, planet.

The houses are vast. Enormous. Everybody seems to have at least two iPods, three cars, four bathrooms, five bedrooms and six cinema-size televisions. Even if it's not all paid for, even if credit-card debt is massive, it looks good. It *is* good. The houses are solid, cheerful, cosy. Exactly the opposite of France's discreet chateaux and tottering farmhouses, they blaze with light: Ireland doesn't penny-pinch on electricity. The atmosphere is lively, even gleeful, as if all the kiddies are raiding a sweetshop, having a ball. Everything about this energetic, enterprising country shouts success: it's small, but spirited. Dynamic. It has come a long way from its famine days, and demonstrably has no intention of ever tasting poverty again. (Oh, hindsight!) Yet it has known hunger, and consequently retains a warm heart, contributes a lot to Third World charities, enjoys being on the giving rather than receiving end of kindness. Only once did I ever hear it criticised in France.

It was the morning after the 2002 Nice Treaty referendum. Ireland had voted to deny EU membership to any further applicants. I was in the local pharmacy, where my accent betrayed me. The chemist peered over his bifocals in a way that boded no good.

'Ah, yes. Our Irish resident. Madame, you should be hashamed of yourself.'

But it wasn't me! I wasn't there! Couldn't vote! I can't vote anywhere, and I had nothing to do with it!

'I must say, I ham happalled by your country's behaviour. Thirty years hago, Hireland joined the EU, a poor supplicant, as the others are now, and nobody hobjected. Hit went on to massive prosperity. And now hit wants to deny that chance to others in turn. I had no idea the Irish could be so shockingly selfish.'

Disapprovingly, heads nodded. Lips pursed. Mortified, I seized my purchase and decamped, ears burning.

And – phew – shortly thereafter the vote was held again, and reversed. After that narrow squeak, I could venture back out onto the streets of France without a brown paper bag over my head.

Now, maybe I need one in Ireland. People seem to feel terribly sorry for me. How can anyone possibly live in France without having at least 'some little bit of property' back here in Ireland? Would a pied-à-terre not be nice, and wise as well – a good investment, just in case . . . you know . . . ?

I think they mean for when I come to my senses and come home. And maybe they're right. After all, they seem to know a lot about property. Everyone has their little pad in Marbella or Capetown or Miami – or had, then. Not to mention their huge home hacienda, rocketing in value almost by the hour. If I don't buy something soon, I thought, I'll never be able to. (Which just goes to show, never say never: you never can tell what's around the corner.)

And so I set off to do some property-hunting. Not in Dublin, where the prices were cosmic – you'd buy Lithuania for the price of a bungalow – but in the west, within striking distance of Shannon airport. Seven appointments and three extremely disheartening days later, I gave up.

I couldn't afford a shoebox, never mind a house. Even the tiniest apartment in the middle of nowhere was well beyond my budget. It was also crystal clear that no ordinary person on their own could afford to run two houses. A foothold in Ireland was a ludicrous luxury and I was wasting my time, off the Irish property ladder with a thud. I have, I thought, no option but to go back to France and stay there for the rest of my life.

Ah, well. There are worse exiles. And even if the value of my French house wasn't rocketing as fast as an Irish one, whose value seemed to double by dinnertime every day, at least it was a roof over my head. Meanwhile, there were all these massive mansions to admire, with their cobblelock driveways and teak decks, multiple garages housing fistfuls of cars, their fountains and eagles, patios and state-of-the-art security systems.

Naturally, some French houses have security systems too. I'd just never seen or heard them. Whereas here, alarms seemed to ring so often they were simply part of the aural furniture: nobody paid them any attention. Presumably the police reacted to all the false alarms, but nobody else blinked.

Listening to the wailing sirens, to all the kiddies calling their mothers 'mom', reading the designer logos on their billboard bodies, I had the oddest sensation of not being in Ireland at all. Dublin felt more like Chicago or Los Angeles – until, that is, I picked up a copy of the evening newspaper. There seemed to have been a dreadful error in the printing process, because it was written in . . . Polish!?!

Yes. The *Polska Evening Herald*, catering on Fridays to Ireland's new Polish community, which now constituted four hundred thousand, or nearly 10 percent of the population.

In an Italian restaurant, our waiter was Romanian. Our taxi driver was Nigerian. The supermarket cashier was some kind of Slav. The hospitals were heavily reliant on Filipino nurses. Dublin now had dedicated shops serving the black, Arab, Oriental and European sectors of Irish society, selling couscous steamers, mealie, harissa, vanilla vodka and sari fabric by the metre.

I'm not in Los Angeles after all, I thought. I'm in Birmingham.

Visiting the country formerly known as home is turning out to be fun. City life, once so stressful, is now a merry whirl of shopping and larking about, as if I were a tourist. In some respects I *am* a tourist, gaping at so much new development, visiting the new wing of the National Gallery, eating in one of the fleets of restaurants that have mushroomed, it seems, virtually overnight. Unlike France, Ireland has no real indigenous cuisine, but it's experimental and adventurous, doing everywhere else's with enormous enthusiasm. The experience of eating out – the pace, the presentation, the ambience – is completely different to the sometimes solemn French experience. There's less stilted reverence, brisker service, brighter décor and a noisier atmosphere. And if the experience is sometimes less refined, so is the prim-and-proper decorum. In France, food is the focus, whereas in Ireland it's conviviality that counts: the laughter and banter, the fun amongst friends. If France lives to eat, Ireland eats to live. Go to a restaurant with the right people, and a wonderful time is had by all. Gradually, I reacclimatised to the concept of going out for a drink, as if drinking were an end in itself. In France drinking is inextricably entwined with eating, and in Ireland I kept reaching for the fork that wasn't there.

Other things were frankly shocking, particularly on television, where the level of obscenity was astonishing – although nobody seemed to notice. Aghast, I saw my nearly nonagenarian mother watch unblinking as two 'm . . . f . . . ing' characters all but disembowelled each other – perhaps it's a mercy that her hearing is now erratic. On the soaps, everybody was 'bleedin' warnin'' everybody else, fingers stabbing each other's chests, voices and faces contorted with aggression, *roight*? In Temple Bar, girls wearing leather coats open over only underwear cracked whips as they handed out their cards to passing youths. Little girls, as young as eight or nine, were wearing tattoos, jewellery and cosmetics: nail polish, perfume, earrings, the whole adult works. A traditional-music session in a Mayo pub was reduced to a Roman orgy by a bunch of lap-dancing women out on a hen night, and a when a friend confided the latest sexual practices amongst thirteen-year-olds, I was stunned: if you don't know what a 'rainbow' or a 'snowball' is, trust me, you don't want to know. Ireland, it must be said, has not been backward in coming forward.

Or maybe this isn't Ireland at all. Maybe it's Miami, or Bangkok?

ᕯᕗ

With the Christmas spending spree over, Ireland collapses coma-tose for a full week before revving up again to plan its summer holidays. This year, it is going, seemingly en masse, to Dubai. Or Florida, Egypt or Australia – anywhere sunny apart from the traditional Canaries, which are now 'so yesterday'. Spain is out, too: Ireland has 'done' Spain. And Ireland itself seems to be ruled out: nobody mentions visiting Cork, Kerry, Galway or Donegal, which apparently will be left to Americans and to the French, who love fishing in Connemara. During the first weeks of January, Irish travel agencies are inundated, and warnings are issued: Book now or miss the boat!

It can't be the sun that's enticing everyone abroad, can it? I'm afraid to ask. After all those reports of sweltering summer, tropical temperatures . . . ? No, they must all be going on cultural tours. Meanwhile, it's time for me to head back into exile, divided as to whether this visit 'home' has been comforting or unsettling. Some people maintain that nobody should visit 'home' for at least two years after moving abroad (although I'd now been in France for nearly three) because otherwise the graft will never take. You can't move forward as long as you're looking back.

As the plane takes off out over Dublin Bay, I wait for the little punch of nostalgia, watching the green patchwork fields evaporate below . . . in spite of everything, Ireland is still 'home' in so many ways. Ireland is warm and witty, and it's where all the reference points still are, it's where you don't have to finish your sentences because everyone knows what you mean. It's where an entire group of people collapses in laughter for no apparent reason, but they know why and so do you. It's where the mere word 'Bertie' or 'Biffo' can reduce a whole table to tears of hilarity. Ireland is spontaneous and scandalous and (at this point in time) a big, brash spender, much amused by its own reputation as the 'Rip-off Republic'. It's smiley and sociable and, unlike France, doesn't take life so very seriously. Plus, it has lots of plug sockets and the lights don't snap off after sixty seconds.

The plane banks out over the bay, and yes, I feel a pang. Feel torn, divided, not quite ripped up by the roots, but very unsure whether I'm coming or going. Is it possible to love one country, yet be *in* love with another? If I were going back to a French husband and children, or indeed an Irish husband and children who'd moved with me, would this all be so much easier? Perhaps it's going back alone that makes me feel ambivalent? Single people know better than to lament their lot (because then we'd never be invited anywhere, would we? In fact, then we'd be French), but yes, life alone can be hard anywhere. Yes, it would be wonderful to have someone to share it with. As the saying goes, a trouble shared is a trouble halved, and a pleasure shared is a pleasure doubled. I'm loving France, but not loving living there single-handed.

Really, I will have to do something about it. Somewhere on this planet, surely there must be at least one nice man who'd jump at the chance to join me *chez les frogs*? It is time to find the elusive Monsieur Hulot.

And then, barely an hour later, the plane is coming down over the green fields of France, landing in appropriately foggy Beauvais. At immigration, to my astonishment, the official recognises me. On the way out, there had been a query about something and he'd helped with it. Now, he beams.

'Ah, our Irish lady is back! Welcome home, madame!'

Home? Isn't that supposed to be where the heart is? I hadn't realised that schizophrenia could be an occupational hazard of moving to France, but maybe it is. Maybe it's even time to start blurring the boundaries and considering dual nationality.

I'm confused. But happy to be home. If only I could be sure where that is.

15.

Fast Track

'Don't take it personally,' the SNCF advises new recruits, 'it happens to most TGV drivers sooner or later.'

I've been visiting friends near Montpellier and am now aboard a Train Grande Vitesse, which is rocketing back to Paris at five hundred kilometres per hour. As in a plane, there is little sensation of speed. People are idly dozing, chatting, reading, nibbling on the picnics without which no French citizen ever ventures forth. The SNCF runs arguably the best train service in Europe, bar Switzerland's, and the TGV is its great success symbol. Punctual to the minute, smooth, quiet, laptop-friendly, blissfully comfortable: the 8.15 to Limerick Junction this is not. The passengers wear the relaxed look of punters sure of arriving in comfort, bang on time for their Christmas shopping, dinners, appointments, onward connections; the couple beside me are heading to Roissy for a flight to India. On arrival, I have another train to catch, back to Normandy from the Gare St Lazare, which means a quick Métro dash across Paris. Time is tight, but of course I will make it. The TGV's punctuality is legendary, and we are already halfway there.

Suddenly, like some cosmic arrow, another TGV bullets by in the opposite direction, showering up stones, or something that causes a series of startling thuds. Our train rocks, lurches, gropes for its grip on the tracks as sparks fly past the windows. There is a sickening sense of being sucked into a horror movie as the train brakes, wavers, squeals and screams to a halt, already many miles past where the driver applied the brakes only seconds ago. Totally silent, eerily composed, every passenger grips a table or armrest, inhaling air, sitting bolt upright, refusing to panic. A stoic lot, the French. Shaken but not stirred – just deathly pale.

The train stops, and it is as if terror takes human form, racing down the aisles, touching everyone so that they remember, belatedly, to gasp, to release the huge lungfuls of air they have gulped. Clearly there has been some terrible disaster, possibly involving the other train – but what is it? Nobody seems to be injured, but neither has anyone the faintest idea what's wrong.

Abruptly, the swish, shiny TGV service reverts to twentieth-century mode. There is a very long, very enigmatic silence. And finally a man's voice, hoarse, quavering. 'We apologise for this . . . this . . . there has been . . . a . . . human . . . incident . . .' Trembling with tears, the voice falters and vanishes, its owner audibly traumatised. Across the aisle, a man nods with sudden comprehension.

'A suicide. Someone's jumped under our wheels.'

What? But how can he know this? How can everyone be nodding in agreement, as if it's already a fait accompli, before a word of explanation has been forthcoming?

'Poor guy.' The man means the driver. 'Today was his turn. Just hope it doesn't unhinge him.' His tone is philosophical, and a murmur of sympathy makes its way down the carriage. Unknown to me until now, TGV drivers are regularly afflicted by people throwing themselves under their high-speed wheels in the desperate conviction that this is the most instantaneous method of death available. In the winter weeks, figures rise, and drivers brace themselves.

Today, it's our unknown driver's turn to find out whether he can handle this most horrific of occupational hazards. Or is his life, too, about to be devastated?

Our fellow passenger, a former SNCF employee, knows the drill. 'The driver's not allowed to move. He'll be in shock and the rule is that he has to wait for the emergency services to arrive. He'll be sedated and interviewed later, whenever he's coherent. We won't be going anywhere until a new driver comes. Which could take hours.'

We are in the pitch-black, bleakest middle of nowhere, on some kind of plain that looks like the Bog of Allen. The lights and heating go off. It's surreal, like being entombed in a freezer. We know we're in central France, about two hours south of Paris, but that's all. As word of the suicide spreads to become fact, an elderly lady turns transparent and buries her face in her handkerchief; someone else sobs with shock and sadness. My own reaction takes the form of an absolute, imperative need for fresh air. Fumbling my way out into the corridor, I find all the smokers already gathering. Rules or no rules, they say, they can't handle this nightmare. 'Haven't had a puff in five years,' one woman says, 'but sorry, give me one, would you?' Someone does, but her hands are shaking so much that the cigarette has to be lit for her.

In the carriages, nobody moves, nobody speaks. But out in the corridor, the smokers begin to revive, to pass round ciggies and lighters, to talk, to speculate as to where we are and how long this is going to take. There has been no further word from the cabin. On my mobile, I text a friend at his desk in Dublin. Can he log onto the SNCF website to see if there's any news?

Incredibly, there is. He tells me exactly where we are, and that a ninety-minute delay is expected. This information circulates amidst incredulity: some man in *Dublin* knows what's happening!?

Obviously, then, we are all going to miss our connections, appointments, flights and whatever, but everyone seems resigned, the very thought of shops and dinners suddenly obscene.

'Poor bastard,' someone sighs. They are not referring to the suicide, whose gender remains unknown, but to the driver. 'Some of them crack up, you know. It can even drive them to suicide themselves. They feel responsible – as if anyone could possibly stop a TGV in time.'

Eventually, the emergency crews arrive, men in yellow jackets flashing torches in the darkness outside. There are also blue ambulance lights, more likely for the driver than the victim: the train has travelled several miles past the site of the initial impact.

'That other train was in trouble too. It's a miracle we weren't all killed.' (Later information discloses that yes, it was a very narrow miss.) Some of the passengers are now getting angry with the 'selfish' person who jumped between the two hurtling trains; others are hoping that he or she 'was well anaesthetised, chock-full of whisky or painkillers, or both.'

Precisely ninety minutes later, a new driver announces our departure. During this time, there has been no panic, no chaos, no unseemly behaviour at all. The French, it must be said, are a calm and orderly nation. There has been no black humour either, as would almost certainly be the case in Ireland. I feel hollow with horror, some kind of delayed shock making me long for Ireland, where even in these politically correct times someone might say something so appallingly irreverent you'd have to laugh, and we'd all bond, head off to the bar for 'first aid' to calm our nerves. Irish behaviour would arguably be loud and in terrible taste, but it would be more natural, more comforting, than this forlorn, awful sense of acceptance.

On disembarking in Paris, there's no avoiding the front of the sleek, beautiful train – a tragic sight. Its conical nose looks as if it's been in a fight, peppered with dents, a steel plate hanging loose. Since the demise of Concorde, the TGV has more than ever been France's icon of success; how ironic that for some citizens it should be an instrument of death. From somewhere, a memory floats into my mind, a headline on *Marianne* magazine claiming that seven million French citizens are hooked on antidepressants. Seven mind-boggling million, in this country of peace and plenty.

'Ah well,' sighs a man in a trenchcoat, surveying the battered train, 'they'll have it fixed by tomorrow. The SNCF is well used to suicide damage.'

As, apparently, are its passengers and its drivers, who have to try to harden themselves. It's the only way they can cope. For all France's wealth, for all its beauty, for all its symbols of speed and success, suicide still goes with the territory. Like the drivers, I find myself having to acclimatise to suicides too; incredibly, the next time I travel by train, it happens again.

16.

Shop Till You Drop

Okay, chaps, you can probably pop out for a pint now while we girls dress up and head out for a little retail therapy. We promise not to spend too much if you promise to meet us back in time for the next chapter, fair enough? Which gives you the whole day in the pub (after you've mown the lawn and put up those shelves and fixed that tap), because shopping in France is a major, gruelling challenge. We don't expect to be home before nightfall, and yes, it would be lovely if you'd have a reviving gin and tonic on standby.

My first experience of *le shopping* was in a *centre commercial* roughly the size of an Irish county, so big that I'd even been given the name of the restaurant where, at noon, I would refuel without having to leave the premises. The restaurant where I'd discreetly ask the waiter to place a bucket of ice under the table, into which I could plunge my sizzling feet – before buying new, much bigger shoes. This centre, I was warned, was absolutely vast, a full day's work, and even then it would probably defeat all efforts to conquer it. Oh nonsense, I snorted, it's only a silly shopping centre for heaven's sake, how big can it be? Of course I'll get round it all. I'm Irish, I've had lots of practice at shopping. Wheee, watch me!

Wrong. Oh, so very wrong. It did defeat, comprehensively, it won hands down, I never even heard the referee's whistle. Admittedly, Britain has similarly huge complexes, but by Irish standards this was enormous: a consumer Mecca, a veritable shopaholic's souk. Best of all, I didn't actually *need* anything – which is of course the ideal mode in which to go shopping. No racing round in desperate search of Christmas presents or a spanner or a precisely pale-blue blouse; just blissful browsing, maybe coming contentedly home at the end of the day triumphantly toting an eyeshadow.

Or a ride-on lawnmower. Or a fridge-freezer. Or a new kitchen. The hypermarket that was first port of call – before even hitting the boutiques, the delis, the florists, the opticians, the travel agencies or the toy stores, all under the same roof – was so huge that the floor staff were gliding round on roller skates and the checkouts went on into infinity, their receding numbers like an eye test: I could only count up to about forty before losing sight of them. Trolleys were, clearly, not just for filling up but for jumping aboard and using as scooters when your feet wouldn't take you any further, when you'd bought your computer and television and garden marquee and dozen cases of wine and six-foot shark, but still hadn't reached the bikes or blenders or three hundred varieties of cheese.

So, accompanied by my masochist friend Véronique, I seized a trolley and set off, gazing around like some idiot infant in Santa's grotto, patting my mobile phone to make sure we could summon air-sea rescue when we got lost, as appeared to be inevitable. Maybe Ordnance Survey maps of this hypermarket were available, but if so we missed them, and were soon as comprehensively lost as if we were in some Amazonian jungle (indeed, there actually were flocks of birds flying around up in the roof.) What to buy first? Suddenly we seemed urgently to need stacks of shampoo, and Garfield cartoons, and a kilo of cuttlefish and hey, that foie gras looks heavenly and how about some of this divine asparagus and dear God, those

mangoes are irresistible and yes, it is high time for a new sound system and let's get some CDs to go with it and how convenient, the
DVD players are in the same section, good grief look at that gorgeous pair of sandals and that linen suit is perfect with them, now
there's a sexy swimsuit and wow, raspberry chocolate, really? Oh
what the hell, let's get the lime and tiramisu too . . . black pudding
from the Antilles, we must try that, yes of course with apple sauce
and a skateboard and an iPod and is there really such a thing as
green-tea ice cream? Would that go with lychee liqueur and octopus
and those boots are gorgeous and how about a new watch and some
lilac paint . . . ?

Next thing it was noon, we'd walked about seventeen miles and
we were wondering whether there might be a pedicure service on
the premises. Also whether we should have brought sleeping bags.
Three hours in, and we'd still barely scratched the surface (now we
knew why hypermarkets are called *grandes surfaces*) of this first shop
in this first section of this hypnotically appalling complex. Never
mind, we could buy sleeping bags, plus pyjamas, toothbrushes and
a tent, all the gear we'd be needing for an overnight stay. Down but
not out, we stopped for lunch – yes, even in a shopping mall it was
delicious – and then, revived, we pressed on to check out the
smaller specialist shops – only about thirty or so of them – for silk
scarves and silver earrings and all those other household essentials.
(As it later transpired, the ten-euro scarves were the same ones that
were on sale in Dublin for seventy euro.) After that, it was time to
hit the big warehouses – Casa and Fly for housewares, Castorama
for hardware, Conforama for furniture, Gémo, Kiabi and Les
Halles for clothes . . . on and on we slogged, thinking that maybe
we should have got this marathon sponsored for charity, and starting to see too why the Third World would hate the First, because
the entire place was a monument to unbridled consumer avarice.

And it wasn't even Paris, with its lush, shiny, *endless* shopping; it was just a suburban complex, one of hundreds of almost identical complexes all over France. It was eye-popping, it was ludicrous, and it was exhausting. Just before closing time at eight, we conceded defeat, broken in body and spirit. Next time, we swore, we'd buy all we needed in our little village street, toting one wicker basket and stopping when it was full. Exhausted, we headed for the car, pushing our overflowing trolley-ful of insanely indulgent, largely superfluous purchases.

And couldn't see the car anywhere. Ten hours after parking, we hadn't the remotest recollection where we'd left it, amidst the thousands in the car park the size of Andorra. Oh. Whoops. What now?

For a while we slogged on, trundling our teetering trolley, peering into the gathering darkness, realising with horror just how many Renaults are manufactured every year, wondering why every last one of them seemed to be parked in this gargantuan shopping centre. After maybe half an hour, they all looked exactly alike, and our legs and our lower lips were starting to tremble ominously.

Which was the point at which, miraculously, a jeep drew up. Driven by a security patrolman, with the complex's logo on it, it seemed to be circulating in search of precisely such situations as this. Dementedly, I hurled myself at it, babbling our predicament, bleating piteously for help.

The man's smile was comforting, even encouraging. 'Don't worry,' he said, 'happens all the time. We'll find your car. You leave your friend here with the trolley, hop in with me, and we'll go look for it.'

Phew. Hurray. *Merci merci merci, monsieur.* And *merci* again for not pointing out that the rows are numbered. What kind of moron doesn't note that they're in row 4567893/AKG/DFX/201?

'So,' he enquired, as I climbed in beside him, 'what kind of car is it?'

Well hey, that's easy! It's a Renault!

'Uh huh. Okay. That narrows things down. There can't be more than a couple of thousand Renaults here. And what colour is it?'

I can answer that too! It's lime green!

'Right. Admittedly lime green is a popular colour, but the registration is . . . ?'

Why, the registration is . . . ah. Well, you see . . . oh, dear God. With rapidly rising panic, I realised I hadn't the faintest idea what the reg was, except that it ended in '76'. But then so did nearly every other reg on every other car, since '76' stands for the *département* Seine Maritime, population four million. It was a bit like standing in Athlone, peering up to Donegal and down to Cork, saying 'I know it's here somewhere.'

'Oh. Hmm. Well, why don't we drive round for a while, and maybe you'll . . . um . . . just . . . sort of . . . recognise it?'

So we did. Round and round and round, for what felt like hours, up and down row after row, through section after section, in growing silence and grim despair, inspecting dozens, hundreds of lime-green Renaults, even stopping to try the zapper on some of them in the futile hope that – ah! Hurray! Suddenly, belatedly, I remembered the *carte grise*, the logbook drivers have to carry at all times in France. It was in my wallet, and the reg number must surely be on it.

Yes, it was. Plus, with another flash of the blindingly obvious, I remembered that the car also had an 'IRL' sticker on its back window. Surely there couldn't be too many of those?

Heroically, the security man didn't yell 'Why didn't you think of that before, you pathetically stupid but typical foreigner!' Instead he revved up from first gear into second, scooted round for only another fifteen minutes or so and, hey presto, there was the green Renault with the 'IRL' sticker. I experienced one of those movie moments when the hero and heroine run in slow motion from opposite ends of a beach into each other's arms.

Incredibly, the man wouldn't take a tip for his trouble, brushed off all attempts at thanks and even smiled cheerfully, making me blush with shame as I thought of all those remarks people make about the French being unfriendly. This one couldn't have been nicer, nor possessed of more saintly patience.

'Now,' he said, 'do you remember where we left your friend?'

No. Of course not. It seemed such a long time since we'd left her, in some other county, or even country, that she might well have been abducted by aliens by now. Adopted and taken home by kindly strangers, or eloped to Gretna Green…anything seemed possible at this stage. I had to concentrate even to remember what she looked like.

'Then get in your car and follow me,' said my saviour. 'I'm pretty sure it was somewhere near the north entrance. We'll soon have you reunited with her, and your shopping.'

And he did. There poor Véronique eventually was, sitting on a bollard in the dark, huddled against the cold, clutching the trolley and looking resigned to spending the rest of her life in this outer wilderness. Our day of hedonism had turned to hell, and I knew it would be a long, long time before we ever went shopping again.

Back home (hallelujah!) a few nights later, there was a programme on television about shopaholics. It was a disease, they asserted, and nothing could cure them of it.

Oh yes it could. A day in a French hypermarket complex could, and almost certainly would, cure them of it permanently. Aversion therapy. It would leave them whimpering for mercy, screaming at the mere sound of the words *centre commerciale.*

茶

It could be argued that such a shopping binge saves money, because it will be a long time before you can face it again. But, inevitably, Christmas eventually rolled around once more and, recovered from her ordeal, Véronique suggested another excursion. 'Let's go to Paris, just for the day, to see the lights.'

Okay. Just for the lights, then. No shopping, no spending. And not before mid-December. That would be fine, she said, because in France Christmas didn't start in October. Lights wouldn't be twinkling until the festive season was actually in sight. The big stores wouldn't be dressing their windows so early it would only annoy everyone. Mid-December would be perfect.

And so it was: a twinkly, frosty morning that felt Christmassy as we set off on the train. French trains are affordable, comfortable and punctual, and you can park free at the station in reasonable expectation of your car being intact when you return. Furthermore, your journey is unlikely to be interrupted by the 'wrong kind' of snow, or leaves – or anything else – on the tracks. (Of course, as we saw in the last chapter, there is the occasional suicide, and Thursdays are prone to fairly regular strikes.) Our train promised to have us in Paris at precisely 9.58, and that was exactly what it did, quietly and painlessly.

Two minutes later, a church bell was striking ten and we were standing in front of our first Christmas window, belonging to Printemps, filled with dancing elves and singing pixies and flurries of snowflakes, teddy bears trudging off to work with little silver shovels over their shoulders, demented dolls swinging on trapezes, teetering on tightropes with manic grins: all the fun paraphernalia that Parisiens are accused of being too snooty to enjoy. All I can report is that hundreds of them were thoroughly enjoying this, hustling their muffled, chirping toddlers up onto the viewing walkway, laughing and chatting with no evidence of snootiness whatsoever. And then, up to the top floor for morning coffee, because Printemps has a terrific terrace with a stunning view over the city, all for the price of an espresso. In summer, you can sunbathe up there; on a winter evening, you can watch the Eiffel Tower light up and sparkle as the whole city turns into a twinkling jeweller's box.

But today we had resolved not to buy anything in a department store. Today was a day for individual shops, starting at Fauchon with its gilded pyramids of plucked pheasants, salmon studded with black caviar, glazed fruits in rainbow colours like edible jewels, mocha macaroons dusted in chocolate . . . its Christmas windows are enough to make grown epicures weep. (Especially when they glimpse the price of the truffles – per kilo roughly on a par with heroin.) If you have to choose just one art gallery to visit in Paris, let it be Fauchon. And yes, be a shameless tourist and whip out your camcorder. If anyone grins, you can always say you're Japanese.

And if you have to choose just one street, head for the Faubourg St Honoré, because even if you can't afford a stitch of Hermès, it will cheer you up to see their handbags being made, along with gorgeous gloves and all the other lovely leather goods for which they're famed. Yes, you can visit their boutique, along with those of Galliano, Gucci and Chanel, without feeling obliged to buy anything. You just go in, smile politely, inhale the intoxicating aroma of money and stagger back out, swooning.

And then you look up at all the shimmering swags of white

lights, and you are struck by the most brilliant idea: let's have a seasonal glass of pre-lunch champagne at the Café de la Paix, beside the Opéra. Yes, *pink*. It is Christmas, after all! Or should we go to Les Deux Magots and pretend to be Juliette Gréco? Only one glass, though, because you didn't come all this way to lapse into a coma. At least not before you've been to O & Co. on the Ile St Louis to buy olive oil to give everyone for Christmas, or browsed the *quais* for old prints from the hinged bookstalls, or had a stroll around the Marais where the smell of garlic and salami permeates the very walls.

Lunch, when you've finally earned it, has to be a proper festive treat, at La Coupole or La Fermette Marbeuf, or – great on a budget – Chez Clément on the Champs Élysées, snuggled in amidst the trees threaded with their thousands of blue lights. Or of course you could go up to La Tour d'Argent for your pressed duckling (they're all numbered and the millionth was ceremonially served to Jacques Chirac), but don't blame me when you get the bill. Legend has it that, in 1870 when France was at war with Prussia, the chef raided the zoo and served up elephant soup along with other, er, unusual dishes. However, you might prefer to order the Claudius Burdel soup, which – like the Billybi soup at Maxim's – is so perfect it seems almost criminal to eat anything else afterwards.

After lunch, if you insist, there's a Christmas market at Les Halles, just beside the church of St Sulpice, which shot to fame as the site where Silas did his thing in *The Da Vinci Code*. Or an even bigger market at La Défence, packed incongruously into the plaza amidst all the gleaming steel and glass architecture, its fabulous arch illuminated in white. But as we weren't great fans of Christmas markets – how much *glühwein* can anyone drink, how many gingerbread men do you really need? – we went instead to the Rodin museum to see *The Kiss* and *The Gossips*, two sculptures guaranteed to make you sob. (Well, is it Christmas, or not?) And then it was nearly five o'clock, and Paris was suddenly shimmering in that misty-blue way it does, and we decided to do the most unforgivably touristy thing and take a *bateau mouche* trip down the Seine.

Okay, laugh if you like, but I'm sticking to my guns here: when you see Notre Dame's golden glow rippling on the indigo water, when you turn round just in time to see the Eiffel Tower start to shiver and sparkle (on the hour), when you look at La Conciergerie and imagine Marie Antoinette spending her last Christmas in her pitch-black cell behind its ghostly white façade . . . well, you'll be glad you're not in Oxford Street or Henry Street, snapping up the last of the fluorescent Santa hats. If the *bateaux mouches* are delicious on a sunny summer morning, they are truly memorable on a haunting winter's evening. We felt very proud that, so far, we'd done hardly any shopping, and were inclined to do even less.

Naturally, you can go shopping if you want. You can wear yourself to a frazzle whirling round Galeries Lafayette – admittedly, their Galeries Gourmet section is very tempting – and Zara and H&M and all those international chainstores the entire length of the Boulevard Haussmann. You can purr your way down the Rue de Rivoli, or rummage on the Rue St Antoine . . . but why? Why not just buy a bag of chestnuts from a street stall and wander round the Marais, or the Tuileries, or the Luxembourg Gardens, especially if they're filigreed with frost? Or go to the Hôtel de Ville to watch the ice-skaters gliding between the fountains . . . Paris isn't called the City of Light for nothing, and you'll remember your magical evening long after you've forgotten what anyone gave, or got, for Christmas. Besides, you can always do your shopping later, when you get home to your own village – which, after all, is hardly likely to be short of books or perfumes or regional foods, or whatever else you might want. A pre-Christmas trip to Paris would in fact be ruined by serious shopping, by zooming round frantically ticking off a list; in December, the shops are merely a pretext for a gorgeous girls' day out. (I mean, the day is gorgeous, whatever about the girls.)

We could have stayed forever. But unfortunately, we now had our return train to think about, which just left time for a cup of hot chocolate. Not any old chocolate, though: chocolate laced with brandy, in Hemingway's bar at the Ritz. Why? Because the Ritz is on the Place Vendôme, which blazes with beauty after dark, and because anyone can – contrary to popular belief – sashay into this divine hotel, the only credential you need is confidence. And because the oak-panelled Hemingway bar makes the most deliciously snug end to a December day out; once you are installed in your leather sofa you may well have to be winched out of it. Our hot chocolate came heaped with whipped cream, and we watched all the brazenly fur-coated plutocrats' wives tottering in with their glossy bags and perfect parcels, and saw a coiffed spaniel sipping tea from its owner's saucer, and goggled at some Russian woman's ruby bracelet (it could have illuminated Pigalle), and had a thoroughly, addictively good time.

Damn. We knew we should have booked a hotel, and stayed overnight. Only not at the Ritz – at least not until we win *le gros lot.* Once again, we found ourselves in need of pyjamas, sleeping bags and a tent.

17.

Summer Swallows

It's nice to know that your friends will not forget you after you move to France. Especially for the first summer or two, you will in fact see quite a lot of them, arguably more than you might do if you were still in Ireland. You become quite adept at quick changes of bed linen and the proud owner of at least thirty bath towels, thirty sets of sheets, thirty assorted spare jackets, sweaters, pyjamas and tennis shoes, six hairdryers and innumerable mobile-phone chargers, since virtually all your visitors forget theirs and no two are ever alike. You know the schedule of every market in every village by rote and you buy so much wine you feel like getting a T-shirt printed up: 'No I Am Not A Lush, It's For Them'. Your shelves fill up with maps and guidebooks and mysteriously abandoned neckties, you amass tons of Barry's tea and learn to keep a stack of Jiffy bags on standby for posting home the specs, keys, earrings and numerous other forgotten items.

Some of my visitors were horrified by their first sight of Normandy, 'when you could have chosen the Côte d'Azur, or Biarritz, or even Paris!'. There was some veiled suspicion that I'd picked this outpost – the French equivalent of Roscommon or Leitrim – specifically to annoy them, to frustrate their plans for lazing by the pool. I have no pool, and no plans for one; pools cost a fortune to run, and besides, what's wrong with the beach or the garden? Yes, admittedly the beach is a bit stony, but you just wear Crocs. And admittedly, mine is the only garden not frothing with hydrangeas, but let's face it, gardening will never be my forte, anywhere.

So, some people pout a bit at first, but then everyone slowly starts slipping into the Normandy pace, gradually getting to like the lack of glitz, to enjoy not having to dress up for everything, to become quite contented, actually, lazily picking at a salad with a glass of rosé or five, idly listening to the hypnotic drone of the bees foraging in my battered banks of lavender. Some start looking round and murmuring: 'Mmm, this is so relaxing. Maybe it would be kind of nice to have a little holiday home somewhere in this area?'

Eventually, some even start visiting Pierre Yves the estate agent, enthusing about cheap air fares, about orchards and coves and cottages, renovations and satellite dishes, markets and French lessons . . . though this last scarcely seems necessary. Pierre Yves reckons that France will soon be operating entirely in English, and I reckon he could very well be right. Next there are visits to glamorous Deauville – hmm, expensive – to fishy Fécamp, to thatched longhouses and flint townhouses, and Pierre Yves smiles at the growing frenzy of it all.

'I hope your friends will find somewhere to make them happy. And I hope they know what they are doing, because 60 percent of foreigners eventually leave, you know. They tire of doing up houses, tire of the sun, run out of money. Their schedules change, their children want to go to Florida . . . Normandy is very lovely, but it is not very trendy.'

Triumphantly, he beams. For him, not being trendy is a major plus. For Pierre Yves, happiness is built on four simple pillars: 'being healthy, loved, relaxed and solvent'. He doesn't want disgruntled clients overstretching themselves, and I suspect he doesn't want to see his lovely landscape turning into St Tropez either, filling up with sports cars and platinum blondes on mobile phones. Although this would no doubt make him richer, he seems to feel that he earns enough. 'At lunchtime, I close my office, I go home and see my wife, I enjoy my children and my garden and my pets . . . no amount of money can compensate for stress, for life zipping by in a blur.'

However, we continue to visit properties, and then my friends fly back to Ireland to think about them. A week or so later, I come home one day to find the phone ringing, but my hands are full, so it takes a message.

'*Bonjour vous avez un nouveau message du zéro zéro trois cinquante-trois seize dix-huit dix-sept quatre-vingt dix-neuf pour écouter vos messages faites le trente-et-un zéro trois ou si vous souhaitez rétourner au menu principal faites le—*'

Aiieee! Of all the media, the phone is the most difficult to master, since you can't see the person at the other end, can't deduce anything from gestures or facial expressions, or ask the mystery caller to slow down. Especially not when, as now, there's nobody there. It is merely a recording, which wants me to dial 3103 and listen to whatever news has arrived from Ireland.

'Hiya!' chirps a familiar voice. 'Great news! Get the kettle on! We're on our way to buy our house!'

And sure enough, in jig-time Séamus and Kate have arrived, signed the papers and finalised the purchase of their holiday home. Just a little place, to unwind in at weekends. Peace and quiet, a nice view, a barbecue, a spot of wine. Simple stuff. Within a month, the house is habitable, painted and furnished. They can even pick a pear or a chestnut off their very own trees, if there's time.

Because, while the house is affordable, the one thing they are slightly short of is time. By the end of a normal week in Dublin, they have between them worked a hundred hours, sat in twenty hours' worth of traffic, done ten hours of paperwork, repainted their living room this month's colour, supervised fifteen hours of homework, cooked for an army, visited elderly parents, flown to London and back on business, attended four receptions, a birthday party, a conference and a dinner party, and been to the theatre to see That Thing, Whatsit by Whosit. They don't realise how exhausted they are, but it's clear as soon as they arrive, translucent with fatigue: Kate instantly falls asleep on the sofa, while the only thing keeping Séamus's forehead out of his dinner plate is the relentless ringing of his mobile phone. But, heroically, he outlines his plan for their first weekend in their new French home.

'Well, first thing in the morning, we've got to hit the hypermarket, of course, get a telly so we can get True Movies, and I'll just give the office a quick call while Kate does that bit of work on her laptop, and then we can see about putting up those shelves and getting up some curtains and sanding the floorboards, and . . . '

Speechless, I stare at him. Did I once live like this? Did I once babble and jabber and live in terror that, if I stopped long enough to draw one extra breath, the entire universe would disintegrate? Soothingly, I try to steer him towards bed (to which Kate literally has to be carried).

Perplexed, he stares back, and for the first time it strikes me at what very different speeds we now live our lives. To me, Ireland sounds breakneck, while to him France is barely crawling.

But sure enough, the house shaped up, and on their first bank holiday weekend, Kate and Séamus got terrific mileage out of their new *résidence sécondaire*. They left Dublin after work on Friday, flew over, rented a car, got lost in the dark, but still reached their cottage just in time for dinner at midnight. On Saturday, they were up with the sun to drive to their favourite shop near Paris, only two hours away, to buy some lamps they wanted for their Dublin residence (after they figured out how to get off the motorway, having driven past the mystery exit 419 times in both directions and all but shot up the Eiffel Tower). Then they drove back. Zipped over to Fécamp to buy some of the oysters they love. Came home to find a note from the electrician, who'd finally arrived to fix the wiring problem. What a pity they were out, said the note when finally deciphered, but not to worry, the electrician had a window in his diary and would return in six months. The gardener had called too, and mysteriously chopped down the pear tree; just a tiny bit of a language muddle, Kate reckoned.

Kate was cooking dinner for their new neighbours (no, she doesn't speak French, but you have to try to make friends who'll watch your property in your absence) when Séamus's knife slipped on one of the oysters he was opening. *Eh oui*, a nasty gash, actually.

His hand was gushing blood and realistically he needed stitches. Would have got them, too, if he'd known how to find a doctor or where the nearest casualty department was, but sadly he hadn't yet had time to investigate these facilities. As things stood, Kate did a sterling job with a box of Band-Aid and her YSL scarf. Admittedly, the oysters never did get served, but at least Séamus will eventually regain the full use of his hand. And now they know that the French medical emergency number is '15'; by the time they next need to use it, they hope to be able to explain why. Yes, French can be a tricky language, especially over the phone when you're bleeding to death.

The dinner guests? Well, they were a little disappointed to find Kate administering first aid to her husband, the oysters swimming in blood, the casserole burning forgotten on the hob and the house freezing because of the wiring problem (it affects the heating). But never mind: one of them – Jacques – said that he knows a chap who might be able to do something about the roof. Yes, a few slates blew off it in a recent gale, and a bit of weather damage had been done by the time Séamus and Kate heard about it back in Dublin, but Jacques has assured them that, yes, it can be fixed. All in good time.

Sunday was a lovely day. Perfect for the beach, particularly since the church bell opposite their house rings on Sundays for a slightly excessive forty minutes. Séamus just needed to mow the lawn first – yes, hopefully the sheep will be coming soon – and Kate just needed to do a bit of laundry, because they'd loaned the house to friends the previous weekend and rather a lot of laundry had accumulated. The friends had had to leave in a hurry, apparently, and didn't get round to it. Such a hurry, in fact, that one of them knocked over the stereo system with his suitcase on the way out, but never mind, he's promised to replace it. As was becoming evident, laundry, and breakages, and perpetual lawn-mowing are all part of owning a holiday home.

Mmm, the beach was a bit crowded. And it did take a while to get there, what with that four-kilometre bank-holiday tailback and the pressure on parking spaces. And yes, there was rather a stiff sea breeze, but Séamus was happy about that, since he's not quite as keen as Kate on scorching sun. Besides, he couldn't sunbathe comfortably with his hand in that awkward condition. So, rather than join his wife on the sand, he left her stretched out to get her tan while he went for a stroll, and very pleasant it was. Really, it's so wonderful to have a little place in France, to potter amongst the rock pools and watch the children shrimping! Back to nature and all that.

When he returned, Kate was fast asleep. Out cold, her novel untouched beside her. How relaxed and comfortable she looked, lying there soaking up the rays. Séamus was quite touched, she looked so sweet and fetching in her designer swimsuit, the prettiest girl on the whole beach.

Sadly, that evening, poor Kate didn't look quite so fetching, nor relaxed or comfortable either, because alas she'd got just the tiniest touch of sunstroke. That deceptive breeze had convinced her that it was cooler than was actually the case, and now she couldn't bring her arms down to touch her sides, nor bear to sit down, because the backs of her thighs were just slightly scorched. This was unfortunate, because they were now facing the two-hour drive back to the airport for their flight home. However, Séamus did his best. Got her a pack of frozen peas to sit on. Slathered her in yogurt, which he'd heard was good for sunburn, even if it did seem a slightly smelly remedy. Put cushions under her arms to support them – apparently it's very tiring to keep them raised for more than a few minutes – and off they set for the airport.

Alas, there was rather a lot of traffic making its way home from the beach. All those foreigners! So it took longer than usual to get to the airport, and they were just a tad stressed by the time they got there, but as it turned out they weren't late for their flight at all. In fact they had plenty of time, after Séamus discovered he'd left the wallet containing his passport back at the house. By the time they'd driven back to get it, and then back to the airport again, the flight had long gone and they were booked on the next, leaving at dawn. In theory, anyway. In reality, it didn't leave till noon because, well, planes do occasionally go techie, *n'est-ce pas*? And it could have been worse: they did get nearly an hour's sleep on the flight, before dashing straight to their offices on touchdown back home. Although it was a bank holiday, a couple of crises had arisen at work, and they had to deal with one each.

The lamps? No, sadly, they didn't make it. Apparently, Ryanair wanted a hundred euro excess baggage for them, and Séamus threw a tiny tantrum, and they ended up in a bin at Beauvais. He threw another tantrum later, too, when the car-rental company billed him for petrol he is adamant he put in the car. But yes, apart from that, he and Kate had an absolutely delightful weekend in their French holiday home. They should be back again any day now, assuming the air-traffic controllers call off their threatened strike.

Meanwhile, so many other francophile friends have been charmed by the tale of the lovely holiday home that I could set up an agency and spend all day, every day, escorting them to see the solicitor – the solicitor who, unknown to us all, is planning to sell his own Normandy home and move down to 'civilisation' in Cannes. Before leaving, he imparts an interesting snippet of gossip. Have my friends heard about the planned new autoroute extension near their house, the halting site, and the exciting adventure centre to which thousands of kiddies are to be bussed over the summer holidays?

'*Eh oui*, isn't it great to see Normandy livening up! Your friends will have way more fun than they expected.'

18.

Wine and Water

'Oh, no. Please, don't make us go! For God's sake, not to a herring festival.'

Why not? Do we have something against herring?

'No, it's just that we . . . we'd rather . . . '

They'd rather sleep. Bed is the prize all my Irish friends crave when they visit France. More than Paris, more than sunny beaches or divine restaurants, more even than the markets or wine shelves, they want to go to sleep. Sometimes, they can't be prised off their pillows for days on end. This lot, unusually, are actually vertical. Coherent. But rebellious.

'I promise you'll love it. Wrap up warm and off we go.'

Grumbling, grizzling, they trundle out to the car, muttering vehement anti-herring sentiments under their breath. There surely cannot, by any stretch of the imagination, be anything remotely sexy, amusing or even gastronomically alluring about *herring*?

It is a blue-bright winter's day, the sun slicing through swathes of copper trees, the country air carrying a salt tang from the deep Norman harbour of St Valéry, where chalk from the crumbling cliffs has tinted the water an opaque, minty green. (It is this combination of sea and country air, I suspect, that sabotages my visitors, felling them like a scythe.) When we reach St Valéry, the war-ravaged little town is bedecked in flags and, around its high-kicking fountain, a band is assembling, red-cheeked, red-striped, pom-pommed, hoisting a banner proclaiming it to be from Picardie, an hour's drive east.

'Isn't it great,' remarks a white-whiskered, ruddy-cheeked old sea dog who must make his fortune moonlighting as Santa, 'to see a foreign band coming all this way.'

One of my friends, whose French is good enough to chisel under the Cauchois accent, giggles and has to be shushed. Another, noticing the girl members of the band changing from flared miniskirts into warmer trousers, snorts with laughter. 'Glamorous lot, aren't they. Ha!'

It has to be admitted that glamour is not high on today's agenda. Any top designer would surely deny all connection with France if he could see 'la mode' – woolly scarves, boots, mittens and bloodstained aprons. Bloodstained aprons are an inescapable feature of the herring festival, enveloping beefy fishermen's wives as they slap huge crates of the silvery fish onto vast log-fuelled braziers, from which fragrant woodsmoke begins to hiss and curl out over the cliffs.

'My God,' squeaks one of our party in horror, 'those fish are *alive!* They're being burnt *alive!*'

Yes, well, Joan of Arc was too, not far from here in Rouen. Burning things alive goes with the territory. But not all the fish are alive, actually: some are whacked against a handy wall, others swiftly beheaded, before being tossed on the flames. All around us, faces flare with anticipation as the shining fish, mere minutes out of the sea, begin to sizzle and glint on the grills. Begin to give off a delicious aroma, too, as only seafood can when barbecued outdoors on a brisk sunny day, destined for immediate consumption with a *coup de vin blanc* or a bubbling bowl of local cider. One of our party is eyeing the proceedings thoughtfully and has to be plucked away, casting nostalgic looks over his shoulder as we shuffle on into the surrounding market.

'But breakfast was hours ago. Do we not get any . . . ?'

No. Not until we've seen what else is available. Everywhere, chestnuts are roasting, hopping on more huge black braziers, and around a mobile bread oven an eager crowd has gathered. A team works together: a young Vietnamese man rolling doughballs with the dexterity of a juggler, hurling them onto oiled trays which are seized by a sturdy older woman, who shoves them into the oven and settles them with a thrust of a long wooden paddle. The previous batch is just out, crusty and steaming, some loaves the size and shape of footballs, others looking exactly like the logs on which they have been baked. There is something profoundly, reassuringly timeless about them, about this whole pageant, which might be medieval: the herring history of St Valéry wafts back as far as 1234.

My friends' noses begin to twitch, comically and in unison; they look like a bunch of hopeful bunnies. But not yet, not yet.

'What about the smoked oysters?'

None of them has ever tasted a smoked oyster. Even those who've been to the Galway oyster festival haven't seen so many baskets of oysters whipped from their beds of seaweed, shucked open by a fisherman with the skill of a surgeon. Collectively we hold our breath, waiting for the flying knife to slice his fingers off. But no such fun; he has done this before. The sleek oysters huddle into the flames, shrivelling into silvery pouches that will burst on the tongue, gushing salty juices . . .

'I'm starving,' growls one of our group. 'I want . . . '

A sausage, maybe? At the next stall, hundreds of sausages, red and black and cream, dangle from hooks in scarlet nets, some

peppered, some wrapped in leaves, others infused with herbs, garlic, apple, mushroom . . . a little tasting dish is on offer, and fists fly
like pistons, emptying it in a flash. The butcher looks both startled
and impressed, and I grin guiltily.

'Uh . . . Irish.' Well, some explanation of our savagery seems
required. 'We . . . uh . . . we'll take a dozen.'

Beaming, the vendor scoops sausages into a brown paper sack,
handing them over with the enigmatic comment one hears so
often: 'Ah, Irish! Not British, then!'

Immediately the sack is seized and rifled, but in vain. The thick
sturdy skin of the sausages refuses to yield and, possessing no
penknife, we are unable to break one into pieces for immediate
consumption. This proves remarkably frustrating, igniting rebel-
lion in the ranks.

'We are bloody ravenous. Our stomachs are rattling like cas-
tanets. If we don't get something to eat soon, we'll . . . '

But what about the scallops? What about the pumpkins, the
mushrooms fresh in from the forests? Good grief, what about the
cheeses?

The cheeses are stacked to the sky, smelling as if the cows and
sheep from which they came are entombed within their rinds.
Noses are held, brows wrinkled. 'Ooh, dis*gus*ting!' Yes, undeniably
the pong is strong. But visually this stall is a Renoir, lush with every
imaginable colour: gold, copper, caramel, bolts of blue forking
through the Morbier, bronze walnuts studding the Noix. Some,
made with goats' milk, are rolled in black ash; others nestle into
bundles of leaves or cuddle up on beds of straw. The wheels of
Comté are the size of tractor tyres. Again, samples are offered, and
demolished at the speed of light. And suddenly, firmly, my wrist is
gripped.

'That's it. We're eating. Here. Now.'

What? But it's only a silly herring festival. Do we not want to
hasten home to bed and back to sleep?

No, apparently we don't. We don't even want to see the scarves,
or jewellery, or hand-carved rocking horses, the kites or handbags
or banks of chrysanthemums. We are sitting down around a gigan-
tic wooden barrel, plunging forks into our bubbling herrings – two
apiece, served with baked potatoes and chive cream, four euro per
plate – and drinking cider, not out of glasses, but thick ceramic
bowls. After that we will have latticed apple pie, glistening with
apricot jam, heaped with crème fraiche, and we will knock back
bracing shots of calvados, igniting fires in our chests against the
winter chill. We will stamp our feet to the music of the marching
band. We will laugh and punch each other's shoulders and make
plans for next year's herring festival.

'Now,' my friends chortle triumphantly, 'aren't you glad we
made you come to it?'

꙳

My friends leave, and I miss them. Things are quiet without their
chat and laughter. So I decide to make a more determined effort to
find the elusive Monsieur Hulot. Would any of my French friends,
I ask around, know any nice eligible chaps?

To their credit, they try. Heads are put together, calls are made,
and dates are arranged. Hurray! Even if Vanessa Paradis has already
snaffled Johnny Depp, it's heartening to have a reason to dress up
and spritz on my favourite perfume, appropriately called Miracle.

French men don't regard bars as congenial places to meet for
dates. It comes as a pleasant surprise to be invited to restaurants,
where nobody drinks too much and all attempts to go Dutch are
firmly declined. Declined in a surprised and faintly reproving way

that makes me realise that the very offer is a mistake, an American aberration that has not found its way into French culture. When a Frenchman is taking a woman out, he's taking her out, and likes to do so without further ado.

So we sashay off to dinner, and nearly all of the men I meet are very nice, some even bearing flowers. Pleasant, courteous, some of them prove extremely interesting company and we have some lovely evenings, eat some great food, laugh and chat and have a lot of fun. Through them, I learn quite a bit about French work practice (*déontologie*, as it's called), labour law, customs and habits (you must shake hands with your boss and colleagues every morning), and the civil-service practice of *mutation*, or transferring staff to places they don't want to be. In some jobs, I'm informed, people can spend years trying to get back to the area where they grew up, and – while it's technically feasible to apply for postings to yummy areas like the Côte d'Azur – your chances of ever getting there are remote. But there you go: *c'est la vie*.

Even if they sometimes seem a bit like guided tours of the inner workings of the French civil service, these sporadic dates are fun, and I enjoy them. But alas, none of them leads anywhere, and as time goes on, I pick up a few clues as to why this might be.

Frenchmen, it seems, are not very keen on women who have as much to say as they have themselves. Rather than engaging in lively dialogue, they prefer to be listened to, ideally even deferred to. Expressing strong opinions is a mistake, and arguing a point is a definite turn-off. Cracking jokes is another mistake: women are expected to laugh at jokes, not make them. They're expected to offer sympathy if a man feels sorry for himself (messy divorce, lousy job, and so on), not to comment or, worse, to try to cheer him up. Questioning the French system (things like the thirty-five-hour week) goes down badly, and while expressing an interest in cooking evokes interest, it eventually leads to a discouraging discussion of what the date is really all about, which is to say their search for a housekeeper.

The lads, ultimately, are not so much in search of companionship or partnership as they are in search of someone to run their homes and lives. What they are doing over dinner is, effectively, conducting job interviews. Two of them frankly say they need a mother for their orphaned children. All of them express very traditional – albeit valid – views of what they want from a relationship, and I, apparently, am not it. I'm independent, talkative and foreign, and might, they fear, turn out to be something of a loose cannon.

'I really like you,' one of them candidly says, 'but I'd be afraid you might put your career ahead of mine. What I really need is a nice supportive spouse, waiting for me with a kiss and an aperitif in the evenings.'

Which is fair enough. After all, that's exactly what I'd love to find myself. Only I would let him express any number of outrageous opinions, and crack all the jokes he liked. God knows he'd need a sense of humour.

*

Never mind. If I still haven't found Monsieur Hulot, I've learned a lot from these encounters, and one of them is that in France it's possible, indeed expected, to enjoy a date without wallowing in alcohol. Another is that Frenchmen are not, contrary to popular opinion, all experts on wine, or obsessed with it, or even very interested in it. While wine is often a terrifying aspect of France for many of those who come to live here, it's really far more terrifying in other countries – with their wine buffs and clubs and dedicated magazines – than in France itself. Here, you'll scarcely hear a word about it. Virtually nothing about noses or legs or bouquets or anything else – not unless you actually live in a wine region, at any rate, or ask for information.

To the French, wine is very simple. '*Eh oui*, that Burgundy tastes good with that nutty cheese.' Or 'Dunno why, but that Bordeaux isn't half bad with this duck.' Or '*Eh oui*, I like that sweet white with this blue cheese.'

Yes, of course you can go all techie if you must, get into vines and vintages and whatnot, if you happen upon someone similarly enthusiastic and knowledgeable. But you don't have to and, on a day-to-day basis, people rarely do. I've never seen anyone strut their wine stuff, but I have often seen them ask the sommelier or shopkeeper for advice, without the slightest sign of snobbery on either side. *Au contraire*. France produces thousands of wines, and the French know that, try as they might (which they don't), they'll never be able to keep up with it all. Besides, that's what your wine merchant is for, *non*?

One day, on a trip to the Auvergne, I sought advice on wine to take to a picnic. The shopkeeper thought about it.

'And where,' she enquired, 'is this picnic to be?'

Up there in them thar hills, I replied. Half a dozen of us are getting together for a little lunch . . .

'How high up in the hills?'

Er, well, search me. Not all the way up, because we're only ramblers, not climbers. Let's say, um, maybe halfway up? Why?

'Because on the lower slopes, this wine' – flourish of dark rosé – 'will taste best. On the higher slopes, you'd be better off with this lighter, paler one.'

Okay, *merci beaucoup*! I fork over my four euro, and the wine, when we eventually drink it on the lower slopes, tastes like the grapes were personally plucked by the archangel Gabriel. Yet I can't tell any of my eagerly enquiring pals anything about it, because the shopkeeper didn't blind me with a word of science. Nothing about robust richness or silky complexity, hints of heather or leather. All she did was match product to picnic.

In the six years I've lived in France (yes, somehow six lovely years have now slipped by), I've scarcely ever come across a wine bar, wine club or wine buff. Wine is simply something you enjoy with your meals. What could be easier?

The longer you live in France, the more enjoyable it becomes, because without ever realising it, you gradually pick up the idea. One day, you buy a wine because it's on promotion in the supermarket, or because it's sporting a silver medal, or because somebody told you 2001 was a great year in Bordeaux . . . and when you taste it, you find yourself saying 'Ugh! That tastes vile with this ham/melon/fish!'

So now you know. Bordeaux wine from 2001 must have some merit if it's got a silver medal, but it doesn't go with ham, melon or fish. Next time, you'll try it with steak or liver or something else. Until one day, you pair it with the perfect dish and, hey, it's heaven! You may not have learned anything further about it but, unconsciously, your palate has absorbed it. You are becoming an *amateur*, in the true sense.

During the summer, France's wine regions are awash with tourists on wine-tasting excursions. What could be more fun than wandering around from one little vineyard to the next, trying a glass here, a glass there? Except for one problem: how to escape without buying a case everywhere you go? If you visit six vineyards, will you have to buy six cases, whether you want to or not? Will the vigneron take offence if you don't?

No, of course not. The vignerons in any given area all know each other, and their attitude is that any sale is good for the community, even if today's doesn't happen to be mine. Our visitors can't possibly buy every wine they sample. So let them come and try us all and, somewhere along the line, some of them will buy something. If not from me, then from Jacques up the road . . . who by chance is married to my daughter/sister/cousin . . .

So, no point in fretting about the etiquette of it all, then; no worries about having to discuss the finer scientific details (since the vigneron doesn't speak English and you don't speak French). All you have to do is either nod or shake your head – and spit out the samples, naturally, if you are to drive on to the next vineyard, and the next, without losing your licence or embedding your rented Citroën in the aisle of the local church. Many of the growers offer tiny nibbles to help you identify their wine's destiny: garlic sausage, chunks of local cheese, whatever brings out the best in it. Nobody will be remotely upset if you don't happen to like garlic sausage, or the wine proposed with it. The only way you can go wrong is by boring them cross-eyed with your knowledge of structures or tannins or vintages – which, frankly, they haven't time to discuss in detail when they have so many visitors. (Unless, of course, you're visiting Chateau Margaux or a vineyard of similar level.)

Like children, young wines express potential but not much complexity. Older wines, like mature adults, are not to be trifled with, and can sometimes be very impressive. And that's about all there is to the question of vintage, unless you're actually planning to go into business, like my Irish pals who have so bravely bought Chateau Soussac in Bordeaux. Otherwise, you're just having lunch somewhere one day, and suddenly you sit bolt upright and say 'My lord, that Sauternes is *delicious* with that foie gras!' – and thereafter, you know to order Sauternes with foie gras. Just as you learn not to order asparagus in winter, or beef casserole in summer . . . not that they'll be on the menu anyway, in any French restaurant worth its salt. Out of season, certain dishes – *most* dishes – just don't taste right.

୬<

French children scarcely ever learn about wine. They just pick it up as they grow up. In Britain and Ireland, on the other hand, there is an increasing tendency to teach them as they move into their teens. Parents worry about this aspect of their offspring's social education. They say things like 'Darling, would you like to try this wonderful Médoc?' to their mud-encrusted twelve-year-old. Whereupon the mud-encrusted twelve-year-old huddles into the depths of his Xbox and refuses to come out.

Whereas, if the parents handed the kid a glass of Burgundy and said 'Do you think this smells like chocolate?' or 'What food would you eat with that?' they'd probably stand more chance of interesting the youngster. Not that many are going to get interested anyway, before the age of sixteen or seventeen at least, because wine is an adult pleasure and younger kids just feel intimidated, or repelled, or wish their stupid parents would leave them alone. What twelve-year-old is going to say 'Oh, why Mummy, that's exquisite, that must be the 1997 Morgon. Chateau Prat, is it?' (Yes, there is actually a Chateau Prat.)

Still, it can be helpful to start learning early. I know this because, as an eighteen-year-old *jeune fille au pair*, I was once confronted with a glass of wine and a dozen aristocratic French eyes awaiting my reaction to it. All I could think of was my mother's parting advice: 'If you come across any wine in France, remember to dilute it with lots of water.' So I did.

Next thing, grandpa is clutching his chest and the whole table's in uproar. Amidst the gasps of horror, I grasp the awful information

that this wine is a priceless vintage, specially decanted in my honour because it has some kind of Irish connection (the Wild Geese),
and I have made a complete spectacle of myself, not to mention
disgracing my country (again).

That was long ago, but given that wine is now a component of
any young European's life, there's a case to be made for teaching
them something about it in school. Or maybe they do, nowadays?
At the very least, kids should know (or maybe not!) that wine has
got much stronger in recent years, gone up from 9 or 10 percent
proof to 13 or even 14 percent, which makes it a substance not to
be trifled with. Personally, I wish it would revert to its lesser
strength, but somehow doubt that the French oeneology industry
is going to pay much attention to me.

Anyway, even if nobody ever taught you anything, no need to
panic. France does not expect you to sniff and swill and sigh with
joy: 'Ah, the St Emilion, I suspect. From the sunny side of the slope.
Hints of vanilla. Nineteen sixty-nine, wasn't it?' In fact, it doesn't
expect you to do or say *anything*. Three of my French friends don't
even drink wine at all. Just don't like it. It's not compulsory.

Which, however, is not my own approach. I reckon I've personally boosted France's GNP stratospherically just by moving here
and drinking wine. Every spring and autumn, the local supermarkets hold wine fairs – sociable events where you can not only meet
the growers, who travel around the country with their produce, but
other immigrants too. (You can tell how long the latter have been
here by the eagerness with which they permit their plastic cups to
be refilled.) And then there are the locals, papa and his pals out
looking for something serviceable to drink over the winter with
their wives' chicken chasseur. It almost always is papa, because for
some reason, few Frenchwomen take much interest in wine –
certainly not on the stocking-up end. Like the seasons, gender roles

are much more clearly defined here, and sourcing wine belongs to the boys. Don't let that put you off, but if you're a woman you will be treated with every respect and courtesy, not patronised at all. After all, some (foreign) women run very successful vineyards. Plus, if you're a single woman, the wine fairs are great places to meet nice men . . .

And yet, for some completely illogical reason, I always prefer my wine to be opened and poured by a man, whether in a restaurant or at home. If I'm entertaining, I like one of my male guests to take charge of it, and in anyone else's home, I always assume the host will do so. Why? I can't explain it. Maybe I'm just hopelessly traditional at heart. Is it any wonder I've ended up in the time warp that is France?

See, lads? Traditional at heart – not nearly so scarily independent as you might think!

19.

Allez Les Bleus!

Pierre Yves, who sells houses, is stamping round the back garden of a thatched cottage, arms outflung, bellowing over the fence at a herd of cows as if they were the assembled Senate.

'France,' he roars, 'is finished!'

Munching ruminatively, Daisy and Claribelle endeavour to digest this along with a mouthful of poppies. Nobody has told them the World Cup is on, much less that France is through to the final.

'Once,' Pierre Yves continues, 'France had musicians! Once, she had artists! Scientists! Philosophers! Chefs! She had . . . ' – fighting for breath, he clasps his chest – 'she had Escoffier, she had Claude Monet, Erik Satie, Louis Pasteur, Jean-Paul Sartre, Gustave Eiffel . . . great creators, giants of real *talent*! And now . . . now . . . ' For a terrible moment, it looks as if he might burst into tears. 'Now, all she has is *tribalism*! Idiots in stupid hats, painting the tricolour on their *faces*, bawling at giant screens like *savages* . . . '

He is bawling like a savage himself, red as a cider apple, looking as if he too might be 'finished' if he doesn't calm down. Pierre Yves is one of the 50 percent of Frenchmen who fervently believe that, far from being a glorious trophy, the World Cup symbolises the end of civilisation as they know it. For them, the playing fields of soccer finals are, he yells, a 'theatre of war' on which acts of unspeakable hostility and imbecility are currently being enacted. It is the Somme all over again. The hype surrounding the whole thing is *honteux* (shameful), and to actually win would be not an honour but a disgrace. Fulminating, he shoves his paperwork into his pocket and zooms off in a cloud of rage.

Why he's so upset is something of a mystery, since the French team has very little to do with France. As a rule, few of its players are born here, many are employed abroad and, lining up for the pre-match anthem, few can even mime the words of La Marseillaise, much less sing it. On the sidelines of all the qualifying matches, the managers, coaches and assorted minders have had to be festooned in identity tags the size of babies' bibs, presumably so the spectators will know with which team they are associated.

In Pierre Yves's view, 'You Irish are lucky not to be involved.' Informed that Ireland has adopted the Ivory Coast as its surrogate team for the 2006 tournament, he all but twirls to the ground like a falling leaf, aghast. 'But you are crazy!' Perhaps, but not as crazy as we would have been had we qualified to play in this 'disgusting *folly*! This opium of the *people*! This orgy of *nationalism*!'

And nationalist it is, for sure. When I ask my pal Sebastien (who's one of the other, equally fervent, 50 percent) whether he'd rather see the best team win or see France win, he doesn't even hesitate. 'France, of course!' he splutters, floored by the very concept of the question. For his camp – whose 50 percent seems to be in a minority, if you follow me – victory matters much more than quality. As Thierry Henry will later demonstrate, France will go to any lengths to win.

But what France has apparently yet to grasp is that watching the match is, in itself, supposed to be a team effort. For tonight's final, the French are not assembling in bars or congregating around each other's televisions to share pizza and beer, waving tricolour-draped teddy bears, and the giant screen erected in a Paris stadium for the duration of 'hostilities' is drawing far fewer fans than anticipated. As kick-off draws near, there are no reports of anyone being knifed or arrested or any of the other things which, in more clued-in countries, go with soccer finals. The French don't realise that this match is supposed to be all about mayhem and mob rule. Or maybe all that storming and slashing back in 1789 wore them out?

However, in our village, the foreign residents are resolved to watch the clash, en masse. A fistful of us drift to the designated venue and, as the team lines up, all the women are agreed: some of these players are real lean machines. Mmm. One of them, whose shirt says Abidal 3, would definitely not be turfed out of the *lit* for snoring. Whether Abidal 3 is his name, or the destination of some bus in Ghana, is unclear – and one woman further muddies the water by insisting that *abidal* is the French for 'tonsil' – but that's neither here nor there. The important thing is that we all cheer whenever Abidal gets hold of the ball, thereby inciting himself and his chums on to victory and earning ourselves brownie points as model foreign residents. Team captain Zinedine Zidane, it is agreed, has a delicious smile, and he, too, would most definitely be licensed to snore all he liked. After having scored, naturally.

But nobody can be expected to concentrate on soccer for much more than five minutes, and so our attention wanders to the particularly crisp rosé we are sharing, to the mist gently mantling the blue meadows of flax outside the open window, to our own tennis match next Friday – which, obviously, will be far more riveting than any World Cup, or indeed Wimbledon (where the ladies' singles final has just been won by France's Amélie Mauresmo). '*Shh*,' hisses one of our more hypnotised comrades, as if our chatter might distract Franck Ribéry from scoring. But the ball goes into the net and, hey, things are looking good for France.

And they continue to look good, up until the very last minute when, for no obvious reason, Zinedine Zidane suddenly spins round, marches up to his Italian rival Materazzi and head-butts him with all the force of a prize bull. And then, waved off with a red card, marches into the German twilight.

There is a collective gasp. Followed by utterly baffled silence. What on earth has happened? This wonderful player, this national hero, this adored role model, guilty of blatantly foul play in the dying moments of a penalty shoot-out? Even we foreigners are stunned. Unable to answer our mobiles as they start to spew text messages from friends in our various countries – 'Wow, didja *see* that!? Way to *go*!!' – we can only pluck and grasp at each other.

Zidane's outburst is followed, not by the rioting usually so beloved of French youth, but by a deafening explosion of silence. Five minutes later, the match is over, Italy has won, and even the owls are in bed. France pulls its duvet up over its head and endeavours to blot out the entire nightmare. Had the team won, there would have been wild effervescence – somebody in a bar in Paris might have cheered, someone in Marseilles, overcome with emotion, might even have ordered a second pastis – but as things stand the silence is completely, utterly stoic. After all, to run amok might lend credence to Pierre Yves's view that soccer is for mindless hooligans, and everyone is aware that tonight is not the night for spraying magnums, vomiting into fountains or stabbing each other by way of expressing their enjoyment of the game. Glumly, we disperse and sneak home, taking care not to disturb any snoring grasshoppers. Amélie Mauresmo, we remind ourselves, is the first Frenchwoman to win Wimbledon for decades . . . comforting ourselves with this, we wonder what might happen next. Amélie notwithstanding, France could well sink into the mire of its national malady, *la morosité*, maybe even trudge off to have a little existential crisis.

But as things turn out, rising to his status as (then) president, Jacques Chirac rallies, gallantly overlooking the country's bewildering, embarrassing defeat. He announces that, on its return from Germany, the team is to be invited to a knees-up at the Élysée (though there's no mention of inviting the victorious Amélie). Defeat or no defeat, the team is to be fêted and, just as soon as he arrives back in Paris, Zidane will explain what happened, live on television. Clearly, he must have been under unbearable pressure and already France is steeling itself to forgive and forget. Poor Zidane, provoked beyond endurance. What a tragic end to such a brilliant career. Hearts harden against the normally popular Italy, and there are mutterings about cancelling next summer's Roman holidays.

But Pierre Yves will not be watching the festivities in Paris, nor Zidane's explanation either. He will, he announces, be decamping to the impenetrable forests of the Ardennes, where he owns a 'small shack' twelve kilometres from the nearest oasis of so-called civilisation. (A five-bedroomed shack, rumour has it: his houses have been selling at quite a rate.) There he will paint his shutters, go walking with a sturdy stick, read some soothing Descartes and encourage France in its pursuit of real glory: the preparation of his favourite *marmite* for supper. Back here at the ranch, we are getting in some crates of Kro with which to lubricate the televised party at the Élysée, some pizza by the metre and – if we can find any – those clacker things that make lots of noise when you whirl them over your brain-dead head. After all, somebody's got to support the French, even if it's only us foreigners, and even if the Frenchman in question isn't quite as French as, say, Molière or Jean-Jacques Rousseau.

After all, poor Zidane's smile is still divine, and he did get France as far as the final, and he did misbehave only under serious stress. As Sartre might say, were he playing for the Sorbonne, you've got to be philosophical about these things. And besides, there's always next time . . . by which time, France might have grasped what soccer is all about, and put several teams of hooligans into training. After all, if you can't wreck your country by way of celebrating, what's the point of winning?

※

Fast-forward four years, and *plus ça change*. One of France's star soccer players, Thierry Henry, has propelled France into the 2010 World Cup by the simple stratagem of applying his hand to the ball which rightly belonged to his Irish opponent. In a flash, Ireland is out of the finals and France is in. This 'light-handedness' naturally renders all my friends in Ireland absolutely furious, my mobile is popping with texts all night, but when next I meet Pierre Yves he is perfectly sanguine about it.

'Of course. What did I tell you? Only savages play soccer. My son has been asking me to take him to see some of these World Cup matches – in South Africa he says it is – but I have said *non*, we will go to our little *cabane* in the Ardennes as usual, and I will take him fishing, and we will have some – what do the Americans call it? – some quality time together. We will play father and son!'

At which he laughs his head off and I can already see the headlines in the local newspaper: 'Estate Agent's Son (7) Absconds to South Africa'.

However, not all French men and women are proud of what

Thierry Henry did. The day after the match, I visit the village bakery. The assistant goes into a whispering huddle with her boss and next thing a gorgeous cake is produced, boxed, and handed to me 'with our apologies, madame, for the way your country was robbed last night'.

Well, even if it doesn't change things, or comfort Ireland in the least, it has to be said that the cake is delicious. And, as my friends point out, it could be the start of a truly great guilt trip.

'Hurry!' they urge enthusiastically, 'run down to the jeweller's shop, quick, and then the wine merchant's, and then the car showrooms. Get all you can out of that guilt!'

Did France really feel guilty? Yes. An online survey showed that it did, to the tune of 80 percent. But Pierre Yves never uttered a word of apology, because of course he hadn't seen the match, and therefore didn't know that Ireland had made up its mind, en masse, never to set foot in France again. Oh no, no more holiday homes for us, ever again, after that!

Only the property squeeze will not, alas, turn out to have much to do with soccer. In December 2010, I run into Pierre Yves in the village square, and he grimaces sympathetically.

'I hear Ireland has played all its money away.'

Indeed. Pierre Yves may know nothing about football, but his verbal footwork is nifty, and so he wins on points.

20.

No Smoke Without Fire

It is coming up to Hallowe'en. The harvest moon glows fatly full, the chevronned fields are knubbly as tweed, pale cows loom in the mist and recede again. The air smells of dung and smoke, the choir has started rehearsals for Christmas, and all is as it should be.

Until – wham! – David Pujadas reads out the dreadful news on TF2, and France leaps into orbit, aghast.

'Whaat? Ban smoking! But . . . but . . . this is all your fault!'

Eh? *Mine?* Like my name is Marie Antoinette?

'*Oui.* You. Irish, that is. You started all this.'

Actually, we didn't. America started it, and Ireland simply likes to mimic America. Then, bewilderingly, Italy, of all places, fell in line, then Scotland . . . and now, France has decided to introduce prohibition too.

It is mystifying. Thus far, France has refused to be sterilised by political correctness – and besides, it doesn't smoke the way other countries do. Many people like a cigarette with their coffee, but there never seems to be a haze of smoke in a bar or bistro, maybe because the weather so often facilitates eating and drinking outdoors or with the windows open. Cigarettes are expensive enough to discourage indulgence, but not prohibitively so, as in

Ireland. Like chocolate, they're seen as an occasional comfort when the mistral is blowing or your team has been humiliated by Manchester United.

But now – well, as of January – smoking is to be banned, and society is to be divided. Half of it will remain at table after dinner, sipping its coffee while the other half huddles out in the street, puffing and grizzling, each camp nursing growing resentment of the other. It's a very vexed question – one that continues to divide Ireland – and, as a foreigner, you're better off staying out of arguments.

But the French are not so easily put off. 'Has prohibition,' they want to know, 'really worked in Ireland?'

Well yes, it has. Many people have given up cigarettes in favour of Valium, hamburgers, chewing gum, cocaine, or the whole lot. A whole new range of stress-busters has gained popularity. Indeed, murder has gained popularity, to quite a spectacular degree: many of the stress-buster dealers have had hatchets embedded in their heads and bullets whistling through their chests. If the country is somewhat living on its nerves these days, at least its lungs are clearer.

'But what about your famous pubs? Do people still go out to drink and hear music?'

Er, no. Not a lot, nowadays. Pubs have been shutting down in their droves. You're about as likely to find a live giraffe now in an Irish pub as a spontaneous outburst of singing, and many jobs have been lost. But there you go, can't make omelettes without breaking eggs, eh?

Pop-eyed, the French gaze at me. Jobs have been lost? But French unemployment is already rocketing! This will be the end, the drop that made the vase overflow! (Yeah, I know, but that's the way they say it.)

'And what happens to anyone who lights a cigarette in public? Do they go to jail?'

Ah. That I can't answer, because nobody to my knowledge has ever dared light one since the ban was introduced; the atmosphere is so Big Brother, you feel as if the mere thought of a cigarette might be enough to land you in jail. It's like Mao's China, where your own family, friends and neighbours might well turn you in. Some of my non-smoking friends have kindly furnished their garden patios for visiting smoker friends, but this doesn't seem to work in reverse: when they're the guests, the non-smokers expect their hosts to be the ones to go outdoors, apparently not being quite as keen on fresh air as their campaign might have led one to believe. Sometimes, things can get a tiny bit strained.

Thoughtfully, we all sit around mulling on this brave new Ireland for a few minutes. And on the new France to come.

Eventually, Didier rallies. '*Ah non*,' he says with conviction, 'it won't come to that. France will never betray her principle of liberty . . . '

'France,' interjects Aurélie, 'sometimes has no principles. Remember all those people who collaborated with the Gestapo? It'll be the same again, you'll see. Maybe a bounty will be introduced on smokers' heads.'

Hmm. Another thoughtful, somewhat gloomy pause. France may be a very fetching little fairy sometimes, but demonstrably no, she is not to be trusted.

'Well,' sighs Didier at length, 'if they're going to ban cigarettes, can alcohol be far behind? And sunbathing, and cheese, and everything else that might pose a risk?'

Soon, we have compiled a comprehensive list of everything that will now, logically, be banned. Wine, obviously. Cognac. Armagnac. Camembert. Brie. Nougat. Chocolate. Sausages. *Pain de campagne. Brioche.* Jam. Biscuits. Cakes. And do you have any *idea* how much cholesterol your average prawn contains?

Still, that leaves water. And fruit and veg . . .

'*Ah non,*' Paul muses mournfully. 'I knew a chap once who choked on a chunk of raw carrot. Died, he did.'

Oh. Well then, lettuce. Nobody ever died of that – at least, not that we know of. And France will still have her sports, her beloved cycling and swimming and rugby and . . .

Mais non. Somebody knows someone who had a heart attack while cycling. Somebody else cites a friend who was paralysed in a rugby scrum. Didier has a friend who's been in a wheelchair since being knocked over by a big wave at Biarritz ten years ago. (Biarritz is actually notorious for its dangerous waves.) As for walking . . . what, up on those cliffs? But they're lethal! Every bit as dangerous as the roads, with all their screaming motorbikes! And what about abseiling, hang-gliding, canyon rafting in the Gorges de Verdun, rollerblading . . . you could even be playing an innocent game of tennis and a whizzing ball would take your eye out. You could be playing boules, and a badly aimed boule would knock your crown jewels for six. There is no end to the danger, now that we think about it, it lurks everywhere.

Embroidery, then? Knitting? Stamp collecting?

Didier is dubious. Is the gum on stamps poisonous? Might knitting not cause repetitive-strain injury? As for embroidery, you could stab yourself with that needle. Maybe even stab someone else, in a moment of madness. You might even mistakenly stab the health minister, should she happen to be within range. His mother, he says, used to knit on her frequent flights to visit his father, when work separated them in his youth, but today . . . why, they'd lock her up for trying to knit on a plane.

Ah, well. That's modern life for you. Cigarettes banned today, all other risks tomorrow. Not that it will matter much, since who'd want to live in the icy social tundra which will be France when the ban comes in?

Oh, come on. Cheer up. Okay, maybe the tobacconists and bartenders will be out of business, but hey, the psychologists will make their fortunes! And America will be so pleased with France, the new regime will make it feel just like California!

Didier fills another skin and rolls himself a last smoke. And then, unexpectedly, he brightens.

'D'you know,' he says suddenly, 'I have an idea.'

Oh, really? *Qu'est-ce que c'est*, Didier?

'I,' he announces, 'am going to change careers. Give up painting – the pigments may be dangerous – to become an antiques dealer.'

Antiques? Well, as you wish, but what has this got to do with . . . ?

'*Oui*. Antiques. I am going to start amassing suits of armour, and start selling them to the many people who will soon be wearing them to protect themselves from the infinite risks of this world. Yes, indeed. I reckon the armour market is about to go cosmic. I will make my fortune.'

Eh bien. Good luck to you so, Didier. And what will you do with this fortune, once made?

'Why, I will go to live in Brazil, or Argentina, or wherever it is you are still allowed to smoke. Actually, allowed to *live*. Live, you understand, as opposed to merely existing. I would rather live dangerously than exist safely.'

Oh, come now, Didier. There must be some counselling you can get for that non-PC attitude. In fact, says Aurélie, now that it occurs to her, she might well quit teaching for a new career in counselling? Clearly it, like armour, is the coming thing, with lots of money to be made.

Meanwhile, it's getting late, time to wend our way home before, on the stroke of midnight, all the village lighting snaps off. Somebody once missed his step in the dark and fell into a ditch . . . no, not killed, thank God, but very nasty injuries. It's a wonder that ditch has never been filled in.

As we disperse, the huge harvest moon is waning. Contemplatively, Didier looks up at it. 'Do you know, I once knew a chap who was killed by the moon?'

What? Ah now Didier, you're getting paranoid, you're making this up.

'*Non*. I swear it. He left his car at home one night so he could drink at a local party, and he was walking home, and he stopped to admire the beautiful full moon, and a sugar-beet truck came hurtling round the bend on its way to the refinery – they start at three in the morning as you know – and knocked him over like a skittle, and *voilà*, there he was, dead. Poor guy. I liked him. Even though he didn't smoke.'

Soon after, the ban is implemented and French doorways are thronged with smokers discovering the joys of flirting amongst themselves, and my pal Paul is ecstatic.

'Before the ban,' he explains, 'I worked a thirty-five-hour week. Now it takes me so long to trek down from my office to the car park to have my five cigarettes a day, and so long to trek back again, I reckon I'm only working thirty hours. *C'est merveilleux!*'

21.

Lingua Franca

Do you understand the following words? Clown, manager, business? Toast, pizza, hamburger? Cash, email, cool? Bacon, sandwich, cake? Graffiti, square, shopping? Fax, telephone, scanner? Job, boss, whiskey? Theatre, cinema, radio? Concert, parking, weekend? Top model? Success story? Live, gay, football? Quilt, archer, fair play, happy few? Meeting, marketing, album?

Congratulations! Your French is fluent! In the eight years I've now lived in France, so many English and American words have started to 'pollute' the language that the Académie Française is clutching its chest in horror, but the good news for anyone planning holidays or business in France is that you'll only need to learn a few verbs at most.

Which is just as well, since nobody can really be comfortable in any country or situation until they speak the language. Until then, there is the persistently nagging feeling that not only are you missing out on all the fun, or that you might even be the reason for it, but something vitally important might be sailing over your head. Is Mr Maximo merely asking whether you'd like to buy some frozen peas, with all that waving and shouting, or is he trying to warn you of an impending tornado?

Two things will help your struggle in this stormy ocean. Firstly, the French have saintly patience with stammering foreigners. They listen, they wait, they politely restrain their giggles at even the most egregious errors. (Although one pharmacist did collapse under the strain the day I asked for something for a nasty cough, or *toux*. Heading in the right aural direction, I asked if she had something for a nasty *toussaint*, or Hallowe'en.)

The other crutch is the Anglo-American factor. So much English seeps in via films, news clips, financial exchanges, TV programmes, property purchases, music, and so forth, that the French now speak far more English than they realise. *Yeah, mega!* It's everywhere. To the point where a boy band called Phoenix, from Versailles and popular with pre-teens, now actually sings in English. There were mutterings about this, at first, accusations of going too far, people pointing out that if a boy band from, say, Streatham or Cork or Hoboken starting singing in French, everyone would think they were mad. But all the kids love it. 'Multicultural,' they chirp, delighted.

However, Phoenix won't get you through a whole day, much less a life, in France. A certain amount of concentration is required, and a definite dollop of determination. Even if you don't attend the free classes that are laid on for foreigners by many *mairies* or *chambres de commerce*, you'll still pick up a lot effortlessly. All you have to do is stand in the street, and bits of the chatter will stick to you, like sand in a desert, whether you try to catch it or not. After about six weeks, you'll wake up one morning feeling that there's been a bit of a breakthrough: you're now up to buying your baguette or greeting the postman without having to write it all down first. Conversely, after six months you'll hit a wall, breaking out in a cold sweat as you realise that all that went before was, in fact, garbled pathetic rubbish. Swahili for the slow-witted. Your inner ear will now hear every mistake you ever made, and you will want to smuggle yourself out of France wrapped in a beige blanket on the floor of an old 2CV. It's only when your French starts getting really good that you realise how really bad it was before.

It was at this point, just as I was otherwise settling happily in and enjoying *la belle vie*, that I started realising the kind of awful things I'd been coming out with by virtue of picking up slang from French friends who, I suspect, hugely enjoyed the haphazard way in which I grasped its meaning.

In a swish restaurant, instead of politely asking for another glass of wine, I innocently instructed the waiter to 'hit me again'. Attempting to buy mosquito repellent one day, I asked for 'a musketeer'. As for what I suggested a nice teenage lad might like to do with his girlfriend . . . suffice it to say that his mother went all but catatonic with shock, and the episode will haunt me forever. But that's exactly the kind of thing that happens when you reach the slang stage, get cocky, and start strutting your stuff like a teenager in the most hideously fecund phase of adolescence. Slang is a swamp: no matter how curious you might be to see what happens, just don't go there before you're sure of your ground.

After my first full year in France, gaining confidence and remembering that I had acquired a degree in a previous life, had even *taught* French, I suddenly realised all the gruesome mistakes I'd been making, and every solecism started ringing in my ears like the angelus. I yearned to revoke every word I'd ever uttered. Overnight, it all shot downhill and I lost the key to the whole thing – which is, of course, confidence. Up to then, I'd felt that the French were looking marginally less bemused every time I spoke to them. Sometimes their eyes even glimmered with the light of comprehension. But now . . . nothing. *Nada.* All gone.

Don't despair. Everyone hits this wall, like marathon runners at the halfway stage. That miserable moment when you think: (a) I can't do this, (b) it's not even worth trying any more, (c) they're all laughing at me, and (d) let's move to Tasmania. It's a wretched moment, but it's just the darkest hour before dawn: stay with it, and the sun will rise. Soon.

About a week after I hit this wall, a friend picked me up off the floor and persuaded me to come to a dinner party. No, I pleaded, I won't understand them and they won't understand me. I'm sick of having to think out every sentence, and they must be even sicker of waiting for me to string it together. I thought I was much better than I was, but now I can see it was all just a comedy of errors . . .

This is a dangerous moment. Lose your nerve now, and it's gone for good. You will spend the rest of your life in France hovering on the edge of every conversation, never quite sure whether you've grasped its point, never mind its finer points. You will wonder whether you dare tell the mechanic you think the clutch is the problem, or might he think you mean the brake discs? Will he think you're asking him to sell you his first-born, or abscond with him to Hawaii, or is he in favour of vivisection, or what?

Fortunately, my friend was adamant. You will come to this dinner, she asserted, and you will tell your funny story about Michael Flatley and the bottle of wine. (I'd met the dancer in Berlin and blithely drunk his wine like water, not realising it was a 1966 Chateau Latour.)

No, I whined, I won't. Can't.

Then, she said, I will never speak to you again. Unless you change your mind, *au revoir*. Forever. You're not worth bothering with any more.

So I slunk along to the blasted dinner party and, at an opportune moment, was encouraged to tell the tale. Perhaps because it involved wine (and I'd had four glasses by then), the French guests grew quietly attentive as I embarked on a story that made me look a fool in any language.

It's one thing saying hello to the postman. It's quite another relating an entire anecdote to a raptly expectant audience, especially as humour is the most difficult of things to translate. I demurred, stuttered, stumbled . . . and eventually took the plunge, noting that everyone was starting to smile, and then to grin openly, no doubt at my utter imbecility. But suddenly I didn't care, and what was more, the dots seemed to be joining up, there weren't any of those excruciating pauses while I rummaged for the right word. When I finished the tale, they all laughed.

But, incredibly, not at my French. At my story. They understood, and they were amused? Clearly, there must be some misunderstanding. I collared my friend.

'You bribed them, didn't you, or blackmailed them? Warned them to laugh, or paid them?'

But no, she hadn't. She'd actually been amazed herself, she confessed, by the growing fluency with which the story had miraculously emerged. Inwardly cringing, she'd braced herself for the mumbles, the mispronunciations, but there'd been virtually none. The whole thing had been perfectly comprehensible and, even though she'd heard it before, she'd found it funny herself.

It was a defining moment. Conquering K2 could scarcely have been more defining. It was as if my application for membership of an exclusive club, after having been rejected dozens of times, had suddenly been accepted. I was in. I could speak French.

No, you won't get a swelled head. You'll simply catch your mistakes, from now on, in time to correct them. You'll see that subjunctive looming, and you'll field it like Babe Ruth catching a baseball. You'll never – *ever* – remember the gender of every last noun in the French lexicon, but you'll remember 90 percent and guess the rest. If you can't find the precise word you want, you'll have something similar on standby. Magically, like a written recipe turning into a casserole, you'll hear that 'ooh' turning into '*eu*', and one day you'll cough up a proper '*rrrr*', like Garfield on a winter's morning.

It just takes time, is all. Pride goes before a fall, but after you fall, you pick yourself up again, finding that you've learned from your mistake. Gradually, the mistakes become fewer, and the vocabulary grows. Mind you, it's still hugely frustrating when a conversation gets really complex and subtle, and you just don't have that one damn word, that *exact* word you want – the one that's worth a dozen merely passable substitutes. That's when you say to yourself: it's time to go home. Back to Ireland, just for a weekend to friends and family, who understand every syllable I utter.

And then you go back to Ireland and, instead of saying something is 'so-so', you've shrugged the dreaded *bof*. Before you can stop yourself, you've called a pie a *tarte*. A cinema has acquired a ridiculous accent on the 'e', and every second sentence seems to start with '*Beuh* . . . '

And everyone's looking at you wishing you'd go back home where you belong, to France.

❧

'I don't understand it,' wailed an English friend. 'These French lessons just aren't working. The language graft is not *taking*.'

And here's the bad news. It might not. Ever.

Some people simply don't have an ear for languages. Some have an ear for German or Russian or Urdu, but not French. Some take private tuition for two years and still can't ask the barber for a short back 'n' sides. Some freeze when the postman starts babbling about 'the accused', not realising that an *accusé* is merely a delivery receipt. Some spend three-quarters of their classes doodling, or leching after their teacher, or thinking bloody hell, will this ever end?

Others pay close attention and write down every single word, do their homework religiously every night, ingest Ferrar's French Grammar in a gulp – and still can't speak in the street, because they are surgically welded to their pencils, clinging to that trusty Faber as if it were a log in the churning ocean. I know this for a fact, because I've taught English to French students, and they're exactly the same in reverse, frantically jotting down everything I say including 'good morning'.

Look. Some day, you're going to have to let go of that pencil, okay? Whether you like it or not, it's the only way. French is not Latin. It's a living, luscious language, and the idea is to *speak* it. After a year, chuck your pencil, your notebook, your grammar book, your dictionary, your Michel Thomas tapes, your Rosetta Stone and every other tangible aid into the Seine. Think of yourself as a toddler learning to swim: water wings are handy when you're four, cute when you're five, but when you're twenty-five, or thirty-five? As the Americans would say, *puh-leez*.

You are a grown adult, no? So, you can't whip out your notebook every time you go to the hardware store or newsagent and start riffling through it for the relevant page – seventy-four, or was it forty-seven? – while the staff have a hernia trying to stifle their laughter because, for God's sake, you've been in here a hundred times already! Some day, you've got to say your piece, without notes! Walk upright!

'Huh,' says my English pal Norma, 'that's all very well if you're eighteen, or maybe even thirty. But the older you get, the harder it gets . . . in my mind, a rabbit has been a rabbit for decades, it can't just turn into a *lapin* overnight.'

Yes it can. If you *concentrate*. Maybe it'll take a while, but one day a *lapin* will bounce into your brain, if you want it to badly enough. If you love France enough to work hard at it. (Not everyone does: some people are just economic migrants, here for the health care or cheaper housing, with no intention of learning anything.)

'Well yes, I do love France,' concedes one of my anglophone pals, 'but I can't even count up to a hundred. I get stuck after sixty. I can't say the alphabet, didn't even realise it's different . . . '

So, turn on your telly. Yes, *French*! Unplug the BBC! Watch the children's programmes along with all the other beginners. You may feel like a dork, but you will learn to count up to a hundred, and you will learn to pronounce 'A' through 'Z'. Guaranteed.

Still can't let go of your pencil? Okay, here's your punishment. Go out and buy a crossword. Yes, that's right, in French. Your nearest Maison de la Presse will have a whole series of crossword books, graded from one to ten in degrees of difficulty. Buy number one. Go home. Sit down. Get up. Make tea. Sit back down. Sigh heavily. Read clues. Lick pencil.

And stay there until you've solved it, no matter if you're there till three in the morning or next Easter.

After that, you can move on to Scrabble. Mmm, bilingual. You invite your French neighbours in – yes, the ones who want to learn English – and they can play in your language and you can play in theirs and next thing a bottle of wine's nearly empty and, well what do you know, you're all much better than you thought . . . it really isn't rocket science, is it?

'No,' admits Norma. 'I suppose I could do that. Maybe I even *will* do it, because as things stand, when I try to speak to anyone,

I feel like I'm playing tennis without a stick.'

That's the spirit. Mix all the metaphors you like, so long as you *just do it*.

But even if you don't do it, *nil desperandum*. If you wait long enough, the French language will come to you instead. It's not *très speedy*, but it's definitely *en route*. Hang in for another fifty years, and *monsieur le president* will probably be addressin' y'all with a Texas drawl.

22.

À La Recherche du Temps Perdu

In Normandy, my Irish friend Sheila and I have established a tradition of celebrating our birthdays by taking each other out to lunch. Hers is in autumn and mine is in spring, and we look forward to the chance to dress up and go out somewhere nice; often the weather is good enough that we can flaunt our finery and stroll in the soft, silken air after we've eaten.

Today, my turn to be fêted, is such a day. The March sun is shining for the third day in a row, caressingly warm as we emerge from the restaurant to find the nearby newsagent attaching the freshly delivered newspaper headlines to the stand outside his shop. Adjusting the sweater around my shoulders (it's warm, but not scorching), I suddenly think of something so absurd it makes me laugh. Sheila wants to know what's so funny.

'Oh, I was just thinking, after three days of sun, that newspaper headline is probably some doom-and-gloom yelp about droughts and hosepipe bans and farmers demanding heatwave subsidies!'

She gives me one of those looks that says 'Oh, you have such a nasty mind', and giggles at the absurdity of such a notion . . . until the newsagent stands back to reveal the headline: *'Normandy facing summer-long drought!'*

That's all it takes. Three days of mild sun, and France fears the worst. Terror strikes, and the cafés start to hum with anticipation of meteorological horror to come. The previous year, we celebrated my birthday in the riverbank town of La Bouille, which actually lost one of its best restaurateurs to this paranoia. A charming, talented young chef-patron, he said he was moving to the Antilles because 'At least there, they're used to the sun. I won't have to listen to them whining about the unbearable heat every time it shines.'

Being Irish, Sheila and I are of course thrilled when the sun shines. We love bright hot weather, can't get enough of it after our waterlogged childhoods in grey old Ireland. But even now, in early spring, the French are already revving up to grumble.

Throughout April and May, the sunshine continues and increases, gathering warmth as wisteria whizzes up the walls. By early June, it is deliciously hot. The chestnut trees glow with 'candles', fields blaze with fierce yellow rapeseed, apple orchards float on a cloud of blossom, the cows are knee-deep in clover and every lilac tree drips under the weight of its laden boughs. It is like living in one of Monet's landscapes. Picnics and barbecues rev up, everyone's in shorts, gone fishing, out canoeing, zooming to the beach to swim on their lunch hour, windsurfing, cycling, playing tennis long into the slow, fragrant dusk. It is divine.

Already, I have quite a tan. The temperature is in the thirties, and I'm beaming like the Cheshire cat, loving every dazzling drop of sunshine, soaking it up, purring with joy. But the French are not happy. *Eh non.* It is *too* hot. Fanning their fevered brows, they begin to visibly wilt, muttering in the markets, predicting the chaos that will result, the heatstroke, the scorched crops, the shrivelled hydrangeas, the dried-up streams, all the looming disaster that will surely strike any minute now. In the bakery, the bank, the doctor's surgery, everywhere long queues form, it's the same story: too hot! *Pas normal! Insupportable!*

I yearn for a stout hurley with which to smack each and every one of their resolutely miserable skulls. And, after a month of this thankless gloom, apparently the gods yearn for one too, because suddenly – *splat!* At a stroke, summer shuts down. Thick black clouds descend on the horizon and the bright light snaps off. The gleaming, soaring sky collapses, turning charcoal grey as lightning cleaves the clouds and the heavens open. Very heavily, it rains.

And rains, and rains, and rains. Every day, almost non-stop, day and night, violent thunder strikes terror into me and all my neighbours, jolting us awake, turning peaceful dreams into nightmares. I spend a great many nights racing at 4 AM to unplug computers before bolts of lightning reduce them to ash. Our lovely Camelot is washed away as if it were a mirage. Overnight, the potentially drought-stricken farmers are replaced, in café lore, by fishermen who can't fish, tourists flooded out, beachfront restaurants forced to close down, tragic tales of campers' tents being blown away, and vast waves breaking the windscreens of unlucky motorists riskily parked on the seafront to gape aghast at the marine drama. Instead of dying of thirst, the crops are flattened by hammering rain, which pounds them to pulp; the plums that should have been huge and juicy are gnarled and speckled, there isn't even a wasp to be seen. (They have, apparently, swarmed off en masse to their travel agent to book a holiday somewhere sunny.)

The long evenings, so mellow only a month ago, now lie fallow. There's nothing anyone can do with them, no more merry barbecuing or shrimp-fishing or falling asleep to the *thwack* of tennis balls; instead, everyone's watching television with the lights on, huddled into jeans and sweaters, their silks and shorts discarded for winter woollies. The weather forecast is so bad that Météo France only doles it out in small cautious doses, a few days at a time, presumably to avert the mass suicides that might otherwise result. On the evening news, oilskinned tourists are filmed packing up and leaving in droves, drenched and spluttering as they all chorus the same thing into the microphone: 'What a *dreadful* climate! Never again!'

So, are we happy now? The heatwave is over, the temperature has gone from tropical to arctic. Is that better? No more need to worry about the parched roses, about granny's headache, or all that terrible heat and dust. Perhaps Normandy should consider a service of thanksgiving.

Mais non. Of course not. Normandy is absolutely furious. The summer has been a disaster, a deluge, a . . . a . . . !

A punishment? For all that whining and complaining back in June? Even if you don't believe in any kind of god, that's certainly what it looks like: a fitting punishment. The Normans hated all that heat and bright light, never stopped moaning about its dismal repercussions, and so the gods simply switched it off. Clearly these people are happier in the dark, cold and wet.

Mais non. They are never happy. Normandy, formerly outraged by the sweltering summer, is now outraged by the lack of it. Tourism statistics plummet along with the temperature, the souvenir shops bemoan a shocking drop in business, the café owners are at their wits' end as demand for all those iced drinks dries up. As am I, trying to understand all this. What is it, exactly, that everyone wants? Perfection? *En permanence?* Richard Burton warbling about the laws governing climactic nirvana, relayed on France Bleu every morning?

Yes. Apparently that's exactly what's required. Nice warm sunshine, not too hot, regularly sprinkled with just the right amount of rain, a little wind to freshen the air, but no gales or storms, all the way through from Easter to Hallowe'en. Anything else is an affront, a reason to mumble and grumble all the way through spring, summer and autumn, to look the proverbial gift horse in the mouth and focus on its one missing tooth.

I am writing this on 28 August. The rain is drumming on the roof like Ringo Starr, the sky is a steel wall of cloud, the valley below my windy plateau is turning into a lake that will take weeks to drain off. The cows are knee-deep in mud, the beach is deserted, bikes, tennis racquets and swimsuits are stored away in basements and my mind is seizing up with horror at the thought of just how long winter is going to be, given that it started four weeks ago. On 1 August, sharp.

A friend rings from Ireland, and I all but weep down the phone, telling her about our ruined summer. 'Really?' she says, and I can hear the barely contained amusement in her voice. 'Well, I hate to tell you this, but it's lovely here.'

No, I'm not deceived. I know that 'lovely' merely means it hasn't rained today, that there's 'a break in the cloud' that normally hovers over Ireland. I can watch RTÉ's weather bulletins online and see the true picture. But hey, I'm desperate.

'Maybe,' I speculate, 'I'll come over so. Hop on a flight tomorrow. Get some Irish sun.'

'Good idea,' she says warily. 'Who knows, it might last for a few days!'

Of course it won't. We both know that warm weather rarely lasts in Ireland, and that 'hot' is defined as anything over 17 degrees. But 'hot' delights the Irish in a way it never delights the French. It sends them scampering off to the beach whooping with joy, waving their bottles of sun lotion like trophies, revelling in the sheer, simple pleasure of summer. They love it. Even during famously sweltering heatwaves, such as that of 1985, they have never been known to say one bad word about it.

Whereas the French: *ah, non*. It is miserable, it is rotten, it is unbearable . . . whatever the weather. They will be making an official complaint to the government about it, to demand that something be done, that compensation be paid out and action taken to ensure that it never happens again.

And who knows, maybe it never will. Maybe the sun will never again cook Normandy to a crisp. From my window right now, that's certainly how it looks.

See? There *is* a god.

23.

A Matter of Opinion

It is a crystal-clear spring day. Late April, and France is foaming with blossom, engulfed in exuberance. White and lacy, the hawthorn and spyrea embrace like lovers, all but waltzing up the aisle, attended by dancing yellow daffodils, blushing pink tulips and shy, tiny lily of the valley. Overhead, the first swallows swoop and dip, and my sentry blackbird has taken up his station on top of the fir tree, ready to sing, later, the evening aria. You could forgive France almost anything this fine morning, and as I wander up the drive, riffling through the post, I even contemplate for one insane moment forgiving the moles. (If you've ever seen the movie *Caddy Shack*, that's northern France – bring on Bill Murray with the gelignite.)

Amongst the missives in the mail is a newspaper cutting. Sent by an Irish friend who has not relinquished the battle for my soul, it is a follow-up to a survey indicating that the Irish are amongst the happiest of Europeans. This new survey, however, finds Dubliners 'far less satisfied with life than rural dwellers'. Conducted by a brace of university researchers, it cites 'proximity to the sea' as one of the things that make people happiest; it discovers that single people are happier than those who are separated, divorced, or in possession of more than three children, and it says that once people attain an income of around sixty thousand euro, the importance of further earnings 'decreases in terms of well-being'.

The things that make people unhappy are predictable: bad infrastructure, unreliable transport, urban overcrowding, crime, frustration at work, lonely old age. The survey is one of those regular little *agents provocateurs* that editors fire off to get people chatting in the pub, but one line hovers in my mind as I head out to buy fish at the harbour, where the first tourists are strolling around in the sun: 'The environment is a much more significant factor in explaining our happiness than was previously thought – just as important as your job or income.' So concludes Dr Peter Clinch of UCD.

It's hard to disagree. Living in the country, within reach of the sea, is doing me good for sure. Despite having less money than before, and virtually none of what Dr Clinch calls 'employment status', I doubt now if I could ever go back to urban life. Moving to France has meant giving up a lot of material benefits, and it's not all rosy – indeed, there are days when I could cheerfully garrotte the entire French nation with its own red tape – but the quality of life is definitely better, and quality does matter. In fact, it's vital. It's worth giving up urban perks for, and you gradually learn to live with downsides such as the moles, the spectacular storms, the two-hour drive to the airport, the thundering sugar-beet trucks in winter and the maddening lack of competent tradesmen.

But that's just my view. For now. Because I'm coming up to that make-or-break moment when the novelty starts to wear off, and people wonder whether, after all, they really intend to stay abroad for the rest of their lives. After a few years, the adrenalin rush recedes, you start feeling less like a tourist and more like a resident – one from whom France expects a contribution in exchange for all this lovely lifestyle. Some people start seeing their half-full glass as suddenly half-empty. They give up on learning the language, on making friends, on coping with flooded basements and power cuts, and start thinking, increasingly, about . . . maybe . . . making their way home . . . some day?

Well, today I'm not going anywhere. I'm practically drunk, this morning, on the fragrance of all these flowers, the intoxicatingly fresh air, the balmy sunshine. I'd sooner have my nose sliced off with a chainsaw than go back to the urban jungle, with its scratchy irritations, its noise and dirt, its aggression and competition. Rural France is where I'm meant to be. But is everyone? Intrigued by the survey, I decide to conduct a little one of my own. By now, I know quite a number of other foreigners living locally. What do they think? Has moving to Normandy really made them happier?

※

A week later, I'm considering sending my findings to *Le Figaro*. Everyone has jumped at the chance to participate in the casual questionnaire, and their comments disclose some aspects of France, both good and bad, that nobody ever mentions unprovoked.

First, of course, there are the obvious things. Everybody loves French food, full stop. Everybody loves the window displays, the architecture, the languid landscape, the sense of style and flair. Everybody hates French paperwork, French angst, the eternal strikes, and that infuriating Gallic shrug. Everybody adores the markets, the music, the summer fireworks and festivals, the uncrowded roads and the sense of space.

More than anything, it emerges that everybody loves the freedom of not having to trudge off to a tedious job every morning, not having to battle public transport or a megalomaniac boss. Many of the foreigners I've questioned do actually work, but they endorse one of Dr Clinch's findings: 'the self-employed are happiest'. Even though France throws every possible spanner at the self-employed, they still say it's better than what they did before. One man from Belfast describes himself as 'a child of Ceaucescu' – by which he means that his previous career, working for a 'demented' boss in 'horrendous' conditions, has left him 'scarred for life'. If he hadn't moved to France, he says, he would have had a nervous breakdown at the very least, maybe even 'gone screaming round the bend'. Now he runs a B&B, teaches a bit of English in winter, and says that no amount of money would ever lure him back to Belfast, where, apart from his boss, he was 'so *sick* of Ian Paisley and Gerry Adams, ranting on day in and day out, dictating the quality of my entire life . . . I never want to see or hear of either one of them ever, ever again'.

Somebody else – who should possibly have been a painter – says that the most attractive thing about France is 'the church spires'.

Eh?

'Yes, spires. Especially when they're lit up at night, glowing like beacons, all over France. And the plane trees, those lovely dappled corridors of greenery that go on and on for miles . . . I just love the churches and the plane trees. They are the *essence* of France.'

Well, Normandy doesn't actually have plane trees – you have to go further south for those – but it has no shortage of church spires, and suddenly I'm looking at ours and thinking, yes, there *is* something timeless about it, something comforting. Although Catholicism is waning in France, and the little rural churches are poorly attended these days, it would be a terrible shame to lose them. An inestimable loss, when you think about it – and, overnight, we all seem to be thinking about it. The decline in vocations means that it's now common for six or seven parishes to share just one priest, but the church is still the focal point of every village, the place where people are married or baptised or buried, and I wonder about the remark of a friend who reckons that 'any day now, they'll all be pulled down to make way for mosques'.

Will they? And if so, will the mosques exercise the same emotional pull as the old churches? Will their spires glow on winter nights, lighting the way home? Will their crypts be damp and haunting? Will their walls reverberate to the enthusiastic – albeit off-key – singing of their faithful? Will there be plaques commemorating those who fell in the defence of France, and of freedom? Will there be handshakes on Sunday mornings or Saturday evenings, and a quick nip of something reviving in the Café des Sports after baby Benoit has been baptised?

Who knows. But the French landscape is changing for sure, and not always for the better: one of my quiz participants quotes 'urbanisation' as the thing she likes least about living here. 'The paving of everything,' as she puts it. 'The fusspot tidying up of nature. And the fact that everywhere else is urbanising too doesn't make it any better. In fact, it makes it worse – this blind rush to follow what other countries are doing. If France doesn't watch itself, it'll soon be completely concreted over. Tarmacked, synthetic, not a blade of grass left.'

Well, this potential disaster seems relatively remote, given the currently vast agricultural plains of central France, the dying Auvergnat villages where even the cat is twiddling its thumbs. But as if to underscore her viewpoint, a farmer appears on television just a few days later, complaining that he has 'no land'. His region, Brittany, is, he says, 'falling victim to the bulldozer'. This is something of a double entendre, since Jacques Chirac's nickname is *le bulldozer*. Jacques was, and still is, famously sympathetic to farmers (especially in his native Corrèze), but this man wants land for his sheep and, bizarrely, none is available. My friend nods solemnly and says: 'There you are, what did I tell you?'

A chap from Kent says that 'the best thing about France is the public transport. Huge autoroutes, the TGV, always on time, not to mention Métro tickets 60 percent cheaper in Paris than in London. A fifty-kilometre bus ride for two euro. In Britain, that'd cost twenty quid. Marvellous, bloody marvellous.'

Well, yes. Even if autoroutes are expensive, they *are* excellent, and trains are extremely punctual (when the SNCF isn't on strike). My only quibble – being Irish, a child of Ryanair – is about aviation. If a tiny country like Ireland can have flights between Cork, Dublin, Galway, Knock, Kerry, Donegal and Waterford, why can't France have direct links between, say, Marseille and Le Havre? Lille and Bordeaux? Why does everything have to filter between Paris or Lyon? Why are there no hop-on, hop-off shuttles across *l'hexagone*?

'Because,' explains my pilot pal Michel, 'there is no demand.'

Rubbish! Nonsense! Infuriatingly, the French take the view that there's no point in supplying something for which there appears to be no demand, whereas we Irish believe that demand is something you create. Demonstrably *can* create. The day Air France or Ryanair puts on a link between, say, Biarritz and Strasbourg, it'll fill up, you'll see. Ironically, the entire French countryside is scattered with small aerodromes, left over from World War Two and just begging for renovation – assuming, that is, that terrorism doesn't stamp out aviation altogether, because, as Michel says: 'Terrorists already dictate the street furniture, transparent litter bins and so forth, the new non-smiling passport photo, the amount of toothpaste we can bring on a plane . . . maybe some day they'll ground us entirely?'

Other ex-pat views are quirky. Somebody says the best thing

about France is 'a stunning painting I once saw by an artist called Jean Grégoire. A village landscape, cubist . . . unforgettable.' Someone else quotes 'the luminous window displays, the gift-wrapping, the perfect presentation, especially in the *pâtisseries* and *chocolateries*. The way they knot a scarf or dress a table like nobody else. I just adore French *visuals*'.

Somebody trumpets the joys of iced shellfish platters, someone else loves 'the free entertainment' (fireworks, church concerts, heritage days, and so on), and there's even a vote for the *café philo*, where people congregate for a convivial, albeit organised, chat about the state of the nation, or the state of humanity, in France's version of a pub. And one Londoner, who had very mixed feelings about moving here, admits to having been completely seduced by 'family life. Those big picnics you see in summer, with babies, toddlers, parents, grandparents, everyone . . . they all seem so close. There's no generation gap. You sense this wonderful warmth.'

But the devil has advocates too. One woman denounces 'those dreadful Turkish loos' (the shock of which all but hospitalised my visiting mother), another wishes that France would 'neuter its army of stray cats', and there's a definite thumbs-down for 'the screaming motorbikes that drive everyone mad, like mosquitoes. Why are silencers not mandatory?' (Because too many cops, I'd guess, were once that testosterone-fuelled teenager, doing wheelies at the lights.)

The 'diversity of the regions' gets a big vote, as do the 'the clearly defined seasons', and the icons are much loved: the Eiffel Tower, the Millau viaduct, the Arche de la Défense, even Paris's Pompidou Centre. (I loathe it, but am squashed by those who find it 'inspiring'.) And of course the affordable wine is a big plus, as are the low crime rate, the 'serious' educational system, and the 'intelligent cinema, which would be classified arthouse elsewhere but is mainstream here'. They all love doctors who still make house calls, the 'delightful' beaches, the *mediathèques* and *espaces publics* where you can use computers, libraries, research resources and so on, for little or no charge. Some Irish ex-pats lament 'the lack of social spontaneity', but their English counterparts salute 'the refreshing reserve' because 'Friends easily made are easily lost. If a friendship's worth having, it's worth working for. Plus, French neighbours aren't a bit nosy.' (This is very true, you could be dead for a month before they'd notice.)

The downsides to life in this putative paradise encompass 'choking taxes and stifled enterprise', the thirty-five-hour week 'which encourages laziness, dependence and navel-gazing', the 'waste of public funds on fussy nonsense' (this voter means traffic-calming devices but includes the Programme Anti-Morosité – yes, there is such a thing), and the burgeoning insurance industry, which, unsurprisingly, is gaining a grip on the neurotic, worst-case-scenario French mind.

'I hate insurance companies,' growls our man from Kent, 'especially when they ring me in the middle of my dinner wanting to know whether I'm worried about slipping on a bar of soap or falling off a ladder. They should be worrying about whether I'm going to turn up in their offices toting a Kalashnikov.'

What else annoys, in fabulous France? 'The bloody moles, of course' – this battle has reached epic proportions – and 'not being able to vote. My great-grandmother was a suffragette, and now France has robbed me of the vote she fought for, even though I've been a French taxpayer for seventeen years.' (Some foreigners can in fact vote if they fight hard enough for long enough, but getting on the electoral register involves taking out dual citizenship and can be a laborious, soul-destroying process.)

French formality, while considered exaggerated by some, is

overall listed as a plus: 'Much better than American rudeness, or the tacky insolence that's creeping across Britain. The French kiss much more than they swear, which is lovely.' A less enchanted contributor points out that the French spit a lot too, and the men urinate in public, 'which is curiously crass amidst so much courtesy'. But my guinea pigs are really rummaging in the bottom of the barrel to find much else to criticise. Even the low-key nightlife gets a vote: 'No drunken thugs, no puking in the streets.' One woman wishes that the shops would stay open throughout lunchtime, but nobody else seems to want this, 'now that we're into the rhythm of life here'.

Nonetheless, there must be some things that people miss about 'home'?

'Hmm . . . chips? Proper fat, greasy chips? Curry? Darts? Pub quizzes? And our friends, of course . . . though honestly, we see them as much as we ever did. There's nothing we miss enough to lure us back.'

So we're all going to stay in France, then, assuming we don't kidnap Mona Lisa or do anything else that might get us kicked out?

Yes. Oh yes. Everybody says they're definitely staying, 'circumstances permitting'. Indeed, in some cases wild horses wouldn't drag them 'home', wherever it formerly was. One couple have even persuaded their adult children to join them in the Camargue, and, over the years I've been here, I've seen only a handful of disillusioned francophiles wash their hands of France – almost all because they hadn't researched their area or their house before moving, hadn't learned a word of French or were fizzing with an impatient inability to accept that the French lifestyle is, um, French.

And is France proving good for our health?

'Yes,' says the chap who hates the insurance industry, 'especially my mental health. I never knew what a difference it would make to eat real home-cooked food, to sit out in the garden on summer evenings or play boules . . . I've even learned to let the phone take messages, whereas in my previous life I was a slave to it. I'm a different person here in the Sologne. I even gather my own walnuts and can tell a truffle from a toadstool.'

What if someone offered you a job back in Blighty at, say, a hundred grand a year?

'I'd tell them to go find a Frenchman for it!'

Finally, there's the chap just back from a weekend in his native London. 'Hideous,' he says, 'like a failed America. I only wish I'd moved to France sooner. Years ago.'

Why? What's the best thing about it?

'The best thing about France is that it's France.'

24.

Material Girl

'Be careful what you wish for. You might get it.'

That was one sceptic's wry comment when I first mooted moving to France. Another was more optimistic.

'Oh, it'll be gorgeous,' he said. 'Lazing in the sun, surviving on peaches and baguettes . . . how romantic!'

Clearly he'd never tried surviving on peaches and baguettes. But that's what downsizing is all about. Trading a hectic lifestyle for simplicity. You have to make *sure* that simplicity, in all its shapes and forms, is going to suit you, because once you jump off your local property ladder there's no going back. You won't be able to buy so much as a garden shed. A garden *rake*.

Materially, I'd been doing fine back home. I had a good job, a lovely house, lots of clothes and holidays and a new car every few years. It was fun – until it all inexplicably began to itch like a hair shirt. I was exhausted and dispirited, tasting nothing, enjoying nothing any more. No amount of money can compensate for living a life that tastes like sawdust. It's at this point that so many people seem to start thinking about France – where, the myth persists, it is possible to live on peaches and baguettes.

No. It is not. Do not for one moment believe this myth. Peaches may make you healthy, but they are not enough to make you happy. Even if the sale of your house furnishes a temporary cushion, money is going to be an issue for the vast majority of 'economic migrants', as well as for ardent francophiles. Your attitude to it is going to be another. Learning to let go of your previous lifestyle can be amazingly liberating, but it takes time. The first months, or even years, can be spectacularly scary: letting go of anxiety takes even longer to learn than letting go of habits, of expectations, of toys and treats.

France is dazzlingly seductive for the committed consumer. The bakery windows glow like art galleries, the chic shops flaunt their exquisite shoes, handbags and furniture, the restaurants beckon with their iced trays of seafood and champagne, the goodies are endlessly gorgeous. In shops like the FNAC, you can spend an entire day in the books or music section alone. Certain IKEA branches are so big, I recommend that you bring a picnic and a compass. On the autoroutes, Porsches commonly fly by, silver cabriolets being driven by beautiful people to beautiful places. The upmarket resorts of Nice, Deauville and St Tropez purr with Rollers and Beamers. The entire country is chock-full of magnificent chateaux, its wines are divine, its sartorial elegance is legendary. Even now, in the midst of global recession, it remains, very quietly, *very* wealthy. Its temptations are endless.

Which, for anyone trying to downsize, means a battle. Yes, that chocolate cake is a Matisse masterpiece, but you can't afford it! Yes, the Printemps has just got in the most beautiful new bedlinen on the planet, but you can't buy any! Okay, one bottle of wine then, but make it last the week! No, don't even *think* about putting on the central heating, put on a woolly jumper! Anyone moving to France to live the simple life should be warned: your nose will be permanently pressed up against the gleaming shop window.

At first, it's hell. Material guys and girls have to be weaned off their goodies, and that doesn't happen overnight. It is very hard to admit that yes, you were a consumer addict. To admit to your friends that no, you won't be changing your clattering old banger this year, or next year, or maybe not even after that. (One of the most socially divisive things the Irish government ever did was to introduce a car-registration system whereby the car's age is clearly stated, creating a competitive state of mind that can take years to unlearn.)

It's not easy to say 'No, sorry, I'd love to go out to dinner but, um, why don't you come round here instead?' (And then to magic potatoes into gourmet marvels.) Even going to the supermarket hurts, because it will have the latest flat-screen TVs, gorgeous clothes and a deli to die for. You'll feel like the only child at the party who isn't getting any present.

But hey, you're off the hamster wheel! I used to fume in stagnant traffic for twelve hours a week; now I walk round the local lake or by the sea for an hour every morning. Walking is free. And yes, it feels good. It feels great. The fresh air and freedom are absolutely exhilarating, as well as the fitness aspect. Burning your bridges can be wonderfully invigorating. No, there won't be any trendy bistro lunch as a reward for the walk, but my cooking has improved along with my shopping; I can make a delicious meal for two people for a fiver. I've discovered that a fish called *lieu* tastes just as good as cod or monkfish, for less than half the price. I can make a vat of carrot or beetroot soup for a euro – not only is it delicious, it gives you turbocharged energy, and you'll never get 'flu again. I'm still wearing the jeans and sweaters I brought from Ireland, because here in my little hamlet the concept of 'dress to impress' is unknown, and my wardrobe is full of long-redundant little black numbers. (When starvation looms, I can open a vintage-clothing shop.)

But a city dweller must miss the arts, surely? The concerts, the cinema, the galleries? Not necessarily . . . not when you're busy reading the hundreds of books you never had time for before. Not when you make friends with a musician who invites you to rehearsals, or when you've got television programmes as good as *Des Racines et Des Ailes* to keep you entertained on winter nights. Once a month, lots of French art galleries, historic sites, museums and so on open their doors for free; all you've got to do is find out which ones on which days. Morning cinema screenings are half price, and going to the cinema in the morning feels delightfully decadent. When you've winkled them out, you discover that an amazing number of activities cost little or nothing, which adds an extra dimension to what would be a pleasure anyway. Once a spoiled shopaholic, now I get a kick out of finding products that work just as well as the luxury brands.

Nowadays, my treats are laughably modest: magazines in English – admittedly expensive ones like *Vogue*, *GQ* and *Vanity Fair* – and the exotic shower gels for which I have a strange craving. Now and then I go to a concert or a restaurant, but I no longer take them for granted, and, as addictions go, at least these little goodies don't require mortgages.

Let nobody kid themselves. Moving to France (or Spain, or Italy, or wherever) might be a seductive dream, but it has its price tag. You need to try it on for size before committing, spend a month in some crumbling old cottage *in winter*, making the kids eat garlic and green beans because, hey, McDonald's is history now! Sign up for the Alliance Française and see if you really *can* learn French – especially that little-known word *non*, which you will be needing more than any other.

Non, je ne regrette rien. Within weeks of arriving in France,

I was loving the simple life, doing nothing more exciting than walking, cycling, reading, listening to music, swimming at the beach – whatever's cheap or free. A friend gave me a pot of home-made chutney one day, and I was as thrilled as if she'd given me a gourmet hamper. (Okay, sad, but true.) I can't afford aerobics, massages or a personal fitness programme, but I do have a bike, skates, a skipping rope and a village tennis court – even cliffs to climb – if I want high-octane exercise for free. Once a week, we gather to play ping-pong, chess, Scrabble and Boggle in our village *salle des fêtes* – which, I'm not ashamed to admit, amuses me as much as many a star-spangled soirée ever did (especially since the glitterati became the illiterati). Yes, of course I'd love a sleek new car, or to get the garden landscaped, but lack of these things is not fatal. You learn to look at the scruffy garden and cultivate a Gallic shrug.

Ironically, I feel richer than before. Younger, fitter, happier. Here in big-sky country, amidst the creamy cows and golden crops, where the air is so pure we sleep like stones, where the fields of blue flax and red poppies ripple for miles, it would take a lot for anyone to feel truly impoverished. I used to have a lot. Now, less is a lot more.

⁂

French income tax (should you have an income) is relatively low. But it is merely the first of endless taxes whose final total is spectacularly high. There is VAT, at nearly 20 percent, on absolutely everything. There is tax on your house, your water, gas, phone, electricity, petrol, food, insurance, pharmaceuticals and clothing; in some cases, there is even tax on tax. There are autoroute tolls, parking meters, medical bills and emergency repairs, and, as everywhere, there are thieves waiting to rip off the unwary. Especially if the unwary is a single woman, or driving a foreign car.

One day, I was heading for Dinard in Brittany when the car started making one of those alarming *splut-splut* noises. I pulled into a garage. Oh dear, said the owner-mechanic, there's a major problem here. You've wrecked your carburettor with supermarket petrol. That's what comes of not buying petrol from proper garages like mine.

But, I pointed out, supermarket petrol works fine. Everyone's been using it for decades. Anyway, can you fix the car, or what?

He nodded. *Bien sûr.* But it's a big job. Major surgery. It'll cost a thousand euro.

I thought about it. His comment about the petrol was ringing alarm bells.

'No. Too expensive. I'll just have to hope the car holds up until I can get it home to my local mechanic.'

The car did hold up, and eventually came to roost in the workshop of my resolutely cheerless, but honest, *garagiste*. He opened the bonnet. Peered in. Tweaked a rubber pipe.

'*Et voilà.* Just a loose connection. All fixed.'

The ten-second repair was so small that he wouldn't take a centime for it. But how many frantic foreigners have since forked over thousands to that crook in Brittany?

Dashing for a plane another day, I was held to ransom at another garage. Fifty euro, for emergency replacement wipers. The same ones that cost a fiver in the supermarket. The old ones were chucked into a bucket full of similar ones – all destined, I suspected, for vastly profitable recycling. My experience of the French car industry is that it's staffed by a high proportion of licensed gangsters, who regard foreigners (identifiable by their accents) as sitting ducks. Don't be intimidated, and buy all your accessories in supermarkets where possible. Generic products work just as well as fancy brands, at half the price. But a car remains a luxury: some autoroute tolls are all but armed robbery, and parking and speeding tickets are generally acknowledged to be a lucrative rip-off. The only way to avoid speeding tickets in many areas is to drive in third gear, if not first – which generates the permanent feeling that you are following a funeral cortège. Sometimes you'd nearly get further in *reverse*.

On the other hand, some products remain cheaper in France. Wine and cheese, obviously, shellfish for some obscure reason, and hotels. Virtually every village has some little *auberge* which, while not luxurious, is clean and comfortable, and offers excellent value if you don't mind the offhand welcome or the forty-watt bulbs. Even better value – especially if your house-hunting is going to take a month or two, which it should – is to stay in a *gîte*. Apart from economising by cooking your own meals, you can pick up invaluable local tips from the owners about houses for sale: bargain houses, houses that shouldn't be touched with a bargepole, houses that are the subject of domestic dispute or were flooded last winter . . . it is possible to save not only a lot of money but a lot of heartache.

Saving money is, for many, a priority. But it doesn't always happen. I didn't expect to have to replace the washing machine, fridge, computer, dishwasher and car so soon . . . but I did. A storm blew tiles off the roof, they cost a fortune to replace and naturally the insurance only paid a fraction of the bill. Ditto when the computer was assassinated by lightning – twice. A week of ice ripped the surface off the front wall – too expensive to repair, a coat of paint had to suffice – and yet another storm killed the pump in the driveway while I was away, leaving the basement to fill with water for several days. The resulting plumber's bill was cosmic. And how to dry out the basement?

Easy, said the expert I consulted, just install one of our wonderful ventilation systems. See, it's today's special bargain at seven thousand euro. Sign here.

I left nature to take its course, and the basement dried out all by itself. For free.

❧

Money, as the saying goes, only matters when you haven't got any. After a surprisingly short time in France, many of the romantics who envisaged living on tomatoes find that they haven't got any. (Money, that is, anyone can grow tomatoes.) They panic. They sell their houses and return to Ireland, Britain or wherever, sometimes throwing themselves on the mercy of friends or family, bitterly regretting the whole disastrous project that was France. Sometimes even blaming France for somehow failing to fill their pockets with mysterious, magical funds. Whereas all they need to do is visit their local employment exchange, chamber of commerce or *mairie*, to announce their availability to teach English.

France's appetite for English lessons is insatiable. It is acutely conscious of needing this vital commercial skill in today's market-place. Whether it likes learning English is another matter – some students are nakedly resentful – but it has definitely bitten the bullet. Many companies even pay their employees' tuition fees. Sometimes the government even pays. While teaching English may not be the most exciting job in the world, it is a useful fall-back.

No degree, no diploma, no experience? No matter. Language schools such as Wall Street or Berlitz will train you in their own methods, and even offer flexibility in your work schedule. At local level (chambers of commerce, private companies, municipal associ-ations, or – shudder – children's tutorials), you can make use of the excellent material on the BBC website. All you really need to teach English is a smile, a positive attitude, and clear diction.

It's a transitory job, not a career, and as such the pay isn't great. But it's a comforting security blanket for anyone determined to stay in France, it will keep the roof over your head while offering the chance of networking. Many of the students have, by definition, interesting jobs with interesting contacts – which, if you work them well, may lead to something more lucrative in the long term.

Alternatively, many new anglophone arrivals yearn for someone who can set up their computer, satellite dish, home cinema and so on, *in English*. If you're good at technology, just put an ad in your local paper or supermarket, and hey, you're in business.

Until, at least, the *fiscs* start wanting to know about your VAT returns and corporate tax and . . . this is one reason why France has such a high rate of unemployment. As in the Ireland of thirty or forty years ago, enterprise is viewed with suspicion. In one of his solecisms that actually made sense, George Bush famously said that 'The problem with the French is, they don't have a word for "entre-preneur".' And, in a manner of speaking, they don't. Is it any won-der? The paperwork (and advance taxation) required to set up a business is so nightmarish that it's a lot easier to go on the dole. It's a vicious circle, with the authorities retorting that the paperwork relating to unemployment keeps an army of civil servants *off* the dole. Even though the 'Polish plumber' phenomenon has forced France to 'liberalise' some of its employment legislation, the mind-set is still protectionist.

So, whether you're teaching English, or setting up computers, or even making pâté for a living, keep it small, keep it simple, and aim for the 'micro-entreprise' tax category. Simplicity is, after all, one of the attractions of life in France: if you aspire to get rich quick, Tokyo or Manhattan might suit you better.

One day, finally getting my mitts on enough money to butter a baguette, I tried to lodge the cheque in my bank account. Peering at it as if it might be a blueprint for nuclear holocaust, the bank teller sucked his teeth. 'Hmm. Drawn on Barclays? That'll take a month to clear.' A *month*!

Eh oui. Although I was only trying to lodge the cheque, not cash it, the clerk was adamant. A month it would take, and a month it did, even though the nearest French branch of Barclays was barely an hour away.

Yes, France is full of lovely food. You just wouldn't want to be in a hurry to eat it.

❧

But in spite of everything, some people do succeed in accidentally amassing serious money. People like tennis star Amélie Mauresmo, actor John Malkovich, singers Charles Aznavour, Yannick Noah and Johnny Hallyday, all of whom have one thing in common: being forced out of France by the wealth tax.

France currently defines 'wealth' as seven hundred and fifty thousand euro. Anyone worth that much, or more, can expect to be hounded by the government for such vast quantities of ISF (Impôt Sur Fortune) that, in many cases, they simply sell up and leave, sometimes sobbing as they go. Johnny Hallyday, a national icon whose songs regularly top the charts, loathed leaving for Switzerland, but said he had no choice. Should the next government be socialist, chances are that the screw will be turned even tighter. And proper order too, say France's legions of socialists and communists, many of whom have yet to make the connection between enterprise, jobs and money.

This book isn't about politics. Let's not get into a wrangle over fat cats or bolshie agitators or the complexities of European economics. Personally, it's all I can do to keep up when the check-out girl says that will be *cent quatre-vingt dix-sept euro et soixante-treize centimes, s'il vous plaît.* So suffice it to say that you have been warned. If you're truly poor, or disinclined to work (at anything other than the system), or don't understand contraception, France will feed, house, educate, medicate, rehabilitate, counsel and comfort you and your *famille nombreuse.* If you are dynamic or rich, or both, you will be bled dry, or washed away to Guernsey on a tide of taxes. If you're somewhere in the middle, you will muddle along hand to mouth provided you don't make the fatal mistake of (a) trying to better your lot, or (b) protesting about the dozens of dependents with whom the state has saddled you. Even my own modest tax bills would indicate that I seem to be putting triplets through college.

Which is really as much as you need to know. Entrepreneurs apply at their peril.

For years, you had a salary. Steady, secure. Health care too, and a pension plan. None of it seemed very exciting at the time, but now, in retrospect, it seems fabulous. Were you insane to chuck it all in for France?

This question will nibble at you for at least the first year or two of your new life. You will be haunted by memories of money. The heady days when you could just waltz out and buy new shoes, theatre tickets or a Chinese takeaway without even thinking about it. Sometimes, I still whimper when I think of that monthly salary statement all *figured out by somebody else.* I didn't even have to do the maths. Difficult as it is to walk away from regular injections of money, it's even more difficult to walk away from the luxury of having someone else do the paperwork.

Should you? Is it really wise to trade your pension, health care and peace of mind for the charms of Lille on a wet Monday? You will have to hate your current life very much, or love France to the point of insanity, to risk it. Some people thrive on risk, but not all.

After the first euphoric year of living in France (gilded by that gorgeous summer when I became a beach bum), I was hit by a terrible attack of reality. Autumn was drawing in, and what on earth was I going to do next? Although the sale of my Irish house meant that I had no immediate financial problems, I could see one looming, and it became very, very worrying. Suddenly, I was sleeping like a baby only in the sense of waking up screaming in the middle of the night.

But, I reminded myself, you knew that this would happen. You decided that France was worth it. You were going to exchange a busy cosmopolitan life for a quiet rustic one, and you were going to get back your physical and mental health come hell or high water. So far, that's working. So what's the problem?

The problem is the human condition. As soon as we get one thing, we're worrying about not having the other. Now I had my freedom, I was worrying about not having my security.

❧

That was several years ago. Today, I still have no security whatsoever. None of the buffers that used to go with a steady job. If I get run over by a bus, or struck by lightning . . . well, tough. I can't afford the comfort zone of expensive insurance. The only difference between then and now is that I've trained myself to stop worrying about it. As far as is humanly possible, I live in the moment.

You can actually do this. You can train yourself not to worry, the same way you can train a dog not to bite. After I'd done a bit of worrying, I began to realise that (a) it wasn't going to change anything, and (b) it was counter-productive. It was tainting the new life I'd fought so hard for. If it went on, I'd end up worse off than before, which would be pointless and ludicrous. Besides, if bad things could happen, then logically good things could happen too. I might get Alzheimer's, or I might get a contract to write some more books. Might be bitten by a rabid dog or might buy a winning lottery ticket. One night I watched the sun going down and muttered: 'Yeah, okay, but it'll come up again too.'

And it did. Unless you are exceptionally unlucky, there is a fairly even rhythm to life: ups and downs, good and bad, wet and dry. It can't be high summer all the time, nor would one want it to be. As my redundancy money and house money from Ireland began to dwindle, I recognised a learning curve: okay, no Dior handbags (thank God I never craved any!) and okay, things are getting a bit tight, but on the other hand, this is Europe. We're not talking about the street misery of Calcutta. I also grasped one of the main reasons why we worry: we do it because nature abhors a vacuum. We worry when we haven't anything better to do.

Unless you're coming to France to get married, take up a new job or oversee some corporate project, chances are you will have a lot of time on your hands. Once the house is sorted and all the logistics are in place . . . what then? If you have nothing else to occupy your attention, you'll start fretting. Start drinking all that delicious French wine, maybe, at eleven in the morning. Start fighting with whoever is handy. Start building up a head of steam about the hundred and one things that might go wrong and surely will, any day now. Anxiety will become your predominant mode.

But you can ward it off simply by doing something else.

Anything else at all. Watching a movie, weeding the garden, painting a wall (not necessarily your own), reading a novel, whatever: the trick is simply to move your mind elsewhere. My astute estate agent, Pierre Yves, once told me that he rated 'boredom' very high on the list of the things that drive foreigners out of France. And yet, there's no shortage of things to do. Any number of sports, cultural and social facilities, endless charities in need of volunteers. The Restos de Coeur, for instance, will be delighted if you park yourself at a supermarket entrance cajoling shoppers into filling up a trolley-full of groceries for people needier than yourself, while you in turn will be reminded that there's *real* poverty out there. Poverty that makes your petty fussing look pathetic, actually.

I have yet to sign up for the Restos de Coeur. But I did agree to teach two English classes a week for a local association, even though the pay was peanuts. The point was that it furnished me with a social insurance number and got me out and about, meeting some very nice new people. It engaged my mind – not once during those classes did I ever worry about anything (too busy) – and it provided an insight into local life. By letting my students chat and gossip all they liked – on condition they did it in English – I learned a great deal about what was happening in the area. Really I should have been paying them, rather than the other way round.

Teaching was fun, and I gave it up with reluctance only when something else, even more unexpected, happened. Out of the blue, on one of those rare days that bless and validate a risky lifestyle, a commission arrived from London to write two novels. A contract, a cheque, and a promise of more. This didn't mean any kind of long-term security, but it did take care of today and several tomorrows. Not only was this a relief to me, it was also good news for the friends who so kindly seemed determined to do a lot of my worrying for me. (You will find you have two kinds of friends: those who worry about you, and those who envy you, regardless of what sacrifices your move may have involved.)

So, I needn't have worried after all. What a good thing I didn't – or not for long, anyway. It would have poisoned lovely France, and some of the happiest days of my life might have been squandered for nothing. Besides, as the saying goes, 'your health is your wealth', and nothing erodes good health quicker than worry. Anyway, no foreigner will ever be as good at worrying as the French themselves, who have practised for centuries and pride themselves on their mastery of *l'inquiétude*.

❦

Amongst new friends here in Normandy, one is English and in her early seventies, the other French and in his early forties. The English woman moved to France at age sixty-eight, is divorced and has, she candidly says, 'very little' to live on. The French friend is married to a successful vet and enjoys a much higher standard of living.

But is his quality of life higher? My impoverished English pal doesn't consider herself poor at all. 'I just make do and mend,' she says cheerfully, 'and enjoy living in this lovely place. You don't really need much money to enjoy a beach or a sunset or a piece of music, do you?'

The other, wealthier, friend shudders on hearing this. 'I couldn't bear having to "make do and mend" when I'm old. I want plenty of money to cushion my old age. I want to go on nice holidays and eat in civilised restaurants and drive a comfy car.'

Fair enough. So why is he the one who is occasionally prone to anxiety attacks and sleepless nights? After all, he's the one with the security. He has a lot more material goodies . . . and, therefore, a lot more to lose?

There's no particular reason why he should lose any of the things he likes having, or doing. But the mere possibility of losing them is a worry to him.

The other, older, friend doesn't worry at all. She doesn't care whether she ever eats in a posh restaurant, and, the last time she went off on a nice holiday, it was ruined when her handbag was stolen. She's not in any great hurry to go on another one. 'After all, living here is like being on permanent holiday, isn't it?'

Yes, it is. And the quickest way to ruin any holiday is to start mentally packing your bags a week before you need to leave.

⁂

Shock, horror!

Something appalling has happened. The sales are on and, after everything I just said, I've been mysteriously stricken by an attack of must-have. I've blitzed the shops. Inexpensive shops, admittedly, Kiabi and Gémo and Les Halles. In one wicked, wanton afternoon I bought a pair of shoes, a pair of boots, two shirts, new jeans, gloves and a ludicrous bright green scarf.

I needed none of these items. But I wanted them, your honour. I was seized by sheer longing, complete lust. I couldn't help myself. It happens about once every six months. There I am, being all good on a sensible budget, living on twenty euro a day (I mean, is that saintly, or what?), and next thing – *wham!* I have to have, absolutely *must have*, a pink taffeta scarf at all costs. Life simply could not go *on* without that scarf. Or those shoes. Or that dress. Even though there's very little call for them in my neck of the woods, some cosmic force drove me to buy them.

Yes, I know I already have a dress. And shoes. And scarves. That's not the point, your honour. You're not listening. You're a man, you don't understand about clothes or shoes at *all*, do you? No. But you'd understand quick enough if it were a hi-fi, or wi-fi, or iPod or somesuch gizmo, wouldn't you? Flat-screen, high-definition telly? Oh yeah. Well, there we are then. Boy toys for you, a crossover lace top (pale cream on coffee) for me. *Irresistible.*

Yes, all right. I was on probation, and I did promise to behave, and now here I am sinning again. But it *happens*. I can't just shed the consumer habits of a lifetime! I used to have money, you know, I used to buy anything I—

Huh? Very different days now, you say? I'm only allowed one accessory, and that's a tight belt? Do you think one would really suit me? I have tried on a few, but seem to keep losing them. Don't know where they get to. Probably a stack of them under the bed somewhere.

Yes, all right then. I'm pleading guilty as charged. I've been out spending money I'd no business to spend. Sometimes I forget that living in France means resisting everything that is deliciously French. Forget that all these lovely things are only for the natives, for normal people with proper jobs or rich spouses. I just get this rush of blood to the head and start spending as if there were no tomorrow.

Oh well, maybe there won't be any tomorrow. Maybe I'll only get to pirouette round in that new dress once, tonight in front of the mirror, before there's a tsunami or something that'll wash me away on a wave of divine retribution. But see if I care.

Promise never to do it again? Sorry, your honour, no can do.

I've got the shopping gene the same way I've got green eyes and freckles. I can live on fresh air for ages but sooner or later a day comes when, for no apparent reason, I lose the run of myself entirely. As Mae West said: 'When I'm good, I'm very good. But when I'm bad, I'm better.'

If only one could have money *and* France. Now there would be bliss. But for some reason it seems destined never to be. For foreigners, France and funds are mutually exclusive. Take your pick. Meanwhile, if a material girl runs out of money, well, she can always eat her words.

25.

Dancing the Can't-Can't

True story. An Englishman moves to France. He buys a plot of land and, after a while, decides to exploit its small man-made lake by setting up a fishing-holiday business. He will make a living and the area will profit from new tourism.

Ah non, says the *mairie*. Not possible, *m'sieu*.

Why not?

Because the original deeds of the property contain no mention of the lake, which was added later by the person who sold it to you. Therefore, we cannot issue fishing permits for a lake which does not exist.

But it does exist. Look, there it is. That sheet of water just over there, the one with ducks bobbing on it. Water. Fish. Lake. See?

Ah, non. It may exist in practice, *m'sieu*, but it does not exist in theory. On paper, there is no lake. Therefore, there will be no permits. No fishing. No tourism. *Désolé.*

Nothing, absolutely nothing, could induce the *mairie* to acknowledge the existence of the lake, to simply add it onto the paperwork and issue the permits necessary to make a viable business of it. After lengthy wrangling, the Englishman was last seen standing outside the *mairie*, not once but every morning, wrapped from head to foot in red tape. Thus will his life continue, he asserts, until the *mairie* unties the tape.

This is what you are up against in France. No matter how ludicrous the tales you have heard about French bureaucracy, they are probably true. Running your domestic affairs – never mind a business – will consume days, months, years of your life. Your health, your marriage, your solvency and your sanity will all be at risk. For a civilised Western nation, France sometimes bears the most uncanny resemblance to pre-glasnost Russia. To the most backward of banana republics. To a Mickey Mouse cartoon.

One day, I run into a restaurateur new to the area. I ask him how it's going. '*Eh bien*,' he sighs. 'Summer was a nightmare. The tourists all wanted chips and burgers. But now we're back into winter . . . well . . . ' Conspiratorially, he leans forward. 'Can you keep a secret?'

I think so. Hope so. What is it?

Slowly, he smiles, stroking his nose in the manner of the master genius. 'I am going,' he whispers, 'to start serving . . . ssh . . . sshellfish. Under your hat. Don't tell anyone.'

Fingers to lips. A week later, the sshellfish are on view to all the world on their bed of ice in his front window, but *sshh*, it's a secret. No, I still haven't cracked it.

When I visit the bank to pick up my new chequebook, I discover that they have printed the wrong address on it. How bizarre. Why?

'Who knows, madame? *C'est comme ça.*'

C'est comme ça is the most often-used phrase in France, even more than 'My colleague isn't here' or 'Be with you in a minute' or 'Sorry, we're just closing'. If you come from any country in which a shrug is not a solution, you will find France immensely frustrating

– as do the French themselves, often driven to despair by their own maddening inefficiency.

It isn't just the big things that break people's spirits. It's the little ones too. The snow, for instance.

Every time it snows in my area, the electricity goes off. The official explanation for this is that the overhead cables can't take the weight of the snow (despite the proximity of a huge nuclear station supplying power to communities all over Europe). During one of these power cuts – which has, ironically, defrosted the freezer – I meet a woman visiting from Canada.

'Amazing, isn't it,' she says. 'When I left Canada, the temperature was minus twenty and the snow was a metre deep. Yet we had full power. As always. The snow never causes power cuts – after all, it's in cold weather that you most need power.'

A point that appears to have completely bypassed the EDF. Unless maybe its chief executive has a cousin in the candle business?

Equally, when the weather heats up and there's a thunderstorm, my computer is frequently struck by lightning. I'm now on my third, and have learned to unplug it every time I go out (both power and phone lines), after having seen what lightning does to a motherboard: toasts it like a slice of Hovis, is what. It kills televisions too, and pumps, and all sorts of gadgets . . . yes, you can claim on your insurance, but only if you're prepared to do battle into infinity – and even then the one kind of damage you're claiming for will turn out to be the one type you are not, *hélas*, insured for. French banks, insurance companies and tradesmen are all up to international standard on at least one level: their greedy cynicsm. *Eh oui, c'est comme ça.*

In some countries, consumer relations are an industry in themselves. Companies anxious to keep their customers will do whatever it takes to placate them when problems arise. In France, it's war. David versus Goliath. Big business versus the pesky consumer.

I have two mobile phones, one Irish, one French, both run on top-up credit. In Ireland, the credit lasts until it's all used up. Even though months elapse between my visits to Ireland, all I have to do is switch the phone back on, and the credit is reactivated by a brisk American voice. ('Yew hev uhleven yewro an twenny cenz . . . ')

In France, mobile credit lasts for a fixed duration, depending on the price of the *mobicarte*. If it's not used up within this time-span, it expires, forcing you to buy a new *mobicarte*. On average, I calculate that Orange, the operator, plucks two hundred and fifty euro from my pocket every year in unspent credit, *on top* of what I spend on calls. Two hundred and fifty euro in exchange for nothing whatsoever, legally extracted by force. *C'est comme ça.*

French efficiency is indeed unparallelled. Nobody can screw up as comprehensively, as magisterially or as insouciantly as the French can. Why is this? From where did they get their inability to run the proverbial booze-up in a brewery? If they can construct excellent breweries, why can't they run them? This is, after all, the country that built the magnificent Viaduc de Millau, A380 Airbus, Concorde, Arc de Triomphe . . . but now, the *triomphe* seems chiefly to consist in defeating the consumer.

Personally, I blame the parents. While other European, American and Australian teenagers get weekend and summer jobs, thereby earning the money for iPods while learning responsibility, French teenagers very rarely stack shelves, mow lawns or man supermarket checkouts on weekends, much less during the lengthy school holidays. While Irish youngsters busily stockpile funds for their next booze blitz on Gran Canaria or their next pair of designer jeans, their French counterparts anxiously copy out Voltaire in copperplate.

Not all, of course. Nor all the time. Now and then, they will prune a rose bush, if *maman* asks nicely. They do look up from their navels at mealtimes. But somehow the concept of energy, of dynamism, of earning their keep beyond a certain age, seems to elude them. There is a film called *Tanguy* about a student who, at the age of twenty-eight, still lives at home with *maman* and *papa*, who pamper him like a prize poodle. On the whole, French families are small, and French children are much indulged. So long as they put in the study hours – all that Corneille to read, all that Rousseau! – they are rarely expected to further exhaust themselves. As a result, the workplace, when it finally arrives, often comes as a shock to their delicate sensibilities.

Naturally, they do everything in their power to cushion the blow. They invest vast energy in devising labour-saving devices such as the thirty-five-hour week and the *pont*, or bridge, which can turn bank holidays into four- or even five-day events. (If a bank holiday falls on a Friday or Monday, they will endeavour to get nearly a week out of it, and the month of May is pretty well a thirty-one-day holiday.) Until he graduates (reluctantly, after an agreeably lengthy career as a student, with a car and apartment bankrolled by papa), a middle-class Frenchman has little need of drive, initiative or pocket money. Over and over, you hear French mothers lamenting their lazy, 'good-for-nothing' sons, even while cooking their meals, doing their laundry, completing their paperwork and all but blowing their noses for them. (As in most countries, the girls are less spoiled and more enterprising – at least until the creaking 'system' beats it out of them, with its punitive attitude towards endeavour.)

One lovely sunny evening, five of us were lucky enough to spot a table just coming free at a busy restaurant on the waterfront. No maître d' was in sight, there was nobody to welcome or seat us, so we had to make a snap decision: quick, let's sit down at that table before somebody else does!

We installed ourselves, and a waitress appeared. Marching up, she launched into a furious tirade. How *dare* we sit down! How *dare* we not wait to be seated! How *dare* we not present ourselves properly and process our request for a table!

No problem. We obliged her by leaving and moving to another premises across the road, where we formally requested a table.

'Oh,' said the waitress, 'I don't think we have one.'

Yes you do, look, there's one over there, just vacated.

'*Eh oui* . . . but I'd have to clear it.'

And your point is? Feel free, mademoiselle, feel free! Eventually she did, but you'd deliver a baby quicker than she delivered our menus. A full hour elapsed before any food was served, during which one of the children in our group went all but hypoglycaemic from hunger. Not even a basket of bread was offered while we waited, and waited, and waited.

When we were leaving, the manager asked whether everything had been all right, and we said yes, everything had been fine apart from the catatonic, time-warp service.

'*Eh oui*,' he nodded, unsurprised. 'The problem is, you see, things get so busy at dinner time.'

No kidding! Restaurants get busy at dinner time? Silly us, you can tell we're foreigners, can't you, thinking that restaurants get busy at five in the morning!

When they're open at all, that is. One day, at high noon in a pretty Provençal village, a restaurateur put up a sign: 'Closed for Lunch'. *Eh oui*. A restaurant. Closed. For lunch. (This, it transpired, is one of the spin-offs of the thirty-five-hour week: staff gone home for their nap.)

The French tourism season opens on 1 July and ends on 31 August, even if those dates happen to be midweek or in the middle of a heatwave. Incentive tourism, which extends Ireland's season all year round, has yet to be invented; apparently nobody considers the country's plethora of swimming pools, bowling alleys, ice rinks, riding schools, tennis courts, gourmet restaurants, and so on, to be of any interest to tourists outside the eight weeks of summer. Golf, which saved Ireland's bacon, is only barely starting to catch on. Often, France is reminiscent of the snoozing rural Ireland of the 1960s, blissfully unaware of its potential, a sleeping beauty waiting to be woken with a kiss.

Some day, perhaps, its prince will come. But meanwhile, I've given up on the garage that said yes, it could do an emergency repair on my car, bring it in at eight next morning. At 8 AM, I arrived and was invited to fill in a stack of paperwork. That was three years ago. I am still waiting for somebody to take the paperwork and fix the car.

Three years have also elapsed since I first started searching for a company that could replace a broken Velux blind. Someday, if I live long enough into the century – or send off to Taiwan – perhaps a new blind will be got.

But at least I've got my money back on the new television that had to go in for repairs two months after purchase, struck dumb with a sound problem. It went in, and simply never came back. Not only could the shop that sold it to me not find it, they couldn't even contact the repair centre – which to the best of my knowledge has yet to answer its phone, four years later.

I did promise not to talk about plumbers, so I won't. Suffice it to say that I once went five weeks without heating or hot water, scouring all of Normandy for assistance (I even rang a radio station in despair) and was informed by the last in the series of hand-wringingly hopeless plumbers that it was a miracle the overheating thermostat hadn't blown not only my house, but the entire village, sky high. Five weeks later, a neighbouring house was indeed blown apart by its exploding boiler.

On the bright side, I'm no longer waiting for the new jacket replacing the one with the defective buttons: the shop sorted that on my fourth visit. Nor for my new glasses: the optician produced those on my sixth visit. Nor for the Air France plane ticket that went missing in Florence – no, madame, no trace of your booking! And, *hélas*, now the flight is full, you will have to find some other way of getting back to Paris.

So I raced to Florence train station, queued up until the clerk closed her window, queued again at a different window and, after two hours, finally secured a ticket to Paris. It was an urgent trip and, with time running out, I hastened back to my hotel to get my luggage, only to find an aggrieved message from Air France.

'We have your plane ticket here for collection! Are you returning to Paris on this flight or not? If not, please let us know immediately, other people wish to buy the seat.'

No, no explanation for the confusion, hassle or panic. No apology. Just a ticket flung across the counter, when I finally collapsed gasping into their office, with a filthy look as if to say: 'These damn customers would drive you mad!'

Even those whose job it is to smooth life in France seem to find the challenge overwhelming. One day, two policemen walked into the classroom where I was teaching English, seized me by either arm and marched me away, to the incredulity of my goggling students.

What had I done to provoke arrest? I'd arrived from Iceland, it was explained in the police station, and been teaching without a work permit. Iceland is not in the EU, madame – which makes you an illegal immigrant.

No, Iceland isn't. But Ireland is. I'm Irish. So let me go!

Eventually they did, but only after hours of wrangling and a final desperate call to the Irish embassy. An apology? A lift back to work? Hah! Away with you, foreign filth, before we clap you in the cooler!

Whatever country you come from – even if it's Mali, Colombia or Botswana – it is unlikely to have prepared you for the slagheap of administrative muddle that is France. Proudly sitting on top of this heap, at its very apex, is a company called Free.fr, a so-called internet service provider.

For a while, my internet connection worked fine with Free. And then one day it didn't. I rang Free to tell them this. After twenty premium-rate minutes in a call queue, somebody answered. Ah, he said, you must write to us. By registered post. No, we don't do email.

So, since the nature of their own business appeared to have escaped them, I wrote by hand. I registered the letter. I waited. In the meantime, I amused myself by installing a smoke alarm, the sight of which nearly sent a visiting electrician into cardiac arrest. What's that? Really? The stupid gadgets you foreigners waste your money on! And I painted the kitchen, wasting more money on French paint, which dribbled down the walls like milk. Finally, five coats and three weeks later, back came a letter from Free. Consult our website, it said, for advice on how to reconfigure your computer!

No mention of how to consult their website when they're blocking access to it. No mention of reimbursing my massive phone bill, which now resembled Nicolas Sarkozy's. No mention of the hours and hours and *hours* I was wasting on this farce.

Next step. Consult a citizen's advice bureau. A very nice consumer counsellor expressed disgust, and got on the case. Don't worry, he beamed, I will sort out this nonsense.

Three weeks later, he wrote to say no, actually, sorry, he couldn't sort it out. I must write to Free and . . . but I'd already written to Free. He knew this. He had a photocopy of their pointless response. Ringing the CAB, I asked to be put through to him.

'Oh,' chirped a voice, 'sorry! That counsellor resigned just this very morning!'

Furious as I was, I couldn't blame him. Given a choice of trying to sort out French consumer complaints, or retiring to spend the rest of his days up a tree humming La Marseillaise, he hardly had much option.

Does the consumer have any defence against all this inefficiency? Only one, in my experience: *never* sign up to pay for anything by direct debit. If you do, money will be taken from your account whether or not you are happy with the product or service – indeed, whether or not you ever receive it – and you will have no recourse whatever. Given that the system breaks the hearts of the long-inured natives, what it can do to struggling immigrants hardly bears thinking about. France is a most lovely country, but nobody with anything less than the most robust constitution should even think of tackling it.

Shock horror. The Polish plumber has arrived. Nobody has yet seen him, but his spectre stalks the land, striding in like a colossus from Poland to snatch the bread from hard-working French mouths. Rumour has it that he will not only work far more than thirty-five hours a week, he will do the job in half the time for half the price, and will turn up long before French plumbers can even consult their diaries to see whether they might have a window next November.

Overnight, the nation begins to buzz with anxiety. And, soon thereafter, a news bulletin announces partial, tentative reforms of French labour laws. Some are to be 'liberalised' – which, roughly translated, means that old protectionist policies are to be ditched in a desperate attempt to make France, and its workforce, 'competitive'. Henceforth, enterprise, skill, imagination, overtime, commitment and other such offences will be less severely punished. To start with, the rules governing hiring and firing are to be relaxed: employers will no longer be obliged to take unsuitable staff to the grave with them, while employees will be free to bid *adieu* to any boss not to their taste.

Reeling, France digests this, reaching for a glass of calvados to buffer the blow. It looks as though the nation's traditionally socialist leanings are about to suffer a mortal setback. The ugly face of capitalism now lurks, alongside the Polish plumber's, around every corner. Protests are plotted and, a week later, significant chunks of large cities are besieged by the enraged Tanguys, who, en masse, have finally mustered the energy to do a bit of destruction. If there's one thing the French can execute efficiently (apart from monarchs), it's a demo and a spot of window-smashing.

※

I have an acquaintance who, as a committed socialist, sees it as his moral duty to relieve his local supermarket of as many products as possible, unpaid for, every Saturday. This, he says, is to balance out the chain's 'immoral' profits. If prices have to go up as a result of increased security, well . . . so be it. After all, prices are of little concern to him, and the invention of some fiendish American besides. In an ideal world – come the revolution! – all goods will be freely and equally distributed. Meanwhile, he is merely liberating what belongs to the common man, as embodied by himself.

Archaic as it may sound, this view still holds sway in much of France. Which may or may not explain why unemployment is always at 10 percent minimum; there is a feeling of 'entitlement' to many goods and services without actually having to earn or pay for them, and 'entitlement' to jobs without actually having to do them. There is also an unspoken rule that tradesmen are to be paid in cash, and the choice is fairly stark: either the job will be done *au noir*, or it won't be done at all. Terror of taxes (and taxes on taxes) has driven half the workforce underground.

In the year of Nicolas Sarkozy's election (2007), a new word began to circulate. *Le dynamisme* was, demonstrably, rampant elsewhere. Look at Ireland, where they have to import workers to keep up with demand! (True at the time.) Look at the fat-cat British, buying up French holiday houses and raising prices in the process! Look at China, a massive new market ready to crash like a tsunami onto the stock exchange! Clearly, we are going to have to do something to stem this tide of foreign competition. Pierre, pass that calvados again, *s'il te plâit*. We'd better put our heads together and think about this.

After all, thinking beats working any day.

In fairness, France rarely blows its own trumpet. It knows it can be a bit dozy. So it is somewhat surprising when, one morning, a newspaper reports the comments of a leading economist, who sings the praises of the nation's 'unparalleled efficiency'. Of which there have recently been some fine examples.

A registered letter arrives from the local treasury, delivered by the postlady with a grin that says: 'So, dodging your taxes, are you?' Its contents indicate that, since I have failed to pay my poll tax of two years ago, *la belle France* will be obliged to take legal action, as well as levying hefty interest on the original sum.

Bewildered – I normally pay bills on time – I trawl through my financial records. Indeed, they reveal no trace of any cheque having been written or cashed for the sum in question. Now I know why French menus often feature a dessert called a *mystère*. So I trundle down to the treasury, where the desk is staffed by a clerk so sour she is a caricature of the French civil servant: Mona Lisa with PMT.

'You didn't pay,' she says flatly. Whereupon a suspicion suddenly crosses my mind. 'Did you bill me?'

'Oh yes.'

'You're sure?'

'Of *course*.'

'Well, would you mind checking your records, just the same?'

With a huge sigh and a scowl that says 'This is what comes of European union', she delves into the depths of her computer. An exhaustive search – with me standing over her while a muttering queue backs up behind – reveals a surprise. Why no, that bill never did go out, actually!

No explanation is proffered. No apology. Why don't I just pay up now immediately, and as a gesture of goodwill we'll forget the interest?

Meanwhile, the water board also has news. My bill has increased almost four-fold since the last one. Apparently, I have consumed more water than the golf courses of Dubai. I ring to enquire.

'Perhaps you have had guests?'

Occasionally, yes, I have. But none that moved in as permanent housemates. I have not started taking four showers a day, nor washing the car daily, nor set up a Chinese laundry.

'But *alors*, madame. Zere must be a leak. You must get a plumber.'

Really? Well, there's no sign of any leak; for once, the basement actually isn't flooded. But despite lack of evidence, I scout around and get a plumber after barely a month's worth of phone calls. No, he confirms, the basement is not awash. He can find no leak. *Rien.* That will be eighty euro please. I trudge down to the water company's office, where the young clerk wears the blissful expression of one who knows absolutely everything. But still she cannot explain why she has instructed me to get a plumber for a non-existent leak and billed me for Niagara Falls.

Much scratching of heads. Much tutting and lamenting. In a final flash of the blindingly obvious, I invoke the insurance they so resolutely sold me. If there's a leak, should it not be covered?

'But your plumber says zere is no leak.'

Now I begin to grasp France's preoccupation with existentialism. No wonder they love Beckett. 'Then why do you say zere is? Where has all this water gone?'

Hmm. *Curieux*, indeed. Further riffling through files. Phone calls. More calls. And, eventually, daylight.

'Ah yes. Zere was a leak. Year before last. In your driveway. We fixed it on 30 September. You must have been out that day. It's only showing up now on your bill. Your insurance will cover it. Why don't we just call this episode – hah, hah! – water under the bridge?'

Why don't we. After it is conceded that yes, I have been overcharged by almost two hundred euro (plus the plumber). An apology? Eh? What's zat?

The following year, I am overbilled again. This time my water bill has gone up by – brace yourself, Bridget – 1400 percent. There's only one course of action for this, and I take it: I burst out laughing, and frame the bill for the amusement of one and all.

Next, the bank. Where yet another mystery lurks. Zis time, I have vanished altogether. Been erased. There is no trace of either me or my money. The clerk – a.k.a. M. Kafka – informs me that I do not exist.

I beg to differ. I am standing right here. I have stood here before, many times. The bank knows me. *He* knows me. This is my chequebook. So could he produce my account please?

No. Sorry. It is no more. Gone. *Pffttt.* Look, the computer he is blank.

Oh dear. Then we'll have to call in the police, won't we? I am a missing person. Meanwhile, customers, gather round! Look, your bank can do magic! Make you disappear! It has turned me into thin air! Who might be next?

Consternation. Who, indeed? The Normans are *profondement* attached to their money. A wave of anxiety begins to rumble. A manager flies to my side and takes my arm, as if to suggest that it is my marbles, not his, which are rolling down the drain. Sympathetically, he whispers in my ear: 'Madame, please, you are overwrought. I beg you— '

Overwrought, eh? Right so! Find my money, buster, or I will run amok. Flip the lid, throw a major wobbly. Fly in the lads with the Semtex to blow your bloody bank to kingdom come. I'll give you 'overwrought', and you will deeply regret this moment. For ever, amen.

Approximately forty-five seconds later, my account surfaces. Why, it was there all the time! Somebody – uh, the computer – just confused a '3' with an '8', is all! Perfectly understandable, they look so alike!

An apology? A little sedative, perhaps, to calm me down? Let's call it five hundred even? Of course I'm kidding, but the manager's face freezes with shock. '*Ah non, madame,* regrettably we cannot—'

Cannot apologise? Oh. Okay. No problem. Just give me all my money, then. Yes, all of it. Now. Every cent. In cash. Coin, actually. And the loan of a young fella to ferry it to that rival bank across the street in a wheelbarrow.

This time he gets the joke. Oh, ho ho! How droll one is! The Irish, they have such humour!

Only this time he's wrong. I'm not kidding now. If they can't apologise, I'm going to move, so please give me my money. And the young fella.

A pause for thought. Tortured silence. And then: 'Er . . . ahem . . . we are, uh . . . perhaps you would accept, uh . . . ?'

He does try, but he just can't bring himself to say the words 'our apologies'. Perhaps French mouths just don't have the muscles. Very well. Let's say no more, then, about your utter, spectacular, unbelievable incompetence. Unless it happens again – in which case I am both reporting and suing you for malpractice, fraud and embezzlement. Not to mention attempted homicide, because my blood pressure's somewhere north of Mars. Got that?

Yes, the manager conveys that he has got that. Marginally mollified, I return to my original transaction. The clerk – who'd nonchalantly started signalling 'Next, please' – beams. 'So, how are things in Ireland? Will you be going over soon?'

Yes, as it happens I will be going tomorrow. Why?

'Oh, I just wondered . . . is Bailey's cheaper there? My wife loves the stuff. Could you perhaps bring us back a bottle?'

A different bank. A different day. A different clerk. This time, surely, all will be different?

I am toting a small cheque, drawn on an Irish bank, made out in euro. Euro as in Europe, *oui*? We are now all in the eurozone, yes? Just as a dollar means the same thing in California as in Connecticut, a euro means the same thing in France as in Ireland? Or does at time of writing, at any rate.

At arm's length, holding it up to the light, the clerk surveys the cheque.

'But this cheque is drawn on an Irish bank.'

Very good. Right first time. And your point is?

'But Ireland is not in the eurozone.'

Isn't it? Then how come the cheque is printed and written in euro?

'Ah.' Long, speculative pause. How the French love an enigma. After an intrigued and thoughtful interlude, the cheque is passed around for all the staff to shake their heads over, and then somebody is sent on a search mission, and a photo album is triumphantly produced.

'Look, madame. Let me show you some samples of Irish currency. It is nothing like euro currency.'

Which turns out to be startlingly true. The samples in the album, featuring Lady Hazel Lavery, are pound notes approximately forty years out of date. When I recover my powers of speech, I explain this, and the clerk blinks in dubious surprise.

'*Ah, bon?* Really? Well I must say, nobody told us . . . I will have to investigate further.'

And cash the cheque?

Discreetly, he coughs. Alas, things are not quite that simple. The investigation will take six weeks. And then, should the cheque pass muster, there will be – *bien sûr* – 10 percent 'commission'.

Ten percent! For *what*? For verifying that this antediluvian bank doesn't know which countries are in the eurozone?

'But Britain has never been in it, madame . . . and Ireland is in Britain, *non*?'

Now I know why banks are fortified. It's so you don't damage the walls when you bang your head on them. And I know why they're held up so often, too: those hooded guys with the guns probably started out like me, ordinary customers just trying to get their hands on their own money.

Last, but perhaps not least, there is a cry of despair from Paris. As a rule, Paris likes to feel on top of things, especially in matters of *la mode*, but finally it is forced to concede the unthinkable. John Galliano and Stella McCartney from Britain, Karl Lagerfeld from Germany, the American Marc Jacobs . . . not one French designer, bar Christian Lacroix, at any of the major couture houses.

'French talent,' sobs a fashion insider, 'simply isn't *available*.'

Ah, well. Maybe some day Tanguy will reach for his sketch pad and do a little doodle.

26.

And She Walks Upright, Too!

As a concept, France has grasped feminism. Paris has its tally of token women, in business as in politics. But as a practice, a daily reality, most Frenchwomen recoil from the glacial prospect of autonomy and economic independence as they might from exile to Siberia. They love being married and besides, if you manage to produce more than two children, you are fêted as a national heroine. You are showered in money and, should you have a little job just for amusement's sake, you are entitled to . . . oh, about ten or twenty years of parental leave. After all, raising a young Frenchman is an important project, and even the raising of a young French woman has its challenges. Maman's concentration mustn't be interrupted.

However, despite being a maman of four, a woman almost miraculously decided to present herself for election to the 2007 presidency. Yes, of France. Unknown only six months earlier, Segolène Royal was suddenly everywhere: on television, on billboards, on magazine covers, so ubiquitous that it was difficult to buy a facecloth that didn't bear her effigy. Awestruck, France gazed at her good-looking, well-groomed image (yes, her politics are left of centre, but even the left has copped on to the power of haute couture) and wondered how this could possibly be.

Wondered to the point where, one night on TF2, the current-affairs programme *Arène* devoted itself entirely to the phenomenon that is Segolène, entitling its debate *Une Femme Peut-Elle Diriger La France?* (Can a Woman Run France?)

Yes, I might have replied, had anyone asked me. Ireland has had a female president for nearly thirty years. In fact, it has had two. Both ladies – Mary Robinson and Mary McAleese – have been very popular and very efficient, making some of the initially chauvinistic suspicion of Ms Robinson (nearly three decades ago!) look ludicrous. Both highly qualified, experienced lawyers, they were elected without fuss and no, Ireland was not subsequently struck by lightning, a comet, a cruise missile, or even a bedazzled sense of its own audacity. It simply never dawned on anyone to query a candidate's sex as a danger to the nation.

But TF2 was now querying Segolène's. Bear with me here. I am not making this up. The patronising, mind-blowingly idiotic programme went as follows.

'This country,' opined one panellist, 'is *petrified*.' Yes, petrified of Mme Royal, that is, because she . . . well, um, apparently because she lacks a penis. No other explanation is proffered.

'I,' quaked another panellist, 'have never before seen a blonde president' – Segolène had dyed her hair – 'and besides, this lady is image-obsessed!'

Yes, that's what he said – the man who'd never envisaged a blonde in the Élysée.

Another old duffer piped up. He – an academic of some kind – had written a book aimed at women entitled *Votre Devoir Est de Vous Taire* (Your Duty Is to Shut Up) and, incredibly, some publisher actually unleashed this tome on the gullible nation. I have never seen it in the shops, but suddenly I understood where

Savonarola was coming from, and made a mental note to bring a box of matches next time I visited my local *maison de la presse*. Not that it matters, of course, what I think of any presidential campaign, because I am not allowed to vote for Segolène, or anyone else. To pay taxes, yes; to exercise all my civic duties, yes; to separate my glass from my plastics, yes. But to vote, no. France only believes in European integration up to a point. After all, if resident Europeans were allowed to vote, the Africans and Arabs might want to too!

On and on droned the dreary, antediluvian debate. Yet another male panellist piped up to voice his worry that Madame Royal's 'menstrual moods might be a problem'.

Yes, that's what the man said. Given that Mme Royal was already fifty-three, his fears seemed somewhat neurotic. I found myself wondering what he might do should he ever board a jet for Australia which, after take-off, turned out to be piloted by a woman. A normal, healthy woman, in full menstrual flight? Would he demand a parachute, wrench open the door and throw himself out somewhere over Somalia? What if he should be whipped into hospital for emergency surgery, only to find his surgeon a woman of, say, thirty-five or forty? Would he leap off his trolley and sprint down the corridor in his lace-up paper gown, bellowing for the police?

'Or,' mused another panellist (honestly, this is gospel), 'she might get pregnant.'

In which case, Mme Royal would indeed become the focus of some attention. Not just for producing a fifth child – itself something of a miracle in France – but for doing it at fifty-three, while the rudderless nation collapsed around baby Royal and sank without trace to the bottom of the ocean. Clearly, the man's fears were well founded.

In case it sounds as if this panel was composed exclusively of men, let me point out that in fact it included one Geneviève de la Fontenaye, who famously runs France's annual Miss France contest. Alas, I can't tell you what Geneviève thought of Segolène's prospects, or talents or anything else, because Geneviève did not at any stage of the discussion utter one syllable. She simply sat there, wearing her hat, which is what Geneviève does. Either she was afraid to say 'No, a woman can't run France' or 'Yes, of course a woman can run France, you bunch of idiots', or she was literally dumbstruck by the gaggle of cretins around her.

Another panellist was now anxiously speculating whether 'Mme Royal has had a facelift? She looks young for fifty-three.'

Suddenly, I knew what Mme Royal should do should she find herself installed in the Élysée. She should bring back the guillotine. Round up all these panellists and order an execution, just like they used to do in the good old days. Only now, even better, it can be televised. We can get in some popcorn and enjoy it live.

Finally, this tragic emission petered out. But no sooner had I picked myself up off the floor than another programme came on, this time featuring an actor called Astrid Veillon. Mlle Veillon is young and pretty, and so the interviewer came up with a brilliant question: does she find her youth and good looks a career handicap?

Switching off, I contented myself with imagining her answer. 'Ah well, you know how it is in the movie business. Being young and pretty is even worse than being old and ugly . . . Johnny Depp finds his youth and looks a terrible handicap too. Of course things could always be worse, one might be tall or short, or Jewish or agnostic, or Scots or Hungarian . . . '

Next time I want to find out anything about a female French presidential candidate, I'll watch one of those wildlife programmes about a chimp in a safari park. Has anyone told David Attenborough what he's missing?

As things turned out, Segolène (who, by the way, spent the summer of 1973 as an au pair in Dublin) was not elected. Many believed that this was because of her gratingly nasal voice, which sounded so whiny that even the French couldn't stand it. But not to worry. Since then, she has allegedly taken elocution lessons à la Margaret Thatcher, her voice has softened and she has split from her dreary partner François Hollande (also a politician). She will, she asserts, rally to fight another day. Personally I can't stand the woman, but would like to see her elected, if only because even the most demented of detractors can hardly worry about her becoming pregnant in 2012, at the age of fifty-eight, or how she or France might cope with a baby Royal. Meanwhile, her rival Nicolas Sarkozy was elected and promptly ditched by his wife Cécilia (who refused even to vote for him) and, within weeks, had married singer Carla Bruni, the elegant ex-model who is rumoured to lead him a merry dance. Rumour has it that Carla is bored stiff with life as First Lady, but she does her duty on state or other public occasions, demurely dressing the part – or did up to this morning, anyway, which is about as predictable as Nicolas's wives ever seem to get; by the time you read this, who knows what might have happened. Curiously, Nicolas Sarkozy seems to be one of the very few Frenchmen who actually enjoys the company of spirited, albeit volatile, women. So far, he's married three, indicating that even when they tire of him, he never tires of them.

Feminists (should any remain) be warned. France adores women, but chiefly when they are whipping their *coq au vin* out of the oven, wearing a frilly apron over black stockings and a vast smile of welcome for their Superman husbands. Unless, of course, his name is Nicolas.

27.

Weightwatchers

When I was eighteen, a starving student, I was invited with a friend to the home of a French couple for 'afternoon tea'. Fresh off the ferry from Rosslare, living on oranges, we were even more excited by the prospect of real food than by meeting our first 'frogs'.

Things were superbly formal and we, in our tatty denims, were as daunted as delighted when, eventually, a porcelain pot of Earl Grey appeared alongside a plate of exquisite, *tiny* cakes. Just four minuscule cakes, one each: it was all we could do to restrain ourselves from grabbing our hosts' share. Their swift demise (the cakes, not the hosts) was followed by a long pause, in which we wondered whether maybe the French did things backwards, whether a big fry-up might now be served . . . bacon, sausages, eggs . . . oh yes, *please*!

But no. After an excruciating interval, in which our tummies rumbled audibly, a box of chocolates was produced. Fabulous rich dark chocolates . . . well, we knew what to do with those. No Irish Christmas was ever considered a success until the entire kilo of Quality Street had been scoffed. We dived in. Twice. And then – horror, mystery, diplomatic incident – the box was sealed, removed and put away. Just like that. No apology, no explanation, *rien*. There was nothing left for it but to pretend that we'd had enough anyway, heft our rucksacks back on and leave, muttering scandalised invective about the meanness of the French as we trudged down the long, bleak road. One tiny cake each, and two chocolates! How paltry can you get!

Only years later, when we related the incident to a new French friend, was light shed on it. That wasn't meanness, he asserted, it was simply (a) the standard menu for afternoon tea, and (b) that no French person would ever contemplate eating more than two chocolates. It literally would not cross their minds. Sweets were rich and fattening, and solely for treats. To offer more than two would be to insult the recipient – a subtle suggestion that he or she was a greedy pig of uncontrollable appetite.

It took us a long time to digest this. Only when we both came to live in France did we gradually grasp the vital fact that the French have an entirely different *attitude* to food. An attitude which – despite the most glorious food on every table – keeps them slim. Slim without even trying, dammit – which is why French magazines rarely feature diets, and nobody's ever heard of mad projects such as the Atkins. The French just don't think about food the way other people do – which is to say, virtually 24/7.

An average French meal sounds enormous. *Apéritif* with canapés, starter, main course, salad, cheese, dessert, two or maybe even three wines, possibly a *digéstif* afterwards . . . phew. Yet nobody (bar the genetically or resolutely obese) gets fat. Why?

Because (a) this is the legend, not the reality. The reality is a far lighter meal, maybe only soup for supper (from which the word *souper* comes), the full monty strictly reserved for Sundays or holidays. (b) Big meals mean small quantities of each component, and (c) every meal contains balanced portions of nutrients. Vitamins, proteins, carbohydrates – they're all tucked in there somewhere, which is why there will always be cheese and a salad. If it's one of those vast celebratory meals you see in French films – a wedding or festival, for instance – there might be as many as eight or nine courses, lubricated with numerous wines and chest-clutching shots of calvados. It goes on all day. But between each course, there's music and dancing, nobody starts the next course until they've worked off the last, and the following day you can be sure they're all 'downsizing' on fruit and yogurt, with a swim or a long cycle thrown in. That's simply how they *live*. As one French *maman* remarked to me one day: 'The greatest gifts you can give your child are confidence – so food isn't a crutch – and discipline, so food is never the boss.'

When I first moved to France, food threatened to become the boss. It was so beautiful, I just couldn't seem to stop thinking about it. Nor seeing it either, because it was everywhere, out on the streets, stark naked in every market. Every shop window glowed with goodies, radiating temptation, and I began to feel like an alcoholic in a distillery. One day I stood mesmerised in front of a confectioner's window in Honfleur, gazing at crystallised fruits glowing ruby, emerald, diamond and topaz, until I had to be forcibly dragged away. But then, after a few weeks of this torture, I realised what the solution was: give in. Give yourself one month of unbridled indulgence. Eat anything you like, try everything new, let rip – and then, get a grip. Unless you want to look like the Queen of Tonga, you will wake up one morning finally acknowledging that the party's over: from now on, you are simply going to have to be firm with yourself. And, eventually, enjoy the wonderful gastronomy all the better for not being a slave to it.

Doubtless to counteract all the edible distractions, sports facilities are a priority in France. These widespread facilities are largely financed by household rates, and the French believe in getting value for their money, while the government regards sport as a primary health-care investment. (Indeed, the government might even be taking it a stage too far, as in the case of our mayor, Pierre, who wants to turn the football field into a 'health track'.)

There aren't any pubs. Sure, you'll find a gang of lads sinking beer in any brasserie – but outside the cities, the brasseries close at dusk. Drinking is not a national sport, not regarded as an activity in itself. It's really very difficult to put on a beer belly: you'd have to be utterly determined, and prepared to drink alone. Even more alone than before, now that the smoking ban has cleared Paul and Pierre off the barstools on which they'd been perched since 1868. Instead, people drink at home (by which they mean wine to accompany meals) and many homes have wine cellars – which is a lot less ritzy than it sounds. These cellars are not designed for the kind of clinical, sterile storage currently in vogue amongst wine buffs in London or New York, there aren't any thermometers or climate-controlled fridges. They're just careless corners in dusty basements, strewn with onions and potatoes and strings of garlic, amidst which Pépé vaguely thinks he may have put down some nice Burgundy back in 1965.

Fish and veg, far from provoking pouts, are hugely enjoyed. Vegetables furnish the crucial 'colour component' of a meal and are cooked in endlessly imaginative ways, while fish is a point of national pride. I buy mine direct from the trawlers in the harbour, as does anyone who lives on or near the coast, and there is absolutely nothing penitential about the gorgeous crab, sea bass, cod, whelks or sole on offer. *Au contraire*, their freshness is mouth-watering, an absolute joy. Usually the fisherman will offer to whack the brute's head off for you, thereby providing your little kiddi-winks with a moment of blood-spattered bliss and something to brag about to their peers back in Buncrana or Ballykissangel.

But the French are no saints and yes, despite the public ban, they still smoke. I don't know anyone who'd knock back a whole pack a day, but I know lots of people, mainly women, who insist that their five a day is what keeps off that extra kilo. They'll have one instead of nibbling those olives before lunch, or instead of dessert afterwards. It's their tiny treat, so they don't feel deprived, and attitudes to the occasional puff remain relatively relaxed. One day, a man near me at a café, studying the health slogan on a pack – 'Smoking can endanger your unborn child' – sat back and grinned: 'No it can't, I've had a vasectomy.' In Los Angeles he might almost have been lynched for this irreverence; in Chartres everyone laughed.

Last, but not least, there's the greatest of all incentives to sensible eating: romance. *Eh oui*, the French really are a romantic lot, big into flowers and trysts and mystique. *Le couple* remains vital, even to those who have two or three or – what! – more children. Frenchmen worship women, and love them to look beautiful. Every Frenchwoman knows that, if she doesn't keep her *silhouette*, her man will soon find someone who does. No way is she throwing away her perfectly good husband for a biscuit or a glass of wine. So she sips, she nibbles – never gorges, or binges, or eats between meals. Her marriage is an investment and she works at it, as does her husband. She makes the effort to look good and he, in turn, shows his appreciation. It's a joint project. It is *raisonnable*. (Yes, they do passion too, but only in private: kissing in public is considered distasteful.)

Is it all exhausting, a constant battle against gastronomic indulgence? No, because French children are brought up to regard food as a joy to be managed from the start. Their menu, and their attitude towards food, is balanced from the cradle onwards. Food and drink are disciplined pleasures, ceasing to be pleasurable if they are abused. It would never occur to a French mother to threaten punishment for a child who doesn't eat any part of a meal, nor to make food a reward for compliance, and so French kids don't make those emotional associations. A meal is a necessary and pleasant interlude, no more, certainly not a battleground. French mums just shrug if the menu's not to junior's taste: if you don't like beans or cabbage or whatever, oh well, never mind, *chèri*. There will be something else tomorrow.

Emerging as an adult, the young chrysalis doesn't dive headlong into the first comforting vat of chocolate. He or she instinctively knows – or has learned by example – that feeling fit and looking good is actually a greater comfort. Fitting into nice clothes is far more enjoyable, and attractive, than bulging out of them. Much more enjoyable than stuffing your face with junk, feeling sick, guilty and bloated. No self-respecting *citoyen*, male or female, would dream of letting a chocolate éclair get the upper hand. Nor do they snack between meals, unless you count the children's afternoon pot of vanilla yogurt with *one* plain biscuit. At the cinema, films are not drowned out by the rustle of sweet or crisp wrappers.

Centuries ago, being fat was a success symbol; now it looks more like a failure. While nouvelle cuisine wasn't an unqualified hit in its native France, nor *cuisine minceur* either (most chefs saw both as redundant), the good old days of rich, heavy sauces have faded into the background. Now, you'll be lucky to get a béchamel once a week, or even once a month – and you'll savour it twice as much when it does come along. As for McDonald's . . . certainly, *chèrie*, next time we're stuck on the motorway in a flood in the dark. If José Bovey and his anti-globalisation chums haven't torched it.

Like it or not, that's the French for you: different. They don't regard food as a substitute for sex or love or parental attention, or whatever the gurus say it symbolises. They simply regard it as food. On weekdays, they eat just enough – high quality, low quantity –

and so when they do let rip, they really enjoy it. Until the next time – which will be after a more-than-decent interval.

Yes, it's all most annoying to the spectator. Which may be why those nations that have issues with food have started to sabotage France's status as a happy, healthy eater, slipping regular doses of sugar and salt into the 'convenience' foods which are now plugged on television. Jealousy, no doubt – or maybe just revenge for Agincourt? Whatever it is, the French seem to have twigged it, because they're resisting. Yes, muesli bars for breakfast are now a recognised phenomenon, but I've yet to see a French child eat a whole sack of crisps, refuse their broccoli or scream for sweets (though they scream for plenty else). I've never seen an open box of chocolates in any French home and I've never heard a mother say 'Eat your leeks or you won't get any cake heaped with ice cream and Smarties and syrup'.

Oh God, the confusion caused by that kind of admonition! Maybe the French are so busy figuring out Sartre and Rousseau that they just haven't time to worry about such a conundrum. Or maybe they're too busy cultivating their *tuyaux*, or connections, because high-quality food doesn't just land on the table by magic. Of course you can buy it in the shops, but after a while you get to know where you can lay your hands on the real stuff. You get to know a little man who makes organic cider using apples from his own orchard, a fisherman who can furnish the juiciest sole, a farmer's wife who makes her own foie gras, someone who knows a vigneron in Champagne . . . all in good time, and all in the right season. Yes, strawberries are available in December, but they're only for tourists. You won't find many French eating them. They're purist about food, and it shows.

❦

It's the season of mellow fruitfulness. An orange moon hangs low in the navy sky, the blackberries have been turned into jam, the cartoon-red apples will stuff Sunday's pork roast and, in the misty dusk, a platoon of children is marching up the garden path, clutching trident forks, wearing black eyeshadow and purple lipstick.

Hallowe'en, a huge festival in some countries, hasn't been an unqualified success in France. It's a relatively recent ritual, and the French still aren't quite sure what to make of it. Nonetheless, the local children are toting brooms and baskets, tripping over their Batman capes, witches' hats falling over their eyes, goblin masks askew as they knock on the door. When it's answered, they simply stand there, grinning hopefully. Nobody has explained to them that they're supposed to yell 'Trick or Treat!' – or, as one Irish infant leered at me one year: 'Give us stuff or we'll burn yer house down, ha ha!'

These are cute local kids, I know them by name and a wicker basket is ready for them, filled with brand-name candies as well as walnuts, apples, tangerines, little sacks of dried fruit and mini-bags of chocolate. In Ireland, I learned to dish out goodies to each individual child after once making the mistake of producing the basket, which all but triggered a riot. The little savages dived into it virtually headlong, jostling and yelling, the bigger ones grabbing everything before the smaller ones could even reach into it. So, let's see how the basket fares in France.

Gurgles of delight. The ghosts and goblins peer in, and their purple grins widen. Nobody tries to rip it from my grasp, but the biggest child, aged about ten, pipes up. 'Are we allowed to choose?'

Yep. Two items each, how's that?

That, apparently, is great. Grinning, he spins round, plucks the tiniest infant from the back of their convoy and propels him forward.

'Guillaume's only three. Let him go first.'

Beaming, Guillaume dips in and bags his munchies. Then they all take turns, working from the youngest to the eldest, and I'm astonished: the nuts and fruit are vanishing as fast as the Mars bars, lollipops and toffees. One child actually identifies the contents of his little sack: 'Banana! Coconut! Raisins! Apricots! Yum!' Nobody's fighting, or bursting into tears or accusing or thumping anyone; they simply seem to be having fun. Where I come from, they'd have my arm off up to the elbow by now, but here they seem to have some innate sense of restraint, and seem delighted with what's on offer.

Incredible. Are they, er, kidding? Do they really like dried fruit as much as sweets? I ask and they all nod. One of the girls even insists that she likes fruit better, 'specially the coconut curls'. And then the spokesman pipes up again. '*Merci bien, madame*,' he says before turning to his group with all the authority of Charles de Gaulle: 'Everyone say *merci madame*!'

Which they do, in chorus, before toddling off to the next house, well pleased with their booty. These are not yuppie children, they don't go to expensive schools, they're not called Cosmos or Prunella: they're the offspring of local farmers and fishermen and I've never met such a polite, cheery little bunch in my life. For the first time, the Hallowe'en ritual has been a pleasure rather than an intimidating scrum.

Other groups follow, and by the end of the evening the wicker basket is almost empty. Just a handful of marshmallows and a lone bar of chocolate remain: the apples, tangerines, nuts and dried fruits are all gone.

Which is possibly why the visiting goblins were all such bright-eyed, bushy-tailed little devils, rosy and healthy and carrying scarcely a spare kilo between them.

My English neighbours are equally astonished by this new version of Hallowe'en. 'It was lovely! Nobody seems to have told them it's supposed to be a nightmare! And nobody can have told them that apples are good for them, because they scoffed the lot!'

28.

Home and Away

It is a beautiful October day, bright and brisk with a bite to it, and I am walking around the local lake, smiling at the sixteen little boats bobbing on it with their merrily multicoloured sails; the kiddies have just come in from their sailing lesson. In summer the lake gets crowded, but at this time of year you can walk around it virtually alone. As I walk, a thought strikes me: I must have done nearly a thousand circuits of this lake by now.

It's a lovely lake, as sparkling and serene now as it was the first time I ever saw it, the day I looked out over it wondering whether to buy the house. It's full of wildlife and in addition to its numerous other facilities it now looks as if some kind of floating stage is being installed, perhaps with a view to concerts. It's a great amenity, and an enduring pleasure.

And yet . . . a thousand times? Have I really walked around it that often?

I must have. Because I have kept up my early resolve to walk around it at least twice a week and now, amazingly, I have lived here for almost ten years.

Ten years is a long time. Time to take stock and, perhaps, make some decisions? It's hard to pinpoint why this need to assess and evaluate should suddenly arise, because after all, a decade is just a figure, but for whatever reason, I am surprised to find myself inexplicably unsettled lately, uncertain where life goes from here.

A decade ago, I left an Ireland that had been almost deafened by the roar of the Celtic Tiger. An Ireland that had lots of money, but money that seemed to me to have gone to its head. It was party central, and I was partied out. Was moving to France the right decision?

Yes. Hand on heart, it was. In exchange for a frenetic lifestyle I got peace and freedom and a rhythm of life that has greatly enhanced my quality of life – even, perhaps, its duration. In exchange for a steady salary, I found new challenges and surprises, discovering a resilience I hadn't known I possessed, as well as an optimism that, so far, has actually proven justified. Best of all, I have been blessed by the fact that, while making new friends, I have also kept the old ones. There have been days when France has been maddening, but there have been many more when it has been exquisite, a glowing gift, a joy. Living here has been a very great pleasure, and quitting the rat race has been rejuvenating. Against all the odds, the infamous attic has held up, and to my astonishment I'm somehow still solvent. Haven't gone broke, haven't been deported, haven't stormed off back to Ireland declaring the French to be an intolerable bunch of good-for-nothings. No, they haven't been as exuberant as the Irish, and yes, there is some truth in the old sayings about them: they're not cold, but they can be cool. That said, they are kind and sincere and, overall, helpful people who mean well. I will always be an outsider – let there be no mistake about that – but we live and let live and get along pretty well together, all things considered.

Pierre is still mayor, but no, his projected housing scheme hasn't materialised. Schemes, I have discovered, often remain merely that. The field where village festivals were once held is now a soccer pitch, with artificial grass on which new children play, but otherwise the village remains largely unchanged, the church spire still glowing comfortingly every night. The trees on which black-birds once warbled have grown huge and now block a good deal of sunlight, but at least the eternally barking dog has gone, and the honking goose has been replaced by tranquilly clucking chickens. None of their owners ever did invite me to any of their barbecues or make any other social overtures, but I did make other lovely friends, some French, some Irish, and some English. A cosmopoli-tan crowd, after all, and jollier than it would have been had I stuck to my French-only guns.

Serge Reggiani is dead now, as are Jean Ferrat and Charles Trenet. France's music has changed, become more international and less haunting . . . or am I the only one who has difficulty distin-guishing the singers, and the songs, from each other? At any rate, it's no longer as important to me as it once was, I wouldn't move here for it today. Nonetheless, I've been to some fabulous concerts, and achieved my ambition of seeing George Moustaki perform live. I've been to – and, more importantly, followed – fascinating films, I've danced at great parties, seen fantastic exhibitions, eaten fabu-lous food, celebrated with champagne, shopped in Paris, swum in turquoise water, lazed on sunny beaches, watched dazzling sunrises and blazing fireworks, cuddled new babies, laughed with friends, learned to roller skate (ish), visited magnificent abbeys, played ten-nis, been racing at Longchamp, walked through fields of blue flax and citrus rapeseed, through pink orchards and purple vineyards. I've read, and revelled in, the hundreds of books I never had time for before. I've cycled thousands of kilometres, and dispatched more delicious wine than I dare to think about. France continues to be a marvellous unfolding adventure, and there is no reason why it should not continue to bewitch me for many more years . . . for ever? Or for how long, exactly?

Ah. Ah ha. That's the question. How long can you stay away? How long before you feel the pull of your roots? How long before you start having inexplicable dreams of Slea Head and Claremont beach, of banter and bodhráns, of Galtee sausages and heated, hilarious conversations, of people screeching at each other on *Liveline* and *The Late Late Show*?

H'mm. Well, let's not go too misty-eyed here. As I write, Ireland's not entirely a pretty picture. The overheated economy is royally banjaxed, there are savage cuts on the way, and even my stalwart mother, aged ninety, is feeling the chill wind of a cold climate. The kids are still studded and tattooed; the girls are taller, blonder and more beautiful than before, but look somehow cloned. Crime continues to cause many heartaches, and no, I still wouldn't walk around the city centre at night with the same insouciance I do here. As for the health system – well, reports make it sound like an episode of *M*A*S*H**. Drug dealers routinely shoot each other, and it's a good thing that public transport has improved, because your car stands an excellent chance of being stolen, vandalised, clamped, towed away or burnt out on a sink estate. The weather can still be grey for weeks on end, and—

And yet.

And yet, the hill of Howth on a summer's evening, the bay twinkling far below, the shipping slipping into a necklace of glittering lights. The theme tune to the Ronan Collins show. Chicken and chips after a walk in the Wicklow hills. Art on the DART. U2 at Croke Park. TG4, Galway oysters, Leopardstown, Lisdoonvarna. Irish coffee, which only properly exists in Ireland. *Reeling in the Years*. Walking Portmarnock strand, climbing Slieve League. Turf fires, Eamon Dunphy, black humour, autumn ivy glowing scarlet on Stephen's Green. 'The Fields of Athenry', Dunnes Stores, Grafton Street at twilight. That sense of communal loss and support when something sad happens, when a Gerry Ryan or a Mick Lally dies. The outrage when we're done out of the World Cup, the cheery, tireless fund-raising – and yeah, let's get in a takeaway and light the fire and switch on all the lights we like!

As the saying goes, you can check out but you can never leave. Unless you emigrate very young, you will always remain spiritually attached to the land of your birth. Even if you fall in love with France, or anywhere else, you will still love the country that nurtured and educated you. Its hold is proprietorial, parental, and over time you come to recognise its power.

But is it powerful enough? It must be said that, at the moment, France is doing itself no favours. It's in turmoil, rioting over the proposed raising of the retirement age to sixty-two, while Ireland is stoically accepting that its citizens will have to work on to sixty-eight. Sometimes I feel a strong urge to seize France by its shoulders and shake it – one of the most prosperous nations on earth, has it no idea how lucky it is! Whereas Ireland, with its prosperity in tatters, is swallowing the bitter pill with dignity: there is shock and anger, certainly, but no rioting, no senseless destruction which would only have to be repaired at yet further expense. If it has huge problems, it seems to recognise that some are self-inflicted, and it's too late to exact retribution for the others; ironically, it's the one now doing the Gallic shrug, with a wry smile. Ah sure, the Celtic Tiger years turned out to be expensive, but hadn't we great fun while they lasted!

Ten years ago, on the outside looking in, I saw France as an alluring oasis of civilisation. Now, like any long-term lover of anyone or anything, I know it well, and I know its faults. It's gorgeous, but it's fretful and genetically disposed to an anxiety that sometimes verges on the ridiculous. Its smile is beautiful, but its laugh is restrained. Whereas Ireland . . . ah. There's a lot of truth in that old line: 'when Irish eyes are smiling, they'd steal your heart away'. It occurs to me that the funniest moments of my life, the helpless-with-laughter episodes, have all been in Ireland or with my Irish friends. Things that reduce the French to puddles of nervous self-pity reduce the Irish to tears of laughter. Even at the worst moments – *especially* at the worst moments – the *craic* in Ireland, the cynical wit, can be coruscating.

France does sensational fireworks, but Ireland does verbal pyrotechnics.

Both countries have been good to live in. Each has its merits and demerits. Nowhere is perfect, and this isn't about point-scoring. It's about taking stock after a decade abroad, and trying to figure out what comes next. I've reached a crossroads, and honestly don't know which direction to take. I'm starting to understand how an errant spouse must feel, faced with a choice between marrying the seductive lover she adores or going back to the husband who drives her mad but is still, at the end of the day, her husband. The husband she took for better or worse all those years ago, whose history she shares and who, in some shape or form, she still loves.

If in fact you are happily married, if you live abroad in the context of a strong family unit, this divisive dilemma isn't such an issue. The family is the focus no matter where you go, and the family is a source of strength, sustaining and protective. It fits in everywhere, it affords social status, it generates warmth and security and stability. Whereas, if you're single . . . well, you're on your own, in every sense. Logistically, emotionally, financially, physically, spiritually. My friend Sheila, whose husband was recently away for a fortnight for the first time in their long marriage, phoned one evening gasping with surprise: 'I had no idea! No idea what it's like to come home every evening to an empty house! It was fun for a few days, but now I can't wait for him to come home!'

Home. Such an emotive word. And such a confusing one, for the emigrant.

⁂

It won't go *oik*, will it?

No. I was sure, ten years ago, that France would never degenerate into a land of hoodies, drug dealers and foul-mouthed hooligans. So, now, has it?

No, happily, it hasn't. While life's daily fabric is now woven from a slightly coarser cloth, here as everywhere, the cloth is still raw silk. Everyone still says *bonjour* when they walk into the bakery or the even more beloved pharmacy, they shake hands and exchange kisses. By and large, the teenagers are well behaved, even if there are more empty cans in the fields and ditches than there used to be. Sometimes headlines shriek news of drugs and other crime, but gangsters don't conduct daily war on the streets. There's more graffiti than there used to be, but burglar alarms are still rare. Screaming motorbikes increasingly streak through peaceful villages, but the boy racers are unlikely to rip your handbag from your grasp as they go. People don't sleep with one eye open, parking is still largely free and easy, and the beaches aren't buzzing with jet skis. The pace remains slow, and the general feeling is that – 'hot' areas apart – France still has a long way to go to catch up with the frenzy of many other countries. A lot of money is invested in sports, public transport, communal facilities and the arts, and it pays off. The two-hour lunch is still a fixture, and Sunday shopping is virtually non-existent – two factors that seem to have a crucially soothing effect on the social structure. On sunny days, we 'blow-ins' still have scandalously long lunches on each other's patios, laughing and shooting the breeze and completely in agreement that, yes, we all love living here.

However, the service remains appalling. You can still take root in a shop or restaurant waiting for one thing or another. Bureaucracy and heavy subsidies continue to inhibit initiative, and the state is becoming increasingly nannying, exhorting its citizens to eat their greens and watch their drinking, all but tying their shoelaces for them. And sometimes the citizens behave like children, throwing their toys out of their pram on the slightest provocation. As I write, France is at a standstill because an exceptionally silly strike has shut down fuel supplies, and millions of working hours are being lost while a world-class tantrum is thrown over something that other countries are dealing with like adults.

Yet for all their strikes and protests, the French can be remarkably meek in certain situations. When our local council cancelled the weekly collection of garden rubbish, nobody said boo, even though it means that elderly or otherwise frail people have to heft everything to the dump – no easy feat if you can't drive, or lug a tree stump over your shoulder. And nobody questioned the fact that, despite the reduced service, taxes went up. Naturally, prices have gone up overall: that favourite French delicacy, the five-euro kilo of prawns, now costs twelve euro, the eleven-euro parking fine suddenly became twenty and the chap who charged twelve euro for lawnmowing only last year now charges twenty. Just little things, but bigger than they would be in stronger economic circumstances.

Ten years ago, I found it romantic to close the blue shutters every night and open them every morning; now it's getting a bit, well, déjà-vu. Ditto the economic constraints of having jumped ship, which used to feel amusingly bohemian but now vaguely chafe. Yes, patching and mending gets boring. Yes, it's time for new lighting and tiling and paving and state-of-the-art stuff, yes, bring it all on!

On the home front, Monsieur Hulot has yet to materialise, leaving me socially handicapped, aware of the many gatherings to which I am not invited because I haven't a husband – thereby making it even harder to meet one. Also leaving me at the mercy of workmen, who, when it comes to ripping off the single woman they see as a soft target, are every bit as adroit as their counterparts in other countries. Being single can be trying anywhere, and now it's beginning to colour my life in France, to throw a gauzy shade across all the lovely sunshine.

On the other hand, as a career woman with a hectic social life in Dublin, I was run ragged. I never expected to end up making my own blackberry jam from my own fruit, waving a sticky spoon and bopping round the kitchen singing in French in a stripy apron. I never expected to enjoy cooking so much, to sleep late on a rainy morning or to go swimming on a whim – no boss, no bus, no pressing schedule! Financially, I moved to France with my breath in my fist, so to speak, and yet my anxiety proved groundless. I may starve yet, because France is a bottomless money pit, but at least food has appeared on the table for the last ten years. As everywhere, the recession is taking its toll, but it's less acute in France and anyway, the passing of time has demonstrated the futility of worrying, of wasting today on what may or may not happen tomorrow. While I'm now coveting certain material pleasures, I've yet to lose any sleep over them.

Would I do it all again? Oh yes! Emphatically. Despite some misgivings, misunderstandings and muddles, despite sometimes missing out on friends' milestone events in Ireland, I've loved my decade in France. Most mornings, I wake up with a smile for no particular reason, and yes, my soul does sing in its shower. If I laugh less loudly here, I shed fewer tears too: there's less battle to be done. There's an equilibrium, a harmony, and an often quite profound contentment. As experiments go, this one can be declared a shining success, yielding a great sense of achievement. The only question is: what now?

It's late October. The harvest moon is huge, 'sailing on ghostly galleons' as the poem goes, its orange light silhouetting a bat flitting across the garden. Up in the silver birches, thousands of stars sparkle through the black filigree of the bare branches, a lone owl hoots into the night and there is soft scuffling in the grass: a mole, probably, or a hedgehog. In the kitchen, a plaited blue basket overflows with freshly picked apples, mushrooms and walnuts. Across the way, over in Marian's field, his sheep are draped in wisps of mist, the night so silent their munching is all but audible. From somewhere on the coast, a foghorn faintly sounds.

It's time to go to bed, and sleep on it.

❧

I wake up dreaming of some barmy drama in the post office on Inisbofin Island. This is absolutely insane: I've never been on Inisbofin and have no idea whether it even *has* a post office. But clearly, at some subliminal level, Ireland and I must be trying to communicate about something.

'Come back, Paddy Reilly, all is forgiven'?

Can people who've had a lover's tiff with their country kiss and make up with it? Forgive and forget, have a big hug and start over? Can they really rediscover each other, and take each other back? Even if they do, will they be able to live together again? Can they work out a new, stronger, better relationship?

According to economist David McWilliams, the Irish diaspora

should come back. Of course it should, without a second thought! It will renew and regenerate the country and be welcomed with open arms, David says. But is he right? I can remember a time when returned emigrants were treated very coolly. Their absence, if not quite treasonable, certainly indicated disaffection, and nobody wanted to hear a word about how great life was 'away'.

Okay, we won't talk about how great it can be 'away', then. But the prospect of returning to the mother ship is scary, and raises many questions. Starting with the very simple one: why?

Ties. Tugs. Heartstrings. Evocative sounds and smells, a shared past, lovely landscapes, the celebrated lilt of Irish laughter. All of these things colour the reality – which is that the country's up the creek, a financial shipwreck for which nobody seems to even recognise, never mind accept, responsibility. On the plus side, the collapse might make a house an affordable possibility, but on the minus side, it almost certainly means a lower standard of living. Work could be hard to find; even from this distance, I've already felt the tightening of belts. Pensions, medical care, social services, public safety . . . all of these things have been eroded by the financial crisis to a much greater degree than they have in France. I don't know anyone here who's actually lost their job, but I know several in Ireland, middle-class people who are suddenly struggling, frightened, verging on panic. Until recently, Ireland was almost exhaustingly exuberant; now it's gazing awestruck at the debris of a hooley that spun wildly out of control.

You'd have to love your country a whole heap to go back to that kind of nightmare. And what exactly is the impetus for going back? Is it true love, or might it simply be itchy feet? Might I have a low boredom threshold, a growing awareness of having 'done' France, made it work, made the point? Does this happen to every migrant everywhere, at some stage, do they just get restless? Is there anything actually wrong with France, seriously wrong enough to drive me out?

All over the world, thousands of Irish emigrants must ask themselves all these questions every day. Is Ireland still the kind of country where we want to raise our children? If we do, will they have a future in it? Does it have a warm welcome for us black sheep? Can we cope with the possibility of unemployment, social upheaval, a severely weakened economy with little prospect of improvement? Will a nostalgic night in a pub, with a pint and a turf fire and maybe a tin whistle, be enough to lure us back to ghost estates, dole queues and severely straitened old age? Will we feel safe? Will we feel ripped off? Will there be defibrillators in every village? Will the *craic* compensate for the climate? Will the new cuts and raised taxes prove unmanageable, or are things not as bad as they look?

And what about the life we'd be leaving behind? The one we worked so hard to build up, the friends we made, the house we bought, the job we got, the children's subsidised skiing and swimming lessons, the way we don't worry about letting them walk or cycle home alone, the way they love shrimping on that beach all summer?

It's a tough decision. Head over heart, mind over matter. Some will feel the inexorable pull of home and emotions may start running high, while others, more pragmatic, will tackle it with just a hint of flint. Yes, of course Ireland is 'home' and of course we'd love to live there if we could, but . . .

On any logical basis, I can't persuade myself that returning to Ireland would improve my quality of life. But I am increasingly aware of one thing: my windy Norman plateau is starting to feel ever so slightly remote, in every sense. I've been here ten years now, done it, got the T-shirt. It's still lovely, leisurely and very laid back, but at an age when many people are starting to contemplate retiring, I curiously find myself revving up again, starting to crave a bit of buzz, a flash of the bright lights, the kind of pace you don't find in the sleepy French countryside. Ironically, just as the music winds down in Ireland, I'm ready for action, sensing resurgent energy after this long and refreshing break, something new to contribute if only I could figure out exactly what it might be.

Which means . . . what? A change of pace, clearly, and of direction too? Stay in France, but move to Cannes, Cherbourg, Paris? Would La Rochelle furnish enough stimulus, or do I need Galway? Strasbourg or Skerries? Deauville or Dublin or Dingle? The more I ponder their various pros and cons, the more confusing it gets. And then sometimes I think I must be off my rocker, gazing in despair around the basement full of junk, the stacks of stuff, the four fully furnished bedrooms: who in their right mind would contemplate moving house at all if they didn't absolutely have to? Moving house is notoriously stressful, and if you're not sure where you want to go, or why, it borders on certifiable insanity. The gods might even punish this kind of ingratitude – the apparently long-term inability to appreciate so many blessings, so much tranquillity, so much beauty?

Would a holiday help? Maybe a month in Mayo or Mulhuddart would cure this confusion. A knees-up in Monte Carlo, a blast of Los Angeles, a dose of Dubai, some slash-and-burn shopping in New York? Maybe after that I'd totter back shattered to this lazily lovely countryside, count my blessings and cycle off into the tangerine-tinted sunset?

But no. Instinctively I sense that tourism is not the answer. Indeed, it may even be part of the question, because for years now I've felt like a tourist, enjoying an extended visit to France without ever truly belonging to the country. On the plus side, this exonerates me from the kind of responsibility I always somehow felt for Ireland: whatever France's woes, they are not of my making nor within my powers of solution. Being a foreigner is, in many ways, quite liberating. Sometimes nowadays I even pretend not to speak French, because playing the hapless tourist can oil clogged wheels. However, being foreign does leave you on the wrong side of some glass ceiling, eternally looking in without fully fitting in. You are an observer, a hurler on the ditch.

Do I want to grab my hurley, go home and jump back into the ditch? Abandon the life I've built here, the hazy lazy days of summer, the soaring notes of spring, the rich depths of autumn, the white glare of winter? Bid *adieu* to everyone who's been so kind, so friendly, so much fun? Get off the sun lounger and back onto the hamster wheel? Start queuing for buses again, commuting, searching and paying for parking when, as things stand, I'm only short of wandering down to the village for croissants in my pyjamas?

No! Don't do it!

Would you think I was nuts to go back to Ireland? Or would you think me nuts to stay here? What would you do, if you lived in a beautiful country whose only crime was that it wasn't your country?

It's not acute homesickness. I'm not breaking out in a rash or floods of tears or anything. Most of the time it's scarcely perceptible, just a tiny throb under the skin, and much of the time I don't feel any pain at all. Most of the time, I feel great. But, like a toothache, might it get worse if the first little pangs are not addressed and treated?

Ah, *la belle France*. Who would have thought it would turn out to be such a conundrum? Or am I just an ungrateful strap who needs a good slap? Maybe I should go out and get a job, some ghastly job that would make me realise how lucky I am and leave me too tired to think about any future whatsoever, anywhere.

Would I miss France, if I left?

Yes. Oh, yes. I'd miss it in the way you'd miss George Clooney, say, if for reasons beyond comprehension you were engaged to him and then felt you had to break it off. Sorry George, but I'm going to marry the boy back home! The boy who's lost all his money and drinks too much and has a sore head . . . but the one I've known all my life, the one I grew up with, the one who gets my jokes and makes me laugh. A naughty feckless kid, but freckled and red-haired, with an adorable, unforgettable smile.

Or maybe he's not a kid, any more? Maybe Ireland has changed, moved on, grown into a stronger, happier, nicer place? Maybe I have too? Maybe we've both mellowed, and things would work out much better the second time round? By all accounts, the recession has had a softening side effect, there's almost a spirit of the Blitz, of people doing their best to help each other out in these challenging times. And I'm more understanding, too, of so many of the things that seemed to make no sense at the time. France has had a soothing and maturing effect.

Limbo is a strange place to find yourself in the middle of your life. But that's how it feels today, after ten years abroad, albeit ten very happy years, in this most beguiling of countries. Suddenly, I'm standing at a crossroads, with no map and no compass. In an ideal world, there'd be some way to keep a foot in both camps, but I can't see how . . . or would that just be 'chicken' anyway, and a shortcut to schizophrenia?

Eh, oui. France is as beautiful as ever, often quite heartbreakingly beautiful. This morning I stood by the sea watching huge glittering pillars of water blowing across the beach, sculpted by the wind, amazed that after all this time I still have the luxury of spending a morning at the seaside. A little girl ran across the pebbles, playing hide-and-seek with the waves, her pink scarf flying on the breeze, and I thought: such a beautiful, perfect picture. Claude Monet could not have painted anything more beautiful.

And then I got into the little green Renault, and there was Ireland on the radio, laughing its socks off at the latest crazy episode of its soap-opera life.

I looked at the lovely little French girl, and I listened to the laughter wafting over the sea, and I wondered: what would *you* do, if you were me?

Do you think Liz should stay in France or return to Ireland?

Vote and give your views on French Leave's Facebook page . . .

 http://tinyurl.com/4t6chyj

Win a family trip to France courtesy of

Irishferries⚫com™

To enter, go to www.irishferries.com

Closing date 30 September 2011